Chinese phrasebook

Elizabeth Leith
Zhang Yuan

McGraw·Hill

k Chicago San Francisco Lisbon London Madrid Mexico City
New Delhi San Juan Seoul Singapore Sydney Toronto

The McGraw-Hill Companies

ISBN 0-07-148246-6
Reprinted 2008

Editor & Project Manager
Anna Stevenson

Publishing Manager
Patrick White

Prepress
Heather Macpherson

CONTENTS

INTRODUCTION

This brand new English-Chinese phrasebook from Harrap is ideal for anyone wishing to try out their foreign language skills while travelling abroad. The information is practical and clearly presented, helping you to overcome the language barrier and mix with the locals.

Each section features a list of useful words and a selection of common phrases: some of these you will read or hear, while others will help you to express yourself. The simple phonetic transcription system, specifically designed for English speakers, ensures that you will always make yourself understood.

The book also includes a mini dictionary of around 2,500 words, so that more adventurous users can build on the basic structures and engage in more complex conversations.

Concise information on local culture and customs is provided, along with practical tips to save you time. After all, you're on holiday – time to relax and enjoy yourself! There is also a food and drink glossary to help you make sense of menus, and ensure that you don't miss out on any of the national or regional specialities.

Remember that any effort you make will be appreciated. So don't be shy – have a go!

PRONUNCIATION

The Chinese language is called 汉语 ***hànyǔ*** (language of the Han people, the Han being the majority ethnic group in China). It is also sometimes called 普通话 ***pǔtōnghuà***, meaning common or standard language. This language corresponds to that spoken in the central and northern regions of China, and is based especially on the language of Beijing. In the West, it is often known as Mandarin Chinese. It is the official language, used in education and in the media.

Other dialects are spoken in China, but Mandarin Chinese is the common language understood by all Chinese people. In the province of Canton (广东 ***Guǎngdōng***) and in Hong Kong (香港 ***Xiāng Gǎng***) most people speak Cantonese, but Mandarin is, even there, increasingly becoming the language of business.

Chinese is written in characters, composed of various elements known as "strokes". While the dictionary compiled in 1715 during the reign of the Emperor 康熙 ***Kāngxī*** showed 47,021 characters, knowledge of 2,000 to 3,000 is sufficient in order to read the newspapers. In the 1950s the form of the characters was simplified in mainland China, and it is this simplified form that is used today. Taiwan and Hong Kong retain the traditional characters, and of course they are also seen in historical and older literary texts.

In 1958, the People's Republic of China adopted a system of phonetic writing using Roman letters, with the aim of making the characters easier to learn. This transcription system is known as pinyin 拼音 ***pīnyīn***. While some older Chinese people are not familiar with it, young people use this system when they learn Chinese, and it is extremely helpful to foreigners wishing to learn the Chinese language.

In this phrasebook, each phrase in English has a translation using Chinese characters and also has its equivalent in pinyin plus a transcription of the pronunciation using the Roman alphabet, based on approximations to English language sounds familiar to the reader.

For example:
I'd like to book a ticket
我要订一张票。 (Chinese characters)
wǒ yào dìng yīzhāng piào (pinyin)
wo yao ding ee jang peeao (phonetic transcription)

The tones in Chinese

Chinese has four tones, as well as a neutral or unmarked tone, and these tones convey differences in meaning. Pronouncing a syllable with a wrong tone can give rise to confusion. In pinyin the tones are written like accents, above the main vowel of each syllable, and the tone sign gives a guide to pronunciation.

In the diagrams below, the vertical line shows the range of pitch of our voices. The diagram may help you to produce the tones. Try to listen out for them when you hear people speaking and to copy them when you reply.

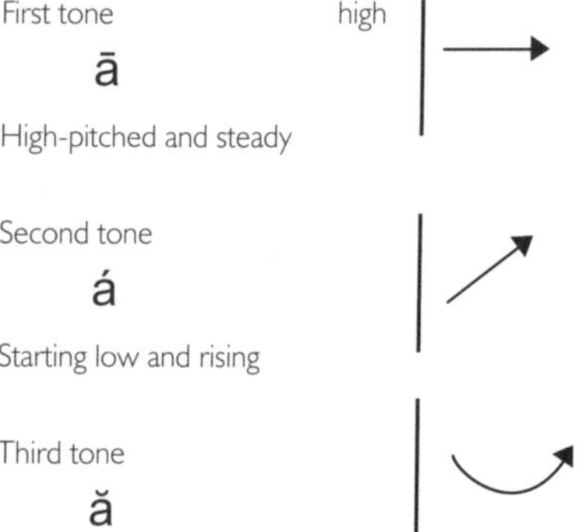

Starting around middle pitch, falling and then rising

Fourth tone

à

Starting high and falling

A syllable in pinyin with no tone is unstressed.

Examples:
妈 *mā* (mother) first tone: flat, but quite high pitch
麻 *má* (hemp) second tone: rising, starting low, ending on a high pitch
马 *mǎ* (horse) third tone: rising-falling
骂 *mà* (to swear) fourth tone: falling
吗 *ma* (marks a question): unstressed

Consonants

Pinyin	Pronunciation	Example	Transcription	Chinese characters
b	b	*bàba*	*baba*	爸爸
c	ts as in ca**ts**	*cài*	*tsy*	菜
ch	ch as in **ch**ild	*chē*	*che*	车
d	d	*dà*	*da*	大
f	f	*fēijī*	*fay-jee*	飞机
g	hard g as in **g**o	*guó*	*gwoe*	国
h	h as in **h**ot	*hái*	*hy*	孩
j	soft g as in **g**eography	*jī*	*jee*	机
k	k	*kě*	*ke*	渴
l	l	*lǎo*	*lao*	老
m	m	*māma*	*mama*	妈妈

n	n	*nǐ*	*nee*	你
p	p	*pá*	*pa*	爬
q	ch as in **ch**ild	*qì*	*chee*	气
r (at the beginning of a syllable)	j	*rén*	*jeun*	人
r (at the end of a syllable)	r	*nǎr*	*nar*	哪儿
s	s	*sān*	*san*	三
sh	sh as in **sh**ip	*shì*	*sheu*	是
t	t	*tīng*	*ting*	听
w	w	*wèi*	*way*	喂
x	sh as in **sh**ip	*xīn*	*shin*	心
y	y	*yào*	*yao*	要
z	**z** as in yar**ds**	*zài*	*zy*	再
zh	**j** as in **j**ar	*zhōng*	*jong*	中

Vowels

Pinyin	Pronunciation	Example	Transcription	Chinese characters
a	a as in f**a**ther	*māma*	*ma-ma*	妈妈
ai	y as in cr**y**	*hái*	*hy*	孩
an	an as in m**an**	*hàn*	*han*	汉
ang	ang	*máng*	*mang*	忙
ao	ow as in c**ow**	*hǎo*	*hao*	好
e	e as in h**er**	*chē*	*che*	车
e (after y)	ay as in **day**	*yě*	*yay*	也
ei	ay as in s**ay**	*hēi*	*hay*	黑

en	en as in brok**en**	*hěn*	*heun*	很
eng	ung as in h**ung**	*péng*	*pung*	朋
er	er as in join**er**	*zhèr*	*jer*	这儿
i	ee as in b**ee**	*bǐ*	*bee*	笔
i (after z, c, zh, ch, s, sh and r)	eu	*shì*	*sheu*	是
ia	ya as in **ya**rd	*jiā*	*jya*	家
ian	yen	*miàn*	*myen*	面
iang	yang	*liǎng*	*lyang*	两
iao	eow	*piào*	*peeao*	票
ie	yay	*jiě*	*jyay*	姐
in	in	*lín*	*lin*	林
ing	ing as in fl**ing**	*píng*	*ping*	瓶
iu	yo as in **yo**lk	*jiǔ*	*jyo*	酒
o	o	*wǒ*	*wo*	我
ong	as in g**ong**	*yǒng*	*yong*	泳
ou	o as in t**oe**	*tóu*	*toe*	头
u	oo	*wǔ*	*woo*	五
uai	why	*kuài*	*kwhy*	快
uan	wan as in s**wan**	*guānxi*	*gwan-shee*	关系
uang	wang	*huáng*	*hwang*	黄
ue	way	*xuě*	*shway*	雪
ui	way	*guì*	*gway*	贵
un	un as m**oon**	*hūn*	*hoon*	昏
uo	woe	*guó*	*gwoe*	国

ü (the two dots are omitted after j, q and x)	as in French **tu**	*lǚ*	*lu*	旅
yi	**ee** when yi forms a complete syllable	*yīdiǎnr*	*ee-dyar*	一点儿

In this book characters are separated for ease of recognition, but in the transcription the parts of a word are linked by a hyphen, eg airport 机场 *jīchǎng jee-chang*

ABBREVIATIONS USED IN THIS BOOK

adj	adjective
adv	adverb
n	noun
v	verb

EVERYDAY CONVERSATION

The formal style of address (您 *nín nin*) is often used, especially in and around Beijing, to show respect but generally only in formal situations, for example to an elderly person or to a senior colleague. It is less common in the south. Often, Chinese people also use the formal "you" with their parents to show their respect.

In China, a person's position or occupation, such as factory director, manager, engineer or teacher, is frequently used as a title to address him or her in preference to expressions such as Mr or Mrs. Surnames always precede the titles. It is considered impolite for a student to address a teacher directly by his or her personal name.

As elsewhere, Chinese names are made up of two parts: the family name (姓 **xìng**) and the given name or names (名。**míng**). In order to avoid offending the person you are speaking to, make sure you know the difference between his or her given and family names: you should use the family name, as the other is used by close family and friends only. In contrast to names in most European languages, where the surname usually follows the given name, family names always precede given names in Chinese. In mainland China, women retain their family names after marriage.

Among groups of people who know each other well, it is common for the older members to be addressed by their surname with 老 ***lăo*** *lao* (old) in front. They would address younger and junior people by putting 小 ***xiăo*** *sheeao* (little or young) in front of the surname. Visitors to China should stick to the polite forms of address, such as 先生 ***Zhāng xiānsheng*** (Mr Zhang), 张小姐 ***Zhāng xiăojiĕ*** (Miss Zhang) and 张夫人 ***Zhāng fūren*** (Mrs Zhang).

It has become common, particularly among men, to shake hands at work-related meetings. Hugging and kissing are not common, although some young people adopt these Western customs.

If you are invited to a Chinese home, it is customary to bring a present. Perfume, make-up and red wine have become particularly popular in recent years. Chinese people also like to exchange business cards (名片 *míngpiàn ming-pyen*) when they meet for the first time. Hold out your own, and take theirs with respect.

The basics

bye	再见 ***zàijiàn*** *zy-jyen*
excuse me	请问 ***qǐngwèn*** *ching-weun*
good afternoon	下午好 ***xiàwǔ hǎo*** *sheea-woo hao*
goodbye	再见 ***zàijiàn*** *zy-jyen*
good evening	晚上好 ***wǎnshang hǎo*** *wan-shang hao*
good morning	早上好 ***zǎoshang hǎo*** *zao-shang hao*
goodnight	晚安 ***wǎn'ān*** *wan-an*
hello	你好 ***nǐ hǎo*** *nee hao*
hi	哎，你好 ***ài nǐ hǎo*** *eye, nee hao*
no	不 ***bù*** *boo*
OK	好 ***hǎo*** *hao*, 行 ***xíng*** *shing*
pardon	请再说一遍 ***qǐng zài shuō yī biàn*** *ching zy shwoe ee byen*
please	请 ***qǐng*** *ching*
thanks, thank you	谢谢 ***xièxie*** *shyay-shyay*
yes	是 ***shì*** *sheu*

Expressing yourself

I'd like ...
我想要 …
wǒ xiǎng yào ...
wo shyang yao ...

we'd like ...
我们想要 …
wǒmen xiǎng yào ...
wo-meun shyang yao ...

do you want ...?
你要 … 吗?
nǐ yào ... ma?
nee yao... ma?

do you have ...?
你们有 … 吗?
nǐmen yǒu ... ma?
nee-meun yoe ... ma?

is there a ...?
有 … 吗?
yǒu ... ma?
yoe ... ma?

are there any ...?
有 … 吗?
yǒu ... ma?
yoe ... ma?

how ...?
… 怎么样?
... zěnmeyàng?
... zeun-me-yang?

why ...?
为什么 …?
wèishénme ...?
way-sheun-me ...?

when ...?
什么时候 …?
shénme shíhou ...?
sheun-me sheu-hoe ...?

what ...?
什么 …?
shénme ...?
sheun-me ...?

where is ...?
… 在哪儿?
... zài nǎr?
... zy nar?

where are ...?
… 在哪儿?
... zài nǎr?
... zy nar?

how much is it?
多少钱?
duōshǎo qián?
dwoe-shao chyen?

what is it?
是什么?
shì shénme?
sheu sheun-me?

where are the toilets, please?
请问，厕所在哪儿?
qǐngwèn, cèsuǒ zài nǎr?
ching-weun, tse-swoe zy nar?

do you speak English?
你说英语吗?
nǐ shuō yīngyǔ ma?
nee shwoe ying-yoo ma?

how are you?
你好吗?
nǐ hǎo ma?
nee hao ma?

fine, thanks
我很好，谢谢
wǒ hěn hǎo, xièxie
wo heun hao, shyay-shyay

thanks very much
非常感谢
fēicháng gǎnxiè
fay-chang gan-shyay

no, thanks
不用了，谢谢
búyòng le, xièxie
boo-yong le, shyay-shyay

yes, please
好，请吧
hǎo, qǐng ba
hao, ching ba

you're welcome
不客气
bú kèqi
boo ke-chee

I'm sorry
对不起
duìbuqǐ
dway-boo-chee

see you later
再见
zàijiàn
zy-jyen

Understanding

请注意 ***qǐng zhùyì***	attention
不要 ***búyào***	do not
入口 ***rùkǒu***	entrance
出口 ***chūkǒu***	exit
免费 ***miǎnfèi***	free
禁止停车 ***jìnzhǐ tíngchē***	no parking
禁止吸烟 ***jìnzhǐ xīyān***	no smoking
开门 ***kāimén (shop)***	open
出故障了 ***chū gùzhàng le***	out of order
已预订 ***yǐ yùdìng***	reserved
厕所 ***cèsuǒ,*** 卫生间 ***wèishēngjiān***	toilets

有 …
yǒu …
yoe …
there's/there are …

如果 … 你介意吗?
rúguǒ … nǐ jièyì ma?
joo-gwoe … nee jyay-ee ma?
do you mind if … ?

请坐
qǐng zuò
ching zwoe
please take a seat

欢迎
huānyíng
hwan-ying
welcome

请等一下
qǐng děng yīxià
ching dung ee-shya
one moment, please

PROBLEMS UNDERSTANDING CHINESE

Expressing yourself

pardon?
请再说一遍，好吗？
qǐng zài shuō yībiàn, hǎo ma?
ching zy shwoe ee-byen, hao ma?

what?
什么？
shénme?
sheun-me?

could you repeat that, please?
请重复一下，好吗？
qǐng chóngfù yīxià, hǎo ma?
ching chong-foo ee-shya, hao ma?

could you speak more slowly?
请说慢一点儿，好吗？
qǐng shuō màn yīdiǎnr, hǎo ma?
ching shwoe man ee-dyar, hao ma?

I don't understand
我不懂
wǒ bù dǒng
wo boo dong

I understand a little Chinese
我懂一点儿中文
wǒ dǒng yīdiǎnr zhōngwén
wo dong ee-dyar jong-weun

I can understand Chinese but I can't speak it
我能懂一些中文，可是不会说
wǒ néng dǒng yīxiē zhōngwén, kěshì bú huì shuō
wo nung dong ee-shyay jong-weun, ke-sheu boo hway shwoe

I hardly speak any Chinese
我几乎不说中文
wǒ jīhū bù shuō zhōngwén
wo jee-hoo boo shwoe jong-weun

do you speak English?
你说英语吗？
nǐ shuō yīngyǔ ma?
ni shwoe ying-yoo ma?

how do you say ... in Chinese?
中文 … 怎么说？
zhōngwén ... zěnme shuō?
jong-weun ... zeun-me shwoe?

how do you spell it?
它怎么写？
tā zěnme xiě?
ta zeun-me shyay?

what's that called in Chinese?
那个中文叫什么？
nà ge zhōngwén jiào shénme?
na ge jong-weun jeeao sheun-me?

could you write it down for me?
给我写下来，好吗？
gěi wǒ xiě xiàlái, hǎo ma?
gay wo shyay shya-ly, hao ma?

Understanding

你懂中文吗？
nǐ dǒng zhōngwén ma?
nee dong jong-weun ma?
do you understand Chinese?

我给你写下来
wǒ gěi nǐ xiě xiàlái
woe gay nee shyay shya-ly
I'll write it down for you

意思是 …
yìsi shì …
ee-seu sheu …
it means …

这是一种 …
zhè shì yī zhǒng …
jeu sheu ee jong …
it's a kind of …

SPEAKING ABOUT THE LANGUAGE

Expressing yourself

I learned a few words from my phrasebook
我从这本手册中学了几个词
wǒ cóng zhè běn shǒucè zhōng xué le jǐ ge cí
wo tsong je beun shoe-tse jong shway le jee ge tseu

I did it at school but I've forgotten everything
我在学校时学过，可是现在都忘了
wǒ zài xuéxiào shí xuéguo, kěshì xiànzài dōu wàng le
wo zy shway-sheeao sheu shway-gwoe, ke-sheu shyen-zy doe wang le

I can just about get by
只能将就对付一下
zhǐ néng jiāngjiu duìfu yīxià
jeu nung jyang-jyo dway-foo ee-shya

I hardly know two words!
我几乎连一个字都不认识
wǒ jīhū lián yī ge zì dōu bú rènshi
wo jee-hoo lyen ee ge zeu doe boo jeun-sheu

I find Chinese a difficult language
我觉得中文很难
wǒ juéde zhōngwén hěn nán
wo jway-de jong-weun heun nan

I can only speak a little Chinese
我只会一些基本的中文
wǒ zhǐ huì yīxiē jīběn de zhōngwén
wo jeu hway ee-shyay jee-beun de jong-weun

Chinese people speak too quickly for me
我觉得中国人说话太快
wǒ juéde zhōngguó rén shuōhuà tài kuài
wo jway-de jong-gwoe jeun shwoe-hwa ty kwhy

Understanding

你发音很好
nǐ fāyīn hěn hǎo
nee fa-yin heun hao
you have a good accent

你中文说得很好
nǐ zhōngwén shuō de hěn hǎo
nee jong-weun shwoe de heun hao
you speak very good Chinese

ASKING THE WAY

Expressing yourself

excuse me, can you tell me where the … is, please?
请问，您能告诉我 … 在哪儿吗？
qǐngwèn, nín néng gàosu wǒ … zài nǎr ma?
ching-weun, nin nung gao-soo wo … zy nar ma?

which way is it to …?
哪条路到 … ？
nǎ tiáo lù dào …?
na teeao loo dao …?

can you tell me how to get to …?
您能告诉我到 … 怎么走吗？
nín néng gàosu wǒ dào … zěnme zǒu ma?
nin nung gao-soo wo dao … zeun-me zoe ma?

is there a … near here?
这儿附近有 … 吗?
zhèr fùjìn yǒu … ma?
jer foo-jin yoe … ma?

could you show me on the map?
您能在地图上给我指出来吗?
nín néng zài dìtú shang gěi wǒ zhǐ chūlái ma?
nin nung zy dee-too shang gay wo zheu choo-ly ma?

is there a map of the town somewhere?
哪儿有本市地图?
năr yǒu běn shì dìtú?
nar yoe beun sheu dee-too?

is it far?
远吗?
yuǎn ma?
ywan ma?

I'm lost
我迷路了
wǒ mílù le
wo mee-loo le

I'm looking for …
我要找 …
wǒ yào zhǎo …
wo yao jao …

Understanding

沿着 … 行进 *yánzhe … xíngjìn* follow …
下去 *xiàqù* go down
上去 *shàngqù* go up
继续行进 *jìxù xíngjìn* keep going
左边 *zuǒbiān* left
右边 *yòubiān* right
一直往前 *yīzhí wǎng qián* straight ahead
拐 *guǎi* turn

您是走路吗?
nín shì zǒulù ma?
nin sheu zoe-loo ma?
are you on foot?

开车要五分钟
kāichē yào wǔ fēn zhōng
ky-che yao woo feun jong
it's five minutes away by car

是左边第一个/第二个/第三个
shì zuǒbiān dì yī ge /dì èr ge /dì sān ge
sheu zwoe-byen dee ee ge/dee er ge/dee san ge
it's the first/second/third on the left

到环岛向右拐
dào huán dǎo xiàng yòu guǎi
dao hwan dao shang yoe gwy
turn right at the roundabout

到了银行往左拐
dào le yínháng wǎng zuǒ guǎi
dao le yin-hang wang zwoe gwhy
turn left at the bank

走下一个出口
zǒu xià yī ge chūkǒu
zoe shya ee ge choo-koe
take the next exit

不远
bù yuǎn
boo ywan
it's not far

就在前边路口
jiù zài qiánbiān lùkǒu
jyo zy chyen-byen loo-koe
it's just round the corner

GETTING TO KNOW PEOPLE

The basics

bad	糟糕 ***zāogāo*** *zao-gao*
beautiful	好极了 ***hǎo jí le*** *hao jee le,* 晴朗 ***qínglǎng*** *ching-lang*
boring	没意思 ***méi yìsi*** *may ee-seu*
cheap	便宜 ***piányi*** *pyen-yee*
expensive	贵 ***guì*** *gway*
good	好 ***hǎo*** *hao*
great	好极了 ***hǎo jí le*** *hao jee le,* 非常好 ***fēicháng hǎo*** *fay-chang hao*
interesting	有意思 ***yǒu yìsi*** *yoe ee-seu*
nice	好心的 ***hǎoxīn de*** *hao-shin de*
not bad	不错 ***bú cuò*** *boo tswoe*
well	好 ***hǎo*** *hao*
to hate	讨厌 ***tǎoyàn*** *tao-yan*
to like	喜欢 ***xǐhuan*** *shee-hwan*
to love	爱 ***ài*** *eye*

INTRODUCING YOURSELF AND FINDING OUT ABOUT OTHER PEOPLE

Expressing yourself

my name's …
我叫 …
wǒ jiào …
wo jeeao …

how do you do!
您好！
nín hǎo!
nin hao!

what's your name?
您叫什么名字？
nín jiào shénme míngzi?
nin jeeao sheun-me ming-zeu?

pleased to meet you!
很高兴认识您
hěn gāoxìng rènshi nín!
heun gao-shing jeun-sheu nin!

this is my husband
这是我丈夫
zhè shì wǒ zhàngfu
je sheu wo jang-foo

I'm English
我是英格兰人
wǒ shì yīnggélán rén
wo sheu ying-ge-lan jeun

I'm from …
我是 … 国人
wǒ shì … guó rén
wo sheu … gwoe jeun

how old are you?
你多大
nǐ duō dà?
nee dwoe da?

what do you do for a living?
你做什么工作?
nǐ zuò shénme gōngzuò?
nee zwoe sheun-me gong-zwoe?

I work
我工作
wǒ gōngzuò
wo gong-zwoe

I'm a teacher
我是老师
wǒ shì lǎoshī
wo sheu lao-sheu

I work part-time
我做半日工作
wǒ zuò bànrì gōngzuò
wo zwoe ban-jeu gong-zwoe

I'm retired
我退休了
wǒ tuìxiū le
wo tway-shyo le

this is my partner, Karen
这是我的伴侣卡伦
zhè shì wǒ de bànlǚ Kǎlún
je sheu wo de ban-lu Kaloon

we're American
我们是美国人
wǒmen shì měiguó rén
wo-meun sheu may-gwoe jeun

where are you from?
你是哪国人?
nǐ shì nǎ guó rén?
nee sheu na gwoe jeun?

I'm 22
我二十二
wǒ èrshí'èr
wo er-sheu-er

are you a student?
你是学生吗?
nǐ shì xuésheng ma?
nee sheu shway-shung ma?

I'm studying law
我学法律
wǒ xué fǎlǜ
wo shway fa-lu

I stay at home with the children
我在家带孩子
wǒ zài jiā dài háizi
wo zy jya dy hy-zeu

I work in marketing
我搞市场营销
wǒ gǎo shìchǎng yíngxiāo
wo gao sheu-chang ying-sheeao

I'm self-employed
我是个体户
wǒ shì gètǐhù
wo sheu ge-tee-hoo

I have two children
我有两个孩子
wǒ yǒu liǎng ge háizi
wo yoe lyang ge hy-zeu

we don't have any children
我们没有孩子
wǒmen méi yǒu háizi
wo-meun may yoe hy-zeu

two boys and a girl
两个男孩、一个女孩
liǎng ge nánhái, yī ge nǚhái
lyang ge nan-hy, ee ge nu-hy

a boy of five and a girl of two
男孩五岁，女孩两岁
nánhái wǔ suì, nǚhái liǎng suì
nan-hy woo sway, nu-hy lyang sway

have you ever been to Britain?
你去过英国吗?
nǐ qùguo yīngguó ma?
nee choo-gwoe ying-gwoe ma?

Understanding

你是英格兰人吗?
nǐ shì yīnggélán rén ma?
nee sheu ying-ge-lan jeun ma?
are you English?

我很熟悉英格兰
wǒ hěn shúxī yīnggélán
wo heun shoo-shee ying-ge-lan
I know England quite well

我们也是在这儿度假
wǒmen yě shì zài zhèr dùjià
wo-meun yay sheu zy jer doo-jya
we're on holiday here too

我很希望哪天能去苏格兰
wǒ hěn xīwàng nǎ tiān néng qù sūgélán
wo heun shee-wang na tyen nung choo soo-ge-lan
I'd love to go to Scotland one day

TALKING ABOUT YOUR STAY

Expressing yourself

I'm here on business
我到这儿出差
wǒ dào zhèr chūchāi
wo dao jer choo-chy

we're on holiday
我们度假
wǒmen dùjià
wo-meun doo-jya

I arrived three days ago
我三天前来的
wǒ sān tiān qián lái de
wo san tyen chyen ly de

we've been here for a week
我们呆了一个星期了
wǒmen dāi le yī ge xīngqī le
wo-meun dy le ee ge shing-chee le

I'm only here for a long weekend
我在这儿只是度一个长周末
wǒ zài zhèr zhǐ shì dù yī ge cháng zhōumò
wo zy jer jeu sheu doo ee ge chang joe-mo

we're just passing through
我们只是路过
wǒmen zhǐ shì lùguò
wo-meun zheu sheu loo-gwoe

this is our first time in China
这是我们第一次到中国
zhè shì wǒmen dì yī cì dào zhōngguó
je sheu wo-meun dee ee tseu dao jong-gwoe

we're here to celebrate our wedding anniversary
我们在这儿庆祝结婚纪念日
wǒmen zài zhèr qìngzhù jiéhūn jìniànrì
wo-meun zy jer ching-joo jyay-hoon jee-nyen-jeu

we're on our honeymoon
我们度蜜月
wǒmen dù mìyuè
wo-meun doo mee-yway

we're here with friends
我们和朋友一起来的。
wǒ mén hé péngyou yīqǐ lái dè
wo-meun he pung-yoe yee-chee ly de

we're touring around
我们到处走走
wǒmen dàochù zǒuzou
wo-meun dao-choo zoe-zoe

we managed to get a cheap flight
我们搞到了便宜机票
wǒmen gǎodào le piányi jīpiào
wo-meun gao-dao le pyen-yee jee-peeao

Understanding

祝您在这儿过得愉快!
zhù nín zài zhèr guò de yúkuài!
joo nin zy jer gwoe de yoo-kwy!
enjoy your stay!

祝您假期愉快!
zhù nín jiàqī yúkuài!
joo nin jya-chee yoo-kwy!
enjoy the rest of your holiday!

这是您第一次来中国吗?
zhè shì nín dì yī cì lái zhōngguó ma?
je sheu nin dee ee tseu ly jong-gwoe ma?
is this your first time in China?

您呆多长时间?
nín dāi duō cháng shíjiān?
nin dy dwoe chang sheu-jyen?
how long are you staying?

您喜欢这儿吗?
nín xǐhuan zhèr ma?
nin shee-hwan jer ma?
do you like it here?

您去过 … 吗?
nín qùguo … ma?
nin choo-gwoe … ma?
have you been to …?

STAYING IN TOUCH

Expressing yourself

we should stay in touch
我们应该保持联系
wǒmen yīnggāi bǎochí liánxì
wo-meun ying-gy bao-cheu lyen-shee

I'll give you my e-mail address
我给你我的电子邮箱地址
wǒ gěi nǐ wǒ de diànzǐ yóuxiāng dìzhǐ
wo gay nee wo de dyen-zeu yoe-shyang dee-jeu

here's my address, if ever you come to Britain
如果你到英国的话，这是我的地址
rúguǒ nǐ dào yīngguó de huà, zhè shì wǒ de dìzhǐ
joo-gwoe nee dao ying-gwoe de hwa, je sheu wo de dee-jeu

Understanding

给我留下你的地址，好吗?
gěi wǒ liúxià nǐ de dìzhǐ, hǎoma?
gay wo lyo-shya nee de dee-jeu, hao ma?
will you give me your address?

你有电子邮箱地址吗?
nǐ yǒu diànzǐ yóuxiāng dìzhǐ ma?
nee yoe dyen-zeu yoe-shyang dee-jeu ma?
do you have an e-mail address?

欢迎你随时到这儿来和我们在一起
huānyíng nǐ suíshí dào zhèr lái hé wǒmen zài yīqǐ
hwan-ying nee sway-sheu dao jer ly he wo-meun zy ee-chee
you're always welcome to come and stay with us here

EXPRESSING YOUR OPINION

Some informal expressions

没意思 ***méi yìsi*** *may ee-seu* I was bored to tears
太棒了! ***tài bàng le!*** *ty bang le!* marvellous!

Expressing yourself

I really like ...
我真喜欢 …
wǒ zhēn xǐhuan ...
wo jeun shee-hwan ...

I don't like ...
我不喜欢 …
wǒ bù xǐhuan ...
wo boo shee-hwan ...

I love ...
我爱 …
wǒ ài ...
wo eye ...

I would like ...
我想 …
wǒ xiǎng ...
wo shyang ...

I really liked ...
我真喜欢 …
wǒ zhēn xǐhuan ...
wo jeun shee-hwan ...

I didn't like ...
我不喜欢 …
wǒ bù xǐhuan ...
wo boo shee-hwan ...

I loved ...
我爱 …
wǒ ài ...
wo eye ...

I would have liked ... if ...
我会喜欢 … 假如 …
wǒ huì xǐhuan ... jiǎrú ...
wo hway shee-hwan ... jya-joo ...

I find it ...
我觉得 …
wǒ juéde ...
wo jway-de ...

it's lovely
令人愉快
lìng rén yúkuài
ling jeun yoo-kwy

I agree
我同意
wǒ tóngyì
wo tong-yee

I don't know
我不知道
wǒ bù zhīdao
wo boo jeu-dao

I don't like the sound of it
听起来不让人喜欢
tīngqǐlái bú ràng rén xǐhuan
ting-chee-ly boo jang jeun shee-hwan

it really annoys me
真让我恼火
zhēn ràng wǒ nǎohuǒ
jeun jang wo nao-hwoe

it's a rip-off
真是敲竹杠
zhēn shì qiāo zhúgàng
jeun sheu cheeao joo-gang

it's too busy
这儿太热闹
zhèr tài rènao
jer ty je-nao

I really enjoyed myself
我玩儿得很愉快
wǒ wánr de hěn yúkuài
wo wanr de heun yoo-kwy

I found it ...
我觉得 …
wǒ juéde ...
wo jway-de ...

it was lovely
令人愉快
lìng rén yúkuài
ling jeun yoo-kwy

I don't agree
我不同意
wǒ bù tóngyì
wo boo tong-yee

I don't mind
我无所谓
wǒ wúsuǒwèi
wo woo-swoe-way

it sounds interesting
听起来有意思
tīngqǐlái yǒu yìsi
ting-chee-ly yoe ee-seu

it was boring
没意思
méi yìsi
may ee-seu

it gets very busy at night
夜里更热闹了
yè lǐ gèng rènao le
yay lee gung je-nao le

it's very quiet
这儿很安静
zhèr hěn ānjìng
jer heun an-jing

we had a great time
我们玩儿得好极了
wǒmen wánr de hǎo jí le
wo-meun wanr de hao jee le

there was a really good atmosphere
这儿气氛真好
zhèr qìfēn zhēn hǎo
jer chee-feun jeun hao

we met some nice people
我们认识了一些好心的人
wǒmen rènshi le yīxiē hǎoxīn de rén
wo-meun jeun-sheu le ee-shyay hao-shin de jeun

we found a great hotel
我们找到一家非常好的饭店
wǒmen zhǎodào yī jiā fēicháng hǎo de fàndiàn
wo-meun jao-dao ee jya fay-chang hao de fan-dyen

Understanding

你喜欢 … 吗?
nǐ xǐhuan … ma?
nee shee-hwan … ma?
do you like …?

你们玩儿得愉快吗?
nǐmen wánr de yúkuài ma?
nee-meun wanr de yoo-kwy ma?
did you enjoy yourselves?

你应该到 … 去
nǐ yīnggāi dào … qù
nee ying-gy dao … choo
you should go to …

我推荐 …
wǒ tuījiàn …
wo tway-jyen …
I recommend …

那是一个漂亮的地方
nà shì yī ge piàoliang de dìfang
na sheu ee ge peeao-lyang de dee-fang
it's a lovely area

没有太多旅游者
méi yǒu tài duō lǚyóuzhě
may yoe ty dwoe lu-yoe-je
there aren't too many tourists

不要在周末去，人太多
bú yào zài zhōumò qù, rén tài duō
boo yao zy joe-mo choo, jeun ty dwoe
don't go at the weekend, it's too busy

评价有点儿太高
píngjià yǒu diǎnr tài gāo
ping-jya yoe dyar ty gao
it's a bit overrated

TALKING ABOUT THE WEATHER

Expressing yourself

have you seen the weather forecast for tomorrow?
你看了明天的天气预报了吗?
nǐ kàn le míngtiān de tiānqì yùbào le ma?
nee kan le ming-tyen de tyen-chee yoo-bao le ma?

it's going to be nice
天气会很好
tiānqì huì hěn hǎo
tyen-chee hway heun hao

it's really hot
天真热
tiān zhēn rè
tyen jeun je

the weather was beautiful
晴朗的天
qínglǎng de tiān
ching-lang de tyen

there was a thunderstorm
下了一场雷暴雨
xià le yī chǎng léibàoyǔ
shya le ee chang lay-bao-yoo

it's very humid here
这儿很潮湿
zhèr hěn cháoshī
jer heun chao-sheu

it isn't going to be nice
天气不会好
tiānqì bú huì hǎo
tyen-chee boo hway hao

it gets cold at night
夜里就冷了
yè lǐ jiù lěng le
yay lee jyo lung le

it rained a few times
下了几场雨
xià le jǐ chǎng yǔ
shya le jee chang yoo

it's been lovely all week
一周天气都很好
yī zhōu tiānqì dōu hěn hǎo
ee joe tyen-chee doe heun hao

Understanding

说是会下雨
shuō shì huì xià yǔ
shwoe sheu hway shya yoo
it's supposed to rain

明天又会热了
míngtiān yòu huì rè le
ming-tyen yoe hway je le
it will be hot again tomorrow

TRAVELLING

The basics

airport	机场 ***jīchǎng*** *jee-chang*
boarding	登机 ***dēngjī*** *dung-jee*
boarding card	登机牌 ***dēngjīpái*** *dung-jee-py*
boat	船 ***chuán*** *chwan*
bus	公共汽车 ***gōnggòng qìchē*** *gong-gong chee-che*
bus station	公共汽车总站 ***gōnggòng qìchē zǒngzhàn*** *gong-gong chee-che zong-jan*
bus stop	汽车站 ***qìchēzhàn*** *chee-che-jan*
car	小汽车 ***xiǎoqìchē*** *sheeao-chee-che*
check-in	登机手续 ***dēngjī*** *dung-jee*
coach	大巴士 ***dàbāshì*** *da-ba-sheu*
ferry	渡轮 ***dùlún*** *doo-loon*
flight	航班 ***hángbān*** *hang-ban*
gate	门 ***mén*** *meun*
left-luggage (office)	行李寄存处 ***xíngli jìcúnchù*** *shing-lee jee-tsoon-choo*
luggage	行李 ***xíngli*** *shing-lee*
map	地图 ***dìtú*** *dee-too*
motorway	高速公路 ***gāosù gōnglù*** *gao-soo gong-loo*
passport	护照 ***hùzhào*** *hoo-jao*
plane	飞机 ***fēijī*** *fay-jee*
platform	站台 ***zhàntái*** *jan-ty*
railway station	火车站 ***huǒchē zhàn*** *hwoe-che jan*
return (ticket)	往返 ***wǎngfǎn*** *wang-fan*
road	路 ***lù*** *loo*
shuttle bus	机场大巴士 ***jīchǎng dàbāshì*** *jee-chang da-ba-sheu*
single (ticket)	单程 ***dānchéng*** *dan-chung*
street	街道 ***jiēdào*** *jyay-dao*
street map	街道地图 ***jiēdào dìtú*** *jyay-dao dee-too*
taxi	出租汽车 ***chūzūqìchē*** *choo-zoo-chee-che*

terminal	终点站 ***zhōngdiǎnzhàn*** *jong-dyen-jan*
ticket	票 ***piào*** *peeao*
timetable	时刻表 ***shíkèbiǎo*** *sheu-ke-beeao*
town centre	市中心 ***shìzhōngxīn*** *sheu-jong-shin*
train	火车 ***huǒchē*** *hwoe-che*
tram	有轨电车 ***yǒu guǐ diànchē*** *yoe gway dyen-che*
underground	地铁 ***dìtiě*** *dee-tye*
underground station	地铁站 ***dìtiězhàn*** *dee-tye-jan*
to book	订 ***dìng*** *ding*
to hire	租 ***zū*** *zoo*

Expressing yourself

where can I buy tickets?
我在哪儿买票?
wǒ zài nǎr mǎi piào?
wo zy nar my peeao?

I'd like to book a ticket
我要订一张票
wǒ yào dìng yī zhāng piào
wo yao ding ee jang peeao

how much is a ticket to …?
一张到 … 的票多少钱?
yī zhāng dào … de piào duōshǎo qián?
ee jang dao … de peeao dwoe-shao chyen?

are there any concessions for students?
有学生优惠票吗?
yǒu xuésheng yōuhuì piào ma?
yoe shway-shung yoe-hway peeao ma?

could I have a timetable, please?
我可以要一张时刻表吗?
wǒ kěyǐ yào yī zhāng shíkèbiǎo ma?
wo ke-yee yao ee jang sheu-ke-beeao ma?

a ticket to …, please
我买一张到 … 的票
wǒ mǎi yī zhāng dào … de piào
wo my ee jang dao … de peeao

is there an earlier/later train/plane?
有早一点儿/晚一点儿的火车/飞机吗?
yǒu zǎo yīdiǎnr/wǎn yīdiǎnr de huǒchē/fēijī ma?
yoe zao ee-dyar/wan ee-dyar de hwoe-che/fay-jee ma?

how long does the journey take?
路程多长时间?
lùchéng duō cháng shíjiān?
loo-chung dwoe chang sheu-jyen?

is this seat free?
这个座位有人坐吗?
zhège zuòwèi yǒu rén zuò ma?
je-ge zwoe-way yoe jeun zwoe ma?

I'm sorry, there's someone sitting there
对不起，有人坐了
duìbuqǐ, yǒu rén zuò le
dway-boo-chee, yoe jeun zwoe le

Understanding

到达 *dàodá* — arrivals
取消 *qǔxiāo* — cancelled
中转 *zhōngzhuǎn* — connections
晚点 *wǎndiǎn* — delayed
开出 *kāichū* — departures *(in station)*
起飞 *qǐfēi* — departures *(in airport)*
入口 *rùkǒu* — entrance
出口 *chūkǒu* — exit
男厕所 *náncèsuǒ* — gents (toilets)
问讯台 *wènxùntái* — information
女厕所 *nǚcèsuǒ* — ladies (toilets)
禁止入内 *jìnzhǐrùnèi* — no entry
售票处 *shòupiàochù* — tickets
厕所 *cèsuǒ* — toilets

票都订完了
piào dōu dìng wán le
peeao doe ding wan le
everything is fully booked

BY PLANE

The CAAC (Civil Aviation Administration of China) oversees everything to do with air travel in China. As well as the national airline, Air China, there are several regional airlines, such as China Eastern, China Southern and Shanghai Airlines, providing domestic flights to all areas of China. In major cities, you can usually pay for your ticket by credit card – but in some smaller cities you may have to use cash.

Expressing yourself

where's the British Airways check-in?
British Airways 的登机手续在哪儿办?
British Airways de dēngjī shǒuxù zài nǎr bàn?
British Airways de dung-jee shoe-shoo zy nar ban?

I've got an e-ticket
我的票是电子票
wǒ de piào shì diànzǐ piào
wo de peeao sheu dyen-zeu peeao

one suitcase and one piece of hand luggage
一个箱子和一件手提行李
yī ge xiāngzi hé yī jiàn shǒutí xíngli
ee ge shyang-zeu he ee jyen shoe-tee shing-lee

what time do we board?
几点登机?
jǐ diǎn dēngjī?
jee dyen dung-jee?

I'd like to confirm my return flight
我想确认回程机票
wǒ xiǎng quèrèn huíchéng jīpiào
wo shyang chway-jeun hway-chung jee-peeao

one of my suitcases is missing
我还差一个箱子
wǒ hái chà yī ge xiāngzi
wo hy cha ee ge shyang-zeu

my luggage hasn't arrived
我的行李还没到
wǒ de xíngli hái méi dào
wo de shing-lee hy may dao

the plane was two hours late
飞机晚点了两小时
fēijī wǎndiǎn le liǎng xiǎoshí
fay-jee wan-dyen le lyang sheeao-sheu

I've missed my connection
我误了中转
wǒ wù le zhōngzhuǎn
wo woo le jong-jwan

I've left something on the plane
我把一个东西落在飞机上了
wǒ bǎ yī ge dōngxi là zài fēijī shang le
wo ba ee ge dong-shee la zy fay-jee shang le

I want to report the loss of my luggage
我要报告我丢失的行李
wǒ yào bàogào wǒ diūshī de xíngli
wo yao bao-gao wo dyo-sheu de shing-lee

Understanding

行李提取处 *xíngli tíqǔchù*	baggage reclaim
登机 *dēngjī*	check-in
海关 *hǎiguān*	customs
候机厅 *hòujītīng*	departure lounge
国内航线 *guónèi hángxiàn*	domestic flights
免税 *miǎnshuì*	duty free
申报物品 *shēnbào wùpǐn*	goods to declare
马上登机 *mǎshàng dēngjī*	immediate boarding
无申报 *wú shēnbào*	nothing to declare
护照检查 *hùzhào jiǎnchá*	passport control

请在候机厅等候
qǐng zài hòujītīng děnghòu
ching zy hoe-jee-ting dung-hoe
please wait in the departure lounge

您要靠窗口的还是要靠通道的座位?
nín yào kào chuāngkǒu de háishi yào kào tōngdào de zuòwèi?
nin yao kao chwang-koe de hy-sheu yao kao tong-dao de zwoe-way?
would you like a window seat or an aisle seat?

您在 ... 转机
nín zài ... zhuǎnjī
nin zy ... jwan-jee
you'll have to change in ...

您有几件行李?
nín yǒu jǐ jiàn xíngli?
nin yoe jee jyen shing-lee?
how many bags do you have?

您的行李是您自己打包的吗?
nín de xíngli shì nín zìjǐ dǎbāo de ma?
nin de shing-lee sheu nin zeu-jee da-bao de ma?
did you pack all your bags yourself?

有人请您把东西带到飞机上吗?
yǒu rén qǐng nín bǎ dōngxi dài dào fēijī shang ma?
yoe jeun ching nin ba dong-shee dy dao fay-jee shang ma?
has anyone given you anything to take onboard?

您的行李超重5公斤
nín de xíngli chāozhòng wǔ gōngjīn
nin de shing-lee chao-jong woo gong-jin
your luggage is five kilos overweight

这是您的登机牌
zhè shì nín de dēngjī pái
je sheu nin de dung-jee py
here's your boarding card

请到 ...号门
qǐng dào ... hào mén
ching dao ... hao meun
please proceed to gate number ...

登机将在 ... 开始
dēngjī jiāng zài ... kāishǐ
dung-jee jyang zy ... ky-sheu
boarding will begin at ...

最后通知 ...
zuìhòu tōngzhī ...
zway-hoe tong-jeu ...
this is a final call for ...

您可以打这个电话号码，查一下您的行李是不是到了
nín kěyǐ dǎ zhè ge diànhuà hàomǎ, chá yīxià nín de xíngli shì bu shì dào le
nin ke-yee da je ge dyen-hwa hao-ma, cha ee-shya nin de shing-lee sheu boo sheu dao le
you can call this number to check if your luggage has arrived

BY TRAIN, COACH, BUS, UNDERGROUND, TRAM

Some big hotels have reservations desks where you can book train tickets. Otherwise you can go to the station or a travel agency, but these are few and far between. In some stations there are counters reserved for foreigners. There are no return tickets. Chinese trains are generally on time, and travel at various speeds. There are four classes: "hard sleeper" (硬卧 ***yìngwò*** *yingwo) with two sets of three bunks per open compartment*, "soft sleeper" (软卧 ***ruǎnwò*** *jwan-wo) with two sets of two bunks in a private, more comfortable compartment*, "hard seat" (硬座 ***yìngzuò*** *yingz-woe*) and "soft seat" (软座 ***ruǎnzuò*** *jwan-zwoe).*

In cities, bus tickets can be bought directly from the driver. The underground is very cheap and generally runs from 5.30am to 11pm. You can buy tickets from the counters before the platform entrance, and they will be punched by a conductor. The advantage of the underground is that the signs are in pinyin, making it the easiest transport system to navigate.

Expressing yourself

can I have a map of the underground, please?
可以给我一张地铁图吗？
kěyǐ gěi wǒ yī zhāng dìtiětú ma?
ke-yee gay wo ee jang dee-tyay-too ma?

what time is the next train to ...?
到 ...的火车下一趟是几点？
dào ...de huǒchē xià yī tàng shì jǐ diǎn?
dao ... de hwoe-che shya ee tang sheu jee dyen?

TRAVELLING

what time is the last train?
末班车几点?
mòbānchē jǐdiǎn?
mo-ban-che jee dyen?

which platform is it for ...?
到 ... 去的火车在几站台?
dào ... qù de huǒchē zài jǐ zhàntái?
dao ... choo de hwoe-che zy jee jan-ty?

where can I catch a bus to ...?
到 ... 去在哪儿上公共汽车?
dào ... qù zài nǎr shàng gōnggòng qìchē?
dao ... choo zy nar shang gong-gong chee-che?

which line do I take to get to ...?
到 ... 去坐哪条线?
dào ... qù zuò nǎ tiáo xiàn?
dao ... choo zwoe na teeao shyen?

is this the stop for ...?
这是 ...车站吗?
zhè shì ... chēzhàn ma?
je sheu ... che-jan ma?

I've missed my train/bus
我误了火车/汽车
wǒ wù le huǒchē/qìchē
wo woo le hwoe-che/chee-che

is this where the coach leaves for ...?
到 ... 去的大巴士是在这儿开出吗?
dào ... qù de dàbāshì shì zài zhèr kāichū ma?
dao ... choo de da-ba-sheu sheu zy jer ky-choo ma?

can you tell me when I need to get off?
您可以告诉我，我什么时候该下车吗?
nín kěyǐ gàosu wǒ, wǒ shénme shíhou gāi xiàchē ma?
nin ke-yee gao-soo wo, wo sheun-me sheu-hoe gy shya-che ma?

Understanding

预订 *yùdìng*	bookings
当天票 *dāngtiānpiào*	day ticket
月票 *yuèpiào*	monthly ticket
售票处 *shòupiàochù*	ticket office
当天票 *dāngtiānpiào*	tickets for travel today
站台通道 *zhàntáitōngdào*	to the trains
周票 *zhōupiào*	weekly ticket

前边一点儿，在右边有一个车站
qiánbian yīdiǎnr, zài yòubian yǒu yī ge chēzhàn
chyen-byen ee-dyar, zy yoe-byen yoe ee ge che-jan
there's a stop a bit further along on the right

请准备好准确的车票钱数
qǐng zhǔnbèi hǎo zhǔnquè de chēpiào qiánshù
ching joon-bay hao joon-chway de che-peeao chyen-shoo
exact money only, please

您得在 ... 换车
nín děi zài ... huànchē
nin day zy ... hwan-che
you'll have to change at ...

这趟火车途经 ...
zhè tàng huǒchē tújīng ...
je tang hwoe-che too-jing ...
this train calls at ...

您得坐 ... 路车
nín děi zuò ... lù chē
nin day zwoe ... loo che
you need to get the number ... bus

两站后(下车)
liǎng zhàn hòu (xiàchē)
lyang jan hoe (shya-che)
two stops from here

BY BICYCLE, CAR AND TAXI

Unless you are working there and have an International Driver's Licence, driving in China is not easy and not recommended. Although private car ownership is growing fast, car hire services are not yet developed everywhere. Car parking provision also varies, but is becoming widespread and standardized in major cities as is the provision of service stations.

In the West, we often have an image of China being full of bicycles. In reality, the Chinese generally only cycle short distances. If you want to hire a bike, ask at your hotel reception desk. However, it can sometimes be cheaper to buy your own than to rent one. Be very careful when cycling in big cities.

Taxis are inexpensive, although there are several types available and the price varies depending on which one you choose (in Beijing a label in the back side window indicates the price per kilometre). Foreigners often find

them the easiest way to get around. You will not be able to haggle over the price, so do check the meter when you get in.

If you hail a taxi and it doesn't stop, it could be that it is not allowed to stop there. Also, some taxi drivers won't pick you up if you are not going in their direction, for example if they are going home or handing the car over to a colleague somewhere else. Taxis are allowed to take three or sometimes four passengers.

Expressing yourself

can you mend my bicycle, please?
请给我修一下自行车，好吗？
qǐng gěi wǒ xiū yīxià zìxíngchē, hǎo ma?
ching gay wo shyo ee-shya zeu-shing-che, hao ma?

where can I put my bicycle?
我把自行车放在哪儿？
wǒ bǎ zìxíngchē fàng zài nǎr?
wo ba zeu-shing-che fang zy nar?

can I borrow a cycle lock?
我可以借用一下车锁吗？
wǒ kěyǐ jièyòng yīxià chēsuǒ ma?
wo ke-yee jyay-yong ee-shya che-swoe ma?

do you have a newer bicycle ?
你们有新一点儿的自行车吗？
nǐmen yǒu xīn yīdiǎnr de zìxíngchē ma?
nee-meun yoe shin ee-dyar de zeu-shing-che ma?

where can I find a service station?
请问，加油站在哪儿？
qǐngwèn, jiāyóuzhàn zài nǎr?
ching-weun, jya-yoe-jan zy nar?

is there a garage near here?
这儿附近有汽车修理厂吗？
zhèr fùjìn yǒu qìchē xiūlǐchǎng ma?
jer foo-jin yoe chee-che shyo-lee-chang ma?

the battery's dead
蓄电池没电了
xùdiànchí méi diàn le
shoo-dyen-cheu may dyen le

I've broken down
车出故障了
chē chū gùzhàng le
che choo goo-jang le

we've run out of petrol
我们没汽油了
wǒmen méi qìyóu le
wo-meun may chee-yoe le

I've got a puncture and my spare tyre is flat
我的车胎扎了，备用胎也瘪了
wǒ dè chētāi zhā le, bèiyòngtāi yě biě lè
wo de che-ty ja le, bay-yong ty yay byay le

we've just had an accident
我们遇车祸了
wǒmen yù chēhuò le
wo-meun yoo che-hwoe le

I've lost my car keys
我的车钥匙丢了
wǒ de chē yàoshi diū le
wo de che yao-sheu dyo le

how long will it take to repair?
多长时间能修好?
duō cháng shíjiān néng xiū hǎo?
dwoe chang sheu-jyen nung shyo hao?

◆ Hiring a car

I'd like to hire a car for a week
我想租一辆小汽车，租一个星期
wǒ xiǎng zū yī liàng xiǎoqìchē, zū yī ge xīngqī
wo shyang zoo ee lyang sheeao-chee-che, zoo ee ge shing-chee

I'd like to take out comprehensive insurance
我想买全包的保险
wǒ xiǎng mǎi quánbāo de bǎoxiǎn
wo shyang my chwan-bao de bao-shyen

◆ Getting a taxi

is there a taxi rank near here?
这儿附近有出租车停车处吗?
zhèr fùjìn yǒu chūzūchē tíngchēchù ma?
jer foo-jin yoe choo-zoo-che ting-che-choo ma?

I'd like to go to ...
我要到 ... 去
wǒ yào dào ... qù
wo yao dao ... choo

I'd like to book a taxi for 8pm
我要订一辆出租车，晚上8点的
wǒ yào dìng yī liàng chūzūchē, wǎnshang bā diǎn de
wo yao ding ee lyang choo-zoo-che, wan-shang ba dyen de

you can drop me off here, thanks
我可以在这儿下车，谢谢
wǒ kěyǐ zài zhèr xiàchē, xièxie
wo ke-yee zy jer shya-che, shyay-shyay

how much will it be to go to the airport?
去机场多少钱？
qù jīchǎng duōshǎo qián?
choo jee-chang dwoe-shao chyen?

Understanding

保存好您的票 *bǎocún hǎo nín de piào*	keep your ticket
租车处 *zūchēchù*	car hire
停车场 *tíngchēchǎng*	car park
满了 *mǎn le*	full *(car park)*
进入车道 *jìnrù chēdào*	get in lane
禁止停车 *jìnzhǐtíngchē*	no parking
其他方向 *qítā fāngxiàng*	other directions
减速 *jiǎnsù*	slow
停车位置 *tíngchē wèizhi*	spaces *(car park)*

我需要你的驾驶执照，它是你另一种身份证，还有你的地址证明和信用卡
wǒ xūyào nǐ de jiàshǐ zhízhào, tā shì nǐ lìng yī zhǒng shēnfènzhèng, hái yǒu nǐ de dìzhǐ zhèngmíng hé xìnyòngkǎ
wo shu-yao nee de jya-sheu zheu-jao, ta sheu nee ling ee jong sheun-feun-jung, hy yoe nee de dee-jeu jung-ming he shin-yong-ka
I'll need your driving licence, another form of ID, proof of address and your credit card

预付款 ¥2,000人民币
yùfùkuǎn liǎngqiān yuán rénmínbì
yoo-foo-kwan lyang-chyen ywan jeun-min-bee
there's a 2,000-yuan deposit to pay

好，上车吧，我把你带到…
hǎo, shàng chē ba, wǒ bǎ nǐ dài dào…
hao, shang che ba, wo ba nee dy dao…
alright, get in, I'll take you as far as …

BY BOAT

The only boat trip you can take on the Grand Canal, which at 1,800 km is the longest man-made waterway in the world, is the tourist ferry between 杭州 Hángzhōu (*hang-joe*) and 苏州 Sūzhōu (*soo-joe*). The 150-km journey takes twelve hours.

Boat trips are also available on some of the lakes, for example 南京 Nánjīng (*nan-jing*), 无锡 Wúxī (*woo-shee*) and 桂林 Guìlín (*gwaylin*).

Expressing yourself

how long is the crossing?
轮渡多长时间？
lúndù duō cháng shíjiān?
loon-doo dwoe chang sheu-jyen?

I'm (feeling) seasick
我晕船
wǒ yùnchuán
wo yoon-chwan

Understanding

只限于步行 ***zhǐxiànyú bùxíng*** — foot passengers only
下一班船在 … 开出 ***xià yī bān chuán zài … kāichū*** — next ferry departure/crossing at …

TRAVELLING

ACCOMMODATION

Big cities and tourist areas have Western-style hotels of at least three stars, and there are many with four and five stars. Most belong to major international chains. It is usually cheaper if you book through a travel agent before you set off.

Small private hotels called 招待所 **zhāodàisuǒ** (*jao-dy-swoe*) are cheaper. They were originally intended for Chinese guests but are now opening up to foreigners. Rooms are quite basic, and in most cases no meals are provided (not even breakfast). Owners rarely speak English, and you will have to pay in cash.

University campuses also offer very cheap accommodation, usually during the long summer break. In big cities, foreign students can often stay in university dormitories (宿舍 **sùshè** *soo-she*) on presentation of an international student card. Some are open to young travellers as well as students.

At most hotels, if you haven't made a reservation beforehand you can negotiate a discount on the price of your room. This can be anything between 10 and 50% depending on the hotel and the time of year.

Youth hostels are still not common in China, but provision is expanding rapidly and hostels can be found in many major cities.

If you want to camp out in the open you will need a special permit, which can be hard to come by. Camping and camping shops are rapidly becoming more popular.

While in China, do as the Chinese do, and drink bottled or boiled water, rather than tap water, and do not have ice cubes in your drink.

The electric current in China is 220V, and there are five different types of plug. Adapters are readily available in Hong Kong and in major cities, but are less easily found in smaller towns.

Note that in China (as in the US), the "first floor" corresponds to the ground floor in Britain.

The basics

bath	（洗）澡 ***(xǐ) zǎo*** *(shee) zao*
bathroom	洗澡间 ***xǐzǎojiān*** *shee-zao-jyen*
bathroom with shower	带淋浴的洗澡间 ***dài línyù de xǐzǎojiān*** *dy lin-yoo de shee-zao-jyen*
bed	床 ***chuáng*** *chwang*
bed and breakfast	住宿加早餐 ***zhùsù jiā zǎocān*** *joo-soo jya zao-tsan*
cable television	有线电视 ***yǒuxiàn diànshì*** *yoe-shyen dyen-sheu*
campsite	野营地 ***yěyíngdì*** *yay-ying-dee*
caravan	旅行房车 ***lǚxíng fángchē*** *lu-shing fang-che*
cottage	乡村房子 ***xiāngcūn fángzi*** *shyang-tsoon fang-zeu*
double bed	双人床 ***shuāngrénchuáng*** *shwang-jeun-chwang*
double room	双人房 ***shuāngrénfáng*** *shwang-jeun-fang*
en-suite bathroom	带洗澡间的卧室 ***dài xǐzǎojiān de wòshì*** *dy shee-zao-jyen de wo-sheu*
family room	家庭房 ***jiātíngfáng*** *jya-ting-fang*
flat	套房 ***tàofáng*** *tao-fang*
full-board	全食宿 ***quánshísù*** *chwan-sheu-soo*
fully inclusive	全包 ***quánbāo*** *chwan-bao*
half-board	半食宿 ***bànshísù*** *ban-sheu-soo*
hotel	饭店 ***fàndiàn*** *fan-dyen*
key	钥匙 ***yàoshi*** *yao-sheu*
rent	房租 ***fángzū*** *fang-zoo*
self-catering	自理膳食 ***zìlǐ shànshí*** *zeu-lee shan-sheu*
shower	淋浴 ***línyù*** *lin-yoo*
single bed	单人床 ***dānrénchuáng*** *dan-jeun-chwang*
single room	单人房 ***dānrénfáng*** *dan-jeun-fang*
tenant	房客 ***fángkè*** *fang-ke*
tent	帐篷 ***zhàngpeng*** *jang-pung*
toilets	厕所 ***cèsuǒ*** *tseu-swoe*, 卫生间 ***wèishēngjiān*** *way-shung-jyen*
youth hostel	青年旅馆 ***qīngnián lǚguǎn*** *ching-nyen lu-gwan*
to book	预订 ***yùdìng*** *yoo-ding*, 订 ***dìng*** *ding*
to rent	租（房）***zū*** *zoo*
to reserve	预订 ***yùdìng*** *yoo-ding*, 订 ***dìng*** *ding*

Expressing yourself

I have a reservation for a room
我订了一个房间
wǒ dìng le yī ge fángjiān
wo ding-le ee ge fang-jyen

the name's …
名字是 …
míngzi shì …
ming-zeu sheu …

do you take credit cards?
收信用卡吗?
shōu xìnyòngkǎ ma?
shoe shin-yong-ka ma?

Understanding

客满 *kè mǎn* full
私人的 *sīrén de* private
前台 *qiántái* reception
厕所 *cèsuǒ*, 卫生间 *wèishēngjiān* toilets
空房 *kòngfáng* vacancies

我看一下您的护照, 可以吗?
wǒ kàn yīxià nín de hùzhào, kěyǐ ma?
wo kan ee-shya nin de hoo-jao, ke-yee ma?
could I see your passport, please?

您填一下这张表好吗?
nín tián yīxià zhè zhāng biǎo, hǎo ma?
nin tyen ee-shya je jang beeao, hao ma?
could you fill in this form?

HOTELS

Expressing yourself

do you have any vacancies?
还有空房吗?
hái yǒu kòngfáng ma?
hy yoe kong-fang ma?

how much is a double room per night?
双人房一个晚上多少钱?
shuāngrénfáng yī ge wǎnshang duōshǎo qián?
shwang-jeun-fang ee ge wan-shang dwoe-shao chyen?

I'd like to reserve a double room/a single room
我要订一个双人房/单人房
wǒ yào dìng yī ge shuāngrénfáng/dānrénfáng
wo yao ding ee ge shwang-jeun-fang/dan-jeun-fang

for three nights
住三个晚上
zhù sān ge wǎnshang
joo san ge wan-shang

would it be possible to stay an extra night?
我可以多住一个晚上吗?
wǒ kěyǐ duō zhù yī ge wǎnshang ma?
wo ke-yee dwoe joo ee ge wan-shang ma?

do you have any rooms available for tonight?
今天晚上有空房吗?
jīntiān wǎnshang yǒu kòngfáng ma?
jin-tyen wan-shang yoe kong-fang ma?

do you have any family rooms?
有家庭房吗?
yǒu jiātíngfáng ma?
yoe jya-ting-fang ma?

would it be possible to add an extra bed?
可以给我们加一张床吗?
kěyǐ gěi wǒmen jiā yī zhāng chuáng ma?
ke-yee gay wo-meun jya ee jang chwang ma?

could I see the room first?
我可以先看一下房间吗?
wǒ kěyǐ xiān kàn yīxià fángjiān ma?
wo ke-yee shyen kan ee-shya fang-jyen ma?

do you have anything bigger/quieter?
你们有没有大一点儿的房间/安静一点儿的房间?
nǐmen yǒu méi yǒu dà yīdiǎnr de fángjiān/ānjìng yīdiǎnr de fángjiān?
ni-meun yoe may yoe da ee-dyar de fang-jyen/an-jing ee-dyar de fang-jyen?

that's fine, I'll take it
行，我要了
xíng, wǒ yào le
shing, wo yao le

could you recommend any other hotels?
您能给我推荐其他的饭店吗?
nín néng gěi wǒ tuījiàn qítā de fàndiàn ma?
nin nung gay woe tway-jyen chee-ta de fan-dyen ma?

is breakfast included?
带早餐吗?
dài zǎocān ma?
dy zao-tsan ma?

what time do you serve breakfast?
早餐在什么时间?
zǎocān zài shénme shíjiān?
zao-tsan zy sheun-me sheu-jyen?

is there a lift?
有电梯吗?
yǒu diàntī ma?
yoe dyen-tee ma?

is the hotel near the centre of town?
饭店在市中心附近吗?
fàndiàn zài shìzhōngxīn fùjìn ma?
fan-dyen zy sheu-jong-shin foo-jin ma?

what time will the room be ready?
什么时候这个房间可以用?
shénme shíhou zhè ge fángjiān kěyǐ yòng?
sheun-me sheu-hoe je ge fang-jyen ke-yee yong?

the key for room ..., please
请给我 … 房间的钥匙，好吗？
qǐng gěi wǒ ... fángjiān de yàoshi, hǎo ma?
ching gay wo ... fang-jyen de yao-sheu, hao ma?

could I have an extra blanket?
可以给我加一条毯子吗？
kěyǐ gěi wǒ jiā yī tiáo tǎnzi ma?
ke-yee gay wo jya ee teeao tan-zeu ma?

the air conditioning isn't working
空调坏了
kōngtiáo huài le
kong-teeao hwhy le

Understanding

对不起，客满了
duìbuqǐ, kè mǎn le
dway-boo-chee, ke man le
I'm sorry, but we're full

我们只剩下一个单人房
wǒmen zhǐ shèngxià yī ge dānrénfáng
wo-meun jeu shung-shya ee ge dan-jeun-fang
we only have a single room available

您住几个晚上？
nín zhù jǐ ge wǎnshang?
nin joo jee ge wan-shang?
how many nights is it for?

请告诉我您的名字，好吗？
qǐng gàosu wǒ nín de míngzi, hǎo ma?
ching gao-soo wo nin de ming-zeu, hao ma?
what's your name, please?

住进的时间是从中午开始
zhùjìn de shíjiān shì cóng zhōngwǔ kāishǐ
joo-jin de sheu-jyen sheu tsong jong-woo ky-sheu
check-in is from midday

早上11点以前结账离开
zǎoshang shíyī diǎn yǐqián jiézhàng líkāi
zao-shang sheu-ee dyen ee-chyen jyay-jang lee-ky
you have to check out before 11am

早餐在餐厅，从 7.30到 9.00
zǎocān zài cāntīng, cóng qī diǎn bàn dào jiǔ diǎn
zao-tsan zy tsan-ting, tsong chee dyen ban dao jyo dyen
breakfast is served in the restaurant between 7.30 and 9.00

您早上要一份报吗？
nín zǎoshang yào yī fèn bào ma?
nin zao-shang yao ee feun bao ma?
would you like a newspaper in the morning?

您的房间还没整理好
nín de fángjiān hái méi zhěnglǐ hǎo
nin de fang-jyen hy may jung-lee hao
your room isn't ready yet

您可先把包搁在这儿
nín kěyǐ xiān bǎ bāo gē zài zhèr
nin ke-yee shyen ba bao ge zy jer
you can leave your bags here

YOUTH HOSTELS

Expressing yourself

do you have space for two people for tonight?
你们今天晚上有两个空床位吗？
nǐmen jīntiān wǎnshang yǒu liǎng ge kòng chuángwèi ma?
ni-meun jin-tyen wan-shang yoe lyang ge kong chwang-way ma?

we've booked two beds for three nights
我们订了两个床位，住三个晚上
wǒmen dìng le liǎng ge chuángwèi, zhù sān ge wǎnshang
wo-meun ding le lyang ge chwang-way, joo san ge wan-shang

could I leave my backpack at reception?
我可以把背包搁在前台吗?
wǒ kěyǐ bǎ bēibāo gē zài qiántái ma?
wo ke-yee ba bay-bao ge zy chyen-ty ma?

do you have somewhere we could leave our bikes?
你们有搁自行车的地方吗?
nǐmen yǒu gē zìxíngchē de dìfang ma?
ni-meun yoe ge zeu-shing-che de dee-fang ma?

I'll come back for it around 7 o'clock
我7点左右来取
wǒ qī diǎn zuǒyòu lái qǔ
wo chee dyen zwoe-yoe ly choo

there's no hot water
没有热水
méi yǒu rè shuǐ
may yoe je shway

the sink's blocked
水池堵了
shuǐchí dǔ le
shway-cheu doo le

Understanding

您有会员卡吗?
nín yǒu huìyuánkǎ ma?
nin yoe hway-ywan-ka ma?
do you have a membership card?

床单、枕套、等都提供
chuángdān, zhěntào, děng dōu tígòng
chwang-dan jeun-tao dung doe tee-gong
bed linen is provided

这个青年旅馆晚上6点再开门
zhè ge qīngnián lǚguǎn wǎnshang liùdiǎn zài kāimén
je ge ching-nyen lu-gwan wan-shang lyo-dyen zy ky-meun
the hostel reopens at 6pm

SELF-CATERING

Expressing yourself

we're looking for somewhere to rent near a town
我们想在城镇附近租一个房子
wǒmen xiǎng zài chéngzhèn fùjìn zū yī ge fángzi
wo-meun shyang zy chung-jeun foo-jin zoo ee ge fang-zeu

where do we pick up/leave the keys?
我们在哪儿拿钥匙?/我们把钥匙搁在哪儿?
wǒmen zài nǎr ná yàoshi?/wǒmen bǎ yàoshi gē zài nǎr?
wo-meun zy nar na yao-sheu?/wo-meun ba yao-sheu ge zy nar?

is electricity included in the price?
价格包括电费吗?
jiàgé bāokuò diànfèi ma?
jya-ge bao-kwoe dyen-fay ma?

are bed linen and towels provided?
提供床单和毛巾吗?
tígòng chuángdān hé máojīn ma?
tee-gong chwang-dan he mao-jin ma?

is a car necessary?
是不是需要开车?
shì bu shì xūyào kāichē?
sheu boo sheu shoo-yao ky-che?

is there a pool?
有游泳池吗?
yǒu yóuyǒngchí ma?
yoe yoe-yong-cheu ma?

is the accommodation suitable for elderly people?
这个住处适合老年人住吗?
zhè ge zhùchù shìhé lǎoniánrén zhù ma?
je ge joo-choo sheu-he lao-nyen-jeun joo ma?

where is the nearest supermarket?
最近的超市在哪儿?
zuì jìn de chāoshì zài nǎr?
zway jin de chao-sheu zy nar?

Understanding

您离开时，房间应保持整洁
nín líkāi shí, fāngjiān yīng bǎochí zhěngjié
nin lee-ky sheu, fang-jyen ying bao-cheu jung-jyay
please leave the house clean and tidy after you leave

这所房子家具俱全
zhè suǒ fángzi jiājù jùquán
je swoe fang-zeu jya-joo joo-chwan
the house is fully furnished

一切都包括在价格里
yīqiè dōu bāokuò zài jiàgé lǐ
ee-chyay doe bao-kwoe zy jya-ge lee
everything is included in the price

在这一带乡下您得有车
zài zhè yīdài xiāngxia nín děi yǒu chē
zy je ee-dy shyang-shya nin day yoe che
you really need a car in this part of the country

CAMPING

Expressing yourself

is there a campsite near here?
这儿附近有野营地吗?
zhèr fùjìn yǒu yěyíngdì ma?
jer foo-jin yoe yay-ying-dee ma?

I'd like to book a space for a two-person tent for three nights
我想订一个放两人帐篷的位置，订三个晚上
wǒ xiǎng dìng yī ge fàng liǎng rén zhàngpeng de wèizhi, dìng sān ge wǎnshang
wo shyang ding ee ge fang lyang-jeun jang-pung de way-jeu, ding san ge wan-shang

how much is it a night?
一个晚上多少钱?
yī ge wǎnshang duōshǎo qián?
ee ge wan-shang dwoe-shao chyen?

where is the shower block?
淋浴房在哪儿?
línyùfáng zài nǎr?
lin-yoo-fang zy nar?

can we pay, please? we were at space …
请给我们结账，好吗？我们在 … 位置
qǐng gěi wǒmen jiézhàng, hǎo ma? wǒmen zài … wèizhi
ching gay wo-meun jyay-jang, hao ma? wo-meun zy …way-jeu

Understanding

每人每个晚上 …
měi rén měi ge wǎnshang …
may jeun may ge wan-shang …
it's … per person per night

您需要什么东西就来找我们
nín xūyào shénme dōngxi jiù lái zhǎo wǒmen
nin shoo-yao sheun-me dong-shee jyo ly jao wo-meun
if you need anything, just come and ask

Chefs in top restaurants can rustle up a real feast with many courses, delightful both to the eye and, of course, to eat. Dining rooms in large establishments offer private rooms, with your own staff to serve you, as well as the public areas.

Smaller local establishments are worth a visit too: you will often be pleasantly surprised by the quality of simple dishes like noodles, dumplings, soup and stews. Here you will be seated at wooden tables alongside Chinese customers, an experience you would miss out on if you stuck to the more upmarket restaurants frequented by tourists.

In hotels, meals are served early: lunch at around midday and dinner no later than 7pm. You can eat later in restaurants. Service is usually fast and customers don't sit around after they have finished.

You can get snacks 小吃 ***xiǎochī*** *sheeao-cheu* until midnight or later, for just a few yuan, from the many street stalls.

Hamburgers and pizza have recently become very popular in China. Unlike in the West, where fast food restaurants can be frowned upon, in China they have a certain prestige.

Remember never to stick your chopsticks in the rice – it is believed to be unlucky in China.

After a meal you often pay at the counter. When eating out as a group the Chinese do not usually split the bill, and there is no tipping.

It is common in China for people to drink boiled water, often hot, from a flask. This comes from the idea in Chinese medicine that hot food and drink can maintain a stable body temperature. China's other favourite drink is tea – there are many different kinds - which is usually drunk unsweetened inbetween meals. Beer is popular too: 青岛啤酒 ***qīngdǎo píjiǔ*** *ching-dao pee-jyo* Qingdao Beer, which is made with spring water to an original German recipe is of a high quality, but there are many other excellent varieties. Wine, both Chinese and imported, is also becoming

more popular, taking over from traditional Chinese spirits which can be up to 70% proof. The most famous alcoholic beverage in China is a potent brew called 茅台酒 ***máotáijiŭ*** *mao-ty-jyo* made from sorghum grain and wheat. It is considered a real honour to be served a glass of ***máotái***! Brandy (白兰地 ***báilándì*** *by-lan-dee*) has recently become popular in China. In big cities and tourist areas, mineral water, fruit juices, fizzy drinks and various beers are all easy to come by.

The basics

beer 啤酒 ***píjiŭ*** *pee-jyo*
bill 账单 ***zhàngdān*** *jang-dan*
black coffee 黑咖啡 ***hēi kāfēi*** *hay ka-fay*
bottle 瓶 ***píng*** *ping*
bread 面包 ***miànbāo*** *myen-bao*
breakfast 早餐 ***zăocān*** *zao-tsan*
coffee 咖啡 ***kāfēi*** *ka-fay*
Coke® 可乐 ***kĕlè*** *ke-le*
dessert 甜食 ***tiánshí*** *tyen-sheu*
dinner 晚餐 ***wăncān*** *wan-tsan*
fruit juice 果汁 ***guŏzhī*** *gwoe-jeu*
lemonade 柠檬汽水 ***níngméng qìshuĭ*** *ning-mung chee-shway*
lunch 午餐 ***wŭcān*** *woo-tsan*
main course 主菜 ***zhŭcài*** *joo-tsy*
menu 菜单 ***càidān*** *tsy-dan*
mineral water 矿泉水 ***kuàngquánshuĭ*** *kwang-chwan-shway*
red wine 红葡萄酒 ***hóng pútaojiŭ*** *hong poo-tao-jyo*
rosé wine 粉红葡萄酒 ***fĕnhóng pútaojiŭ*** *feun-hong poo-tao-jyo*
salad 沙拉 ***shālā*** *sha-la*
sandwich 三明治 ***sānmíngzhì*** *san-ming-jeu*
service 服务 ***fúwù*** *foo-woo*
sparkling water 苏打水 ***súdá*** *soo-da*
sparkling wine 汽酒 ***qìjiŭ*** *chee-jyo*
starter 第一道菜 ***dì yī dào cài*** *dee ee dao tsy*
still water 无汽的 ***wú qì de shuĭ*** *woo chee de shway*
tea 茶 ***chá*** *cha*

tip	小费 ***xiǎofèi*** *sheeao-fay*
water	水 ***shuǐ*** *shway*
white coffee	牛奶咖啡 ***niú nǎi kā fēi*** *nyo ny ka fay*
white wine	白葡萄酒 ***bái pútaojiǔ*** *by poo-tao-jyo*
wine	葡萄酒 ***pútaojiǔ*** *poo-tao-jyo*
wine list	酒单 ***jiǔdān*** *jyo-dan*
to eat	吃 ***chī*** *cheu*
to have breakfast	吃早餐 ***chī zǎocān*** *cheu zao-tsan*
to have dinner	吃晚餐 ***chī wǎncān*** *cheu wan-tsan*
to have lunch	吃午餐 ***chī wǔcān*** *cheu woo-tsan*
to order	点菜 ***diǎn cài*** *dyen tsy*

Expressing yourself

shall we go and have something to eat?
我们出去吃饭，好吗？
wǒmen chūqu chī fàn, hǎo ma?
wo-meun choo-choo cheu fan, hao ma?

do you want to go for a drink?
出去喝酒，好吗？
chūqu hē jiǔ, hǎo ma?
choo-choo he jyo, hao ma?

can you recommend a good restaurant?
你能推荐一个好餐馆吗？
nǐ néng tuījiàn yī ge hǎo cānguǎn ma?
nee nung tway-jyen ee ge hao tsan-gwan ma?

I'm not very hungry
我不太饿
wǒ bú tài è
wo boo ty e

excuse me! *(to call the waiter)*
服务员！
fúwùyuán!
foo-woo-ywan!

cheers!
干杯！
gānbēi!
gan-bay!

that was lovely
菜很好吃
cài hěn hǎochī
tsy heun hao-cheu

could you bring us an ashtray, please?
请给我拿一个烟灰缸，好吗？
qǐng gěi wǒ ná yī ge yānhuīgāng, hǎo ma?
ching gay wo na ee ge yan-hway-gang, hao ma?

where are the toilets, please?
请问，厕所在哪儿？
qǐng wèn, cèsuǒ zài nǎr?
ching weun, tse-swoe zy nar?

Understanding

外卖店盒饭
wàimàidiàn héfàn
wy-my-dyen he-fan
takeaway

对不起，我们十一点停止服务
duìbuqǐ, wǒmen shíyī diǎn tíngzhǐ fúwù
dway-boo-chee, wo-meun sheu-yee dyen ting-jeu foo-woo
I'm sorry, we stop serving at 11pm

RESERVING A TABLE

Expressing yourself

I'd like to reserve a table for tomorrow evening
我要订一张餐桌，明天晚上
wǒ yào dìng yī zhāng cānzhuō, míngtiān wǎnshang
wo yao ding ee jang tsan-jwoe, ming-tyen wan-shang

for two people
两个人
liǎng ge rín
lyang-ge jeun

around 8 o'clock
八点左右
bā diǎn zuǒyòu
ba dyen zwoe-yoe

do you have a table available any earlier than that?
有没有比这个早一点儿的空桌
yǒu méi yǒu bǐ zhè ge zǎo yīdiǎnr de kòng zhuō?
yoe may yoe bee jeu ge zao ee-dyar de kong jwoe?

I've reserved a table – the name's ...
我订了一张餐桌 – 名字是 …
wǒ dìng le yī zhāng cānzhuō – míngzi shì ...
wo ding le ee jang tsan-jwoe – ming-zeu sheu ...

Understanding

已预订
yǐ yùdìng
ee yoo-ding
reserved

几个人
jǐ ge rén?
jee ge jeun?
for how many people?

抽烟吗?
chōuyān ma?
choe-yan ma?
smoking or non-smoking?

什么时间的?
shénme shíjiān de?
sheun-me sheu-jyen de?
for what time?

名字?
míngzi?
ming-zeu?
what's the name?

预订了吗?
yùdìng le ma?
yoo-ding le ma?
do you have a reservation?

在墙角的那张桌子行吗?
zài qiángjiǎo de nà zhāng zhuōzi xíng ma?
zy chyang-jeeao de na jang jwoe-zeu shing ma?
is this table in the corner OK for you?

对不起，现在没有位子了
duìbuqǐ, xiànzài méi yǒu wèizi le
dway-boo-chee, shyen-zy may yoe way-zeu le
I'm afraid we're full at the moment

ORDERING FOOD

Expressing yourself

yes, we're ready to order
好，我们现在点菜
hǎo, wǒmen xiànzài diǎn cài
hao, wo-meun shyen-zy dyen tsy

no, could you give us a few more minutes?
不，我们可以再等一会儿吗？
bù, wǒmen kěyǐ zài děng yīhuìr ma?
boo, wo-meun ke-yee zy dung ee-hwayr ma?

I'd like …
我要 …
wǒ yào …
wo yao …

could I have …?
我想要 … 可以吗？
wǒ xiǎng yào … kěyǐ ma?
wo shyang yao … ke-yee ma?

I'll have that
我吃这个
wǒ chī zhè ge
wo cheu jeu ge

does it come with vegetables?
这个菜也带蔬菜吗？
zhè ge cài yě dài shūcài ma?
jeu ge tsy yay dy shoo-tsy ma?

what are today's specials?
今天的特别菜是什么？
jīntiān de tèbié cài shì shénme?
jin-tyen de te-byay tsy sheu sheun-me?

what desserts do you have?
你们有什么甜食？
nǐmen yǒu shénme tiánshí?
nee-meun yoe sheun-me tyen-sheu?

I'm allergic to nuts/wheat/seafood/citrus fruit
我对坚果/小麦/海味/柑橘类水果过敏
wǒ duì jiānguǒ/xiǎomài/hǎiwèi/gānjúlèi shuǐguǒ guòmǐn
wo dway jyen-gwoe/sheeow-my/hy-way/gan-ju-lay shway-gwoe gwoe-min

some water, please
请给我点儿水，好吗？
qǐng gěi wǒ diǎnr shuǐ, hǎo ma?
ching gay wo dyar shway, hao ma?

a bottle of red/white wine
来一瓶红/白葡萄酒
lái yī píng hóng/bái pútaojiǔ
ly ee ping hong/by poo-tao-jyo

that's for me
是我的
shì wǒ de
sheu wo de

this isn't what I ordered, I wanted …
这不是我点的，我点的是 …
zhè bú shì wǒ diǎn de, wǒ diǎn de shì …
jeu boo sheu wo dyen de, wo dyen de sheu …

could you bring us another jug of water, please?
请再给我们一罐水，好吗？
qǐng zài gěi wǒmen yī guàn shuǐ, hǎo ma?
ching zy gay wo-meun ee gwan shway, hao ma?

Understanding

你们现在点菜吗？
nǐmen xiànzài diǎn cài ma?
nee-meun shyen-zy dyen tsy ma?
are you ready to order?

对不起，没有 … 了
dùbuqǐ, méi yǒu … le
dway-boo-chee, may yoe … le
I'm sorry, we don't have any … left

您喝点儿什么？
nín hē diǎnr shénme?
nin he dyar sheun-me?
what would you like to drink?

怎么样？
zěnmeyàng?
zeun-me-yang?
was everything OK?

一会儿就来
yī huìr jiù lái
ee hwayr jyo ly
I'll come back in a few minutes

您要甜食还是咖啡？
nín yào tiánshí háishì kāfēi?
nin yao tyen-sheu hy-sheu ka-fay?
would you like dessert or coffee?

BARS AND CAFÉS

Expressing yourself

I'd like ...
我想要 …
wǒ xiǎng yào ...
wo shyang yao ...

a Coke®/a diet Coke®
一个可乐/一个健怡可乐
yī ge kělè/yī ge jiànyí kělè
ee ge ke-le/ee ge jyen-yee ke-le

a glass of white/red wine
一杯白葡萄酒/红葡萄酒
yī bēi bái pútaojiǔ/hóng pútaojiǔ
ee bay by poo-tao-jyo/hong poo-tao-jyo

a black/white coffee
一杯黑/白咖啡
yī bēi hēi/bái kāfēi
ee bay hay/by ka-fay

a cup of tea
一杯茶
yī bēi chá
ee bay cha

a cup of hot chocolate
一杯热巧克力
yī bēi rè qiǎokèlì
ee bay je cheeao-ke-lee

the same again, please
请给我再来一个
qǐng gěi wǒ zài lái yī ge
ching gay wo zy ly ee ge

Understanding

无酒精的
wú jiǔjīng de
woo jyo-jing de
non-alcoholic

这是非抽烟区
zhè shì fēi chōuyān qū
jeu sheu fay choe-yan choo
this is the non-smoking area

请您现在付账单，好吗？
qǐng nín xiànzài fù zhàngdān, hǎo ma?
ching nin shyen-zy foo jang-dan, hao ma?
could I ask you to pay now, please?

您要什么？
nín yào shénme?
nin yao sheun-me?
what would you like?

Some informal expressions

我撑死了 ***wǒ chēng sǐ le*** *wo chung seu le* I'm completely stuffed
他喝得烂醉 ***tā hē de làn zuì*** *ta he de lan zway* he's wasted!

THE BILL

Expressing yourself

the bill, please
我们付账单，好吗？
wǒmen fù zhàngdān, hǎo ma?
wo-meun foo jang-dan, hao ma?

how much do I owe you?
多少钱？
duōshǎo qián?
dwoe-shao chyen?

do you take credit cards?
你们收信用卡吗？
nǐmen shōu xìnyòngkǎ ma?
nee-meun shoe shin-yong-ka ma?

I think there's a mistake in the bill
我觉得账单里有个错
wǒ juéde zhàngdān lǐ yǒu ge cuò
wo jway-de jang-dan lee yoe ge tswoe

is service included?
包括服务吗？
bāokuò fúwù ma?
bao-kwoe foo-woo ma?

Understanding

你们是一起付吗？
nǐmen shì yīqǐ fù ma?
nee-meun sheu ee-chee foo ma?
are you all paying together?

是，包括服务
shì, bāokuò fúwù
sheu, bao-kwoe foo-woo
yes, service is included

So great is the variety of food found in China that it is difficult to generalize about its characteristics, but the colourful appearance and aromatic qualities are striking. From large famous restaurants to simple meals created in tiny kitchens you will find much to delight your senses, and discover much that is typical of the region and the people who produce it.

Yet wherever you travel in China you can always taste specialities from other regions.

Perhaps four regional cuisines are best known to the West:

Shandong food – the imperial food for more than 500 years in Chinese history, this food is typical of the northern regions of the country, with lots of grilled, roasted and braised dishes, clean, fresh flavours and characterized by the use of shallots and garlic to give fresh pungent flavours.

Sichuan (or **Szechuan**) **food** – based in the south-western part of China, it is said to have a range of over 5,000 dishes, most of which are highly spiced, characterized by the use of typical Sichuan produce such as chilli, pepper and anise, with ginger, garlic and fermented soya bean also being common ingredients.

Jiangsu (or **Huaiyang**) **food** – this style of cooking is local to the lower reaches of the Yangtze River, but is famous all over China. Cooking methods include braising, simmering and roasting. It uses very fresh seafood and seasonal produce, and is characterized by beautiful artistic presentation. If you travel through China's south-eastern cities of Yangzhou, Suzhou and Nanjing, make sure you don't miss this wonderful cuisine.

Guangdong (or **Cantonese**) **food** – based in the southern areas near Hong Kong, this is perhaps the style most familiar to Westerners. It has mild flavours and a light, crisp and fresh taste. Many cooking techniques are used in this style, but steaming and stir-frying are common. Try its snake dishes or soup for an unforgettable experience when you travel in the south of

China. Make sure you try 点心 ***diǎnxīn*** *dyen-shin*, steamed dumplings filled with all kinds of savoury and sweet fillings and often eaten as a snack.

As for vegetarian food, you can enjoy a whole range of original dishes in which meat is replaced by tofu (豆腐 ***dòufu*** *doe-foo*), bamboo shoots, dried wild mushrooms and many other vegetables.

◆ types of restaurant 饭店种类

小吃店 ***xiǎochīdiàn*** *sheeao-cheu-dyen*	small local restaurant
饭店 ***fàndiàn*** *fan-dyen*	restaurant/hotel
酒店 ***jiǔdiàn*** *jyo-dyen*	restaurant/hotel
饭馆 ***fànguǎn*** *fan-gwan*	restaurant
餐馆 ***cānguǎn*** *tsan-gwan*	restaurant
餐厅 ***cāntīng*** *tsan-ting*	restaurant, canteen
烤鸭店 ***kǎoyādiàn*** *kao-ya-dyen*	restaurant specializing in Peking duck
海味餐馆 ***hǎiwèi cānguǎn*** *hy-way tsan-gwan*	seafood restaurant
包子铺 ***bāozipù*** *bao-zeu-poo*	restaurant specializing in steamed dumplings
面馆 ***miànguǎn*** *myen-gwan*	noodle restaurant
馄饨馆 ***húntúnguǎn*** *hoon-toon-gwan*	wonton restaurant
清真饭馆 ***qīngzhēn fànguǎn*** *ching-jeun fan-gwan*	Muslim restaurant
素菜餐厅 ***sùcài cāntīng*** *soo-tsy tsan-ting*	vegetarian restaurant
快餐店 ***kuàicāndiàn*** *kwhy-tsan-dyen*	fast-food restaurant

◆ preparation and cooking methods 烹调方法

煮 ***zhǔ*** *joo*	to boil
烧 ***shāo*** *shao*	to braise, to roast
片 ***piàn*** *pyen*	thin slices
做饭 ***zuòfàn*** *zwoe-fan*	to cook
火锅 ***huǒguō*** *hwoe-gwoe*	Chinese hotpot
炖 ***dùn*** *doon*	to stew
蒸 ***zhēng*** *jung*	to steam
炒 ***chǎo*** *chao*	to stir-fry
炸 ***zhá*** *ja*	to deep-fry
熏 ***xūn*** *shoon*	to smoke

烤 ***kǎo*** *kao* — to roast
煎 ***jiān*** *jyen* — to shallow-fry

◆ spices and seasonings 调料

大蒜 ***dàsuàn*** *da-swan* — garlic
香料 ***xiāngliào*** *shyang-leeao* — spices
味精 ***wèijīng*** *way-jing* — MSG (monosodium glutamate)
辣酱油 ***làjiàngyóu*** *la-jyang-yoe* — spiced soy sauce
酱油 ***jiàngyóu*** *jyang-yoe* — soy sauce
干辣椒 ***gānlàjiāo*** *gan-la-jeeao* — dried chillies
辣椒 ***làjiāo*** *la-jeeao* — chillies
胡椒 ***hújiāo*** *hoo-jeeao* — pepper
盐 ***yán*** *yan* — salt
糖 ***táng*** *tang* — sugar
醋 ***cù*** *tsoo* — vinegar

◆ breakfast 常见的早餐食品

油条 ***yóutiáo*** *yoe-teeao* — deep-fried strip of dough
麻花 ***máhuā*** *ma-hwa* — deep-fried twisted strip of dough
油饼儿 ***yóubǐngr*** *yoe-bingr* — deep-fried flatbread
黄油 ***huángyóu*** *hwang-yoe* — butter
粥 ***zhōu*** *joe* — thin rice soup
果酱 ***guǒjiàng*** *gwoe-jyang* — jam
蜂蜜 ***fēngmì*** *fung-mee* — honey
鸡蛋 ***jīdàn*** *jee-dan* — egg
炒鸡蛋 ***chǎo jīdàn*** *chao jee-dan* — scrambled eggs
面包 ***miànbāo*** *myen-bao* — bread
酸奶 ***suānnǎi*** *swan-ny* — yoghurt
豆浆 ***dòujiāng*** *doe-jyang* — soy milk
牛奶 ***niúnǎi*** *nyo-ny* — milk

◆ staple dishes 常见的主食

包子 ***bāozi*** *bao-zeu* — steamed stuffed dumpling
豆沙包 ***dòushābāo*** *doe-sha-bao* — steamed bun stuffed with sweet red bean paste
蒸饺 ***zhēngjiǎo*** *jung-jeeao* — steamed stuffed dumpling
饺子 ***jiǎozi*** *jeeao-zeu* — stuffed dumpling
锅贴 ***guōtiē*** *gwoe-tyay* — lightly fried stuffed dumpling

烧卖 **shāomài** *shao-my*	steamed dumpling with the dough gathered at the top
馒头 **mántou** *man-toe*	steamed bread
花卷儿 **huājuănr** *hwa-jwanr*	steamed twisted bread roll
面条 **miàntiáo** *myen-teeao*	noodles
米饭 **mĭfàn** *mee-fan*	cooked rice
糯米 **nuòmĭ** *nwoe-mee*	sticky rice
粥 **zhōu** *joe*	thin rice soup
炒饭 **chăofàn** *chao-fan*	fried rice
蛋炒饭 **dàn chăofàn** *dan chao-fan*	egg-fried rice
炒米粉 **chăomĭfĕn** *chao-mee-feun*	fried rice noodles
豆腐 **dòufu** *doe-foo*	tofu
豆腐干 **dòufugān** *doe-foo-gan*	flavoured dried tofu
酱豆腐 **jiàngdòufu** *jyang-doe-foo*	fermented tofu
方便面 **fāngbiànmiàn** *fang-byen-myen*	instant noodles
牛肉炒面 **niúròu chăomiàn** *nyo-joe chao-myen*	stir-fried noodles with beef
海鲜炒面 **hăixiān chăomiàn** *hy-shyen chao-myen*	stir-fried noodles with seafood
家常豆腐 **jiācháng dòufu** *jya-chang doe-foo*	stir-fried tofu
麻辣豆腐 **málà dòufu** *ma-la doe-foo*	hot and spicy tofu

◆ lamb dishes 羊肉菜

麻辣羊肉 **málà yángròu** *ma-la yang-joe*	hot and spicy lamb
咖喱羊肉 **gālí yáng-ròu** *ga-lee yang-joe*	curried lamb
什锦羊肉片 **shíjĭn yángròupiàn** *sheu-jin yang-joe-pyen*	lamb strips with vegetables
奶羊肉 **năiyángròu** *ny-yang-joe*	kid meat
麻酱羊肉 **májiàng yángròu** *ma-jyang yang-joe*	lamb in sesame paste sauce
烤羊肉串 **kăo yángròuchuàn** *kao yang-joe-chwan*	barbecued lamb on a skewer

◆ beef dishes 牛肉菜

萝卜牛腩 **luóbo niúnăn** *lwoe-bo nyo-nan*	beef stew with spring turnip
红烧牛肉 **hóngshāo niúròu** *hong-shao nyo-joe*	red stewed beef with soy sauce
咖哩牛肉 **gālí niúròu** *ga-lee nyo-joe*	curried beef
什锦牛肉片 **shíjĭn niúròupiàn** *sheu-jin nyo-joe-pyen*	beef strips with vegetables
宫保牛肉 **gōngbăo niúròu** *gong-bao nyo-joe*	fried beef with cashew nuts or peanuts
蚝油牛肉 **háoyóu niúròu** *hao-yoe nyo-joe*	fried beef in oyster sauce
灯影牛肉 **dēngyĭng niúròu** *dung-ying nyo-joe*	strips of spicy beef steamed and then fried
家常焖牛舌 **jiācháng mèn niúshé** *jya-chang meun nyo-she*	braised ox tongue
笋炒牛肉 **sŭn chăo niúròu** *soon chao nyo-joe*	beef fried with bamboo shoots
麻辣牛肉 **málà niúròu** *ma-la nyo-joe*	hot and spicy beef

◆ pork dishes 猪肉菜

咸鱼蒸肉饼 **xiányú zhēng ròubĭng** *shyen-yoo jung joe-bing*	steamed pork burger cooked with salt cured fish
狮子头 **shīzitóu** *sheu-zeu-toe*	large meatball braised with vegetables
椒盐排骨 **jiāoyán páigŭ** *jeeao-yan py-goo*	spare rib fried with spiced salt
糖醋排骨 **táng cù páigŭ** *tang tsoo py-goo*	sweet and sour spare rib
葱爆里脊 **cōng bào lĭjĭ** *tsong bao lee-jee*	quick-fried tenderloin with chopped Chinese onion
火锅猪排 **huŏguō zhūpái** *hwoe-gwoe joo-py*	hotpot spare ribs
咕老肉 **gūlăoròu** *goo-lao-joe*	sweet and sour pork
回锅肉 **huíguōròu** *hway-gwoe-joe*	twice-cooked pork (boiled then stir-fried)
板栗烧肉 **bănlì shāo ròu** *ban-lee shao joe*	braised pork with chestnuts

米粉蒸肉 **mǐfěn zhēng ròu** *mee-feun jung joe* — steamed pork cooked in crushed spicy rice
肉丝炒饭 **ròusī chǎofàn** *joe-seu chao-fan* — stir-fried rice with finely sliced pork strips
肉丝炒面 **ròusī chǎomiàn** *joe-seu chao-myen* — stir-fried noodles with finely sliced pork strips
笋炒肉片 **sǔn chǎo ròupiàn** *soon chao joe-pyen* — stir-fried pork slices with bamboo shoots
宫保肉丁 **gōngbǎo ròudīng** *gong-bao joe-ding* — fried pork with cashew nuts or peanuts
时菜肉片 **shícài ròupiàn** *sheu-tsy joe-pyen* — stir-fried pork with seasonal vegetables
榨菜炒肉丝 **zhàcài chǎo ròusī** *ja-tsy chao joe-seu* — stir-fried pork strips with hot mustard pickle
滑熘肉片 **huáliū ròupiàn** *hwa-lyo joe-pyen* — quick-fried pork slices in thick sauce
青椒炒肉片 **qīngjiāo chǎo ròupiàn** *ching-jeeao chao joe-pyen* — stir-fried pork with green pepper
叉烧肉 **chāshāoròu** *cha-shao-joe* — marinated grilled pork
炸肉卷儿 **zhá ròujuǎnr** *ja joe-jwanr* — deep-fried pork roll

◆ chicken and poultry dishes 鸡菜

红酒锔鹌鹑 **hóngjiǔ jū ānchún** *hong-jyo joo an-choon* — steamed quails in red wine
烧鸡腿 **shāo jītuǐ** *shao jee-tway* — roast chicken thighs
珊瑚榆树鸡 **shānhú yúshù jī** *shan-hoo yoo-shoo jee* — chicken with crab or ham
佛跳墙 **fótiàoqiáng** *fo-teeao-chyang* — stewed chicken, duck, pig's trotters and seafood in Chinese wine
酱爆鸡丁 **jiàng bào jīdīng** *jyang bao jee-ding* — quick-fried diced chicken breast in yellow bean sauce
宫保鸡丁 **gōngbǎo jīdīng** *gong-bao jee-ding* — stir-fried diced chicken breast with cashew nuts or peanuts
红烧全鸡 **hóngshāo quánjī** *hong-shao chwan-jee* — whole chicken stewed in a rich sauce
怪味鸡 **guàiwèi jī** *gwhy-way jee* — whole chicken with peanuts and peppers
沙锅全鸡 **shāguō quánjī** *sha-gwoe chwan-jee* — casseroled whole chicken

香酥鸡 ***xiāngsū jī*** *shyang-soo jee* crispy spiced chicken
白斩鸡 ***báizhǎn jī*** *by-jan jee* sliced cold chicken eaten with spicy sauces
叫花鸡 ***jiàohuā jī*** *jeeao-hwa jee* marinated chicken cooked over a wood fire
辣子鸡丁 ***làzi jīdīng*** *la-zeu jee-ding* stir-fried diced chicken breast with dried chillies

◆ duck dishes 鸭菜

什锦扒鸭 ***shíjǐn páyā*** *sheu-jin pa-ya* braised duck with vegetables
香酥鸭 ***xiāngsū yā*** *shyang-soo ya* crisp spiced duck
葱爆烧鸭片 ***cōng bào shāoyāpiàn*** *tsong bao shao-ya-pyen* quick-fried sliced roast duck with Chinese onion
酱爆鸭片菜心 ***jiàng bào yāpiàn càixīn*** *jyang bao ya-pyen tsy-shin* quick-fried duck slices in bean sauce with Chinese leaf
红烧全鸭 ***hóngshāo quányā*** *hong-shao chwan-ya* whole duck stewed in a rich sauce
樟茶鸭子 ***zhāngchá yāzi*** *jang-cha ya-zeu* smoked whole duck
烤鸭 ***kǎoyā*** *kao-ya* Peking duck

◆ seafood dishes 海鲜

鳝鱼 ***shànyú*** *shan-yoo* eel
香滑石斑球 ***xiānghuá shíbān qiú*** *shyang-hwa sheu-ban-chyo* fish balls
青灰绣球 ***qīnghuī xiùqiú*** *ching-hway shyo-chyo* dark grey fish balls
虾 ***xiā*** *shya* prawns
蟹肉扒芥菜 ***xièròu pá jiècài*** *shyay-joe pa jyay-tsy* crab meat cooked with mustard leaf
百花玳子 ***bǎihuā dàizi*** *by-hwa dy-zeu* scallops cooked with seafood sauce
煎明虾露 ***jiān míngxiālù*** *jyen ming-shya-loo* shallow-fried prawns
龙虾 ***lóngxiā*** *long-shya* lobster
菊花焦鱼 ***júhuā jiāoyú*** *joo-hwa jeeao-yoo* deep fried crispy fish
鱼 ***yú*** *yoo* fish

酸甜醋鱼 ***suāntián cù yú*** *swan-tyen tsoo yoo*	sweet and sour fish
沙锅鱼头 ***shāguō yútóu*** *sha-gwoe yoo-toe*	fish head slow-cooked in an earthenware pot
蛇 ***shé*** *she*	snake
豉椒田鸡腿 ***chǐjiāo tiánjītuǐ*** *cheu-jeeao tyen-jee-tway*	stir-fried frog's legs with fermented black beans and green pepper

◆ soup 汤类

木须汤 ***mùxūtāng*** *moo-shu tang*	soup with pork, beaten egg and wild black fungus
酸辣汤 ***suānlà tāng*** *swan-la tang*	hot and sour soup with chicken
西红柿鸡蛋汤 ***xīhóngshì jīdàn tāng*** *shee-hong-sheu jee-dan tang*	tomato and egg soup
海鲜汤 ***hǎixiān tāng*** *hy-shyen tang*	seafood soup
馄饨汤 ***húntún tāng*** *hoon-toon tang*	wonton soup
汤面 ***tāngmiàn*** *tang-myen*	noodle soup
豆腐汤 ***dòufu tāng*** *doe-foo tang*	tofu soup
玉米鸡丝汤 ***yùmǐ jīsī tāng*** *yoo-mee jee-seu tang*	chicken and sweetcorn soup
鱼翅汤 ***yúchì tāng*** *yoo-cheu tang*	shark fin soup
鸡丝蘑菇汤 ***jīsī mógu tāng*** *jee-seu mo-goo tang*	chicken and mushroom soup

◆ vegetables 蔬菜

什锦菜 ***shíjǐn cài*** *sheu-jin tsy*	medley of vegetables
芦笋 ***lúsǔn*** *loo-soon*	asparagus
茄子 ***qiézi*** *chyay-zeu*	aubergine
蘑菇 ***mógu*** *mo-goo*	mushrooms
大白菜 ***dàbáicài*** *da-by-tsy*	Chinese cabbage
黄瓜 ***huángguā*** *hwang-gwa*	cucumber
苦瓜 ***kǔguā*** *koo-gwa*	type of bitter cucumber
胡萝卜 ***húluóbo*** *hoo-lwoe-bo*	carrots
萝卜 ***luóbo*** *lwoe-bo*	Chinese turnip
拔丝番薯 ***básī fānshǔ*** *ba-seu fan-shoo*	candied sweet potato
土豆 ***tǔdòu*** *too-doe*	potato
竹笋 ***zhúsǔn*** *joo-soon*	bamboo shoots

FOOD AND DRINK

洋葱 ***yángcōng*** *yang-tsong* — onion
西红柿 ***xīhóngshì*** *shee-hong-sheu* — tomato
豆芽 ***dòuyá*** *doe-ya* — bean sprouts

◆ fruit 水果

杏 ***xìng*** *shing* — apricot
菠萝 ***bōluó*** *bo-lwoe* — pineapple
香蕉 ***xiāngjiāo*** *shyang-jeeao* — banana
樱桃 ***yīngtáo*** *ying-tao* — cherry
柠檬 ***níngméng*** *ning-mung* — lemon
荔枝 ***lìzhī*** *lee-jeu* — lychee
桔子 ***júzi*** *joo-zeu* — mandarin
哈密瓜 ***hāmìguā*** *ha-mee-gwa* — melon
椰汁 ***yēzhī*** *yay-jeu* — coconut milk
橙子 ***chéngzi*** *chung-zeu* — orange
西瓜 ***xīguā*** *shee-gwa* — watermelon
梨 ***lí*** *lee* — pear
桃 ***táo*** *tao* — peach
苹果 ***píngguǒ*** *ping-gwoe* — apple
李子 ***lǐzi*** *lee-zeu* — plum
葡萄 ***pútáo*** *poo-tao* — grape
猕猴桃 ***míhóutáo*** *mee-hoe-tao* — kiwi fruit
草莓 ***cǎoméi*** *tsao-may* — strawberry
柿子 ***shìzi*** *sheu-zeu* — persimmon

◆ desserts 甜点

拔丝香蕉 ***básī xiāngjiāo*** *ba-seu shyang-jeeao* — candied banana
拔丝苹果 ***básī píngguǒ*** *ba-seu ping-gwoe* — candied apple
蛋糕 ***dàngāo*** *dan-gao* — cakes
豌豆黄 ***wāndòuhuáng*** *wan-doe-hwang* — pea flour cake
豆沙包 ***dòushābāo*** *doe-shao-bao* — steamed bun stuffed with sweet red bean paste
点心 ***diǎnxin*** *dyen-shin* — pastry

◆ non-alcoholic drinks 饮料

水 **shuǐ** *shway*	water
白开水 **báikāishuǐ** *by-ky-shway*	boiled water
自来水 **zìláishuǐ** *zeu-ly-shway*	tap water
矿泉水 **kuàngquánshuǐ** *kwang-chwan-shway*	mineral water
可乐 **kělè** *ke-le*	cola
果汁 **guǒzhī** *gwoe-jeu*	fruit juice
西瓜汁 **xīguāzhī** *shee-gwa-jeu*	watermelon juice
汽水 **qìshuǐ** *chee-shway*	fizzy drink/lemonade
咖啡 **kāfēi** *ka-fay*	coffee
茶 **chá** *cha*	tea
花茶 **huāchá** *hwa-cha*	jasmine tea
菊花茶 **júhuā chá** *joo-hwa cha*	chrysanthemum tea
乌龙茶 **wūlóng chá** *woo-long cha*	oolong tea (high-quality, semi-fermented black tea)
红茶 **hóngchá** *hong-cha*	black tea
龙井茶 **lóngjǐng chá** *long-jing cha*	Dragon Well tea (renowned, slightly sweet tea)
绿茶 **lǜchá** *lu-cha*	green tea

◆ alcoholic drinks 酒

葡萄酒 **pútáojiǔ** *poo-tao-jyo*	wine
啤酒 **píjiǔ** *pee-jyo*	beer
香槟酒 **xiāngbīnjiǔ** *shyang-bin-jyo*	champagne
茅台 **máotái** *mao-ty*	maotai spirit
五粮液 **wǔliángyè** *woo-lyang-yay*	wuliangye spirit (a famous spirit distilled from five kinds of grain)
黄酒 **huángjiǔ** *hwang-jyo*	yellow millet rice wine
米酒 **mǐjiǔ** *mee-jyo*	rice wine
白酒 **báijiǔ** *by-jyo*	spirit
二锅头 **èrguōtóu** *er-gwoe-toe*	erguotou (a strong spirit, speciality of Beijing)

One of the most popular pastimes for a night out is karaoke: people hire out a private area in a club or big hotel to have a drink and sing the latest hits.

Concerts of Western classical music or traditional Chinese music are also popular, as are dance performances. There are more than 300 regional forms of opera, with performances in virtually every town. The most famous is, of course, Beijing Opera.

Only luxury hotels show films in English. In public cinemas, all films are dubbed into Chinese.

The price and ambiance of nightclubs varies from region to region. Most are open from 8pm to 2am.

If you get the chance, go and watch a gymnastics display or see a play – just make sure you have the plot explained to you first! Plays usually start at around 6.30pm and last an hour or two. The most expensive tickets include refreshments. Chinese theatre is a real display of acrobatics (特技表演 ***tèjì biǎoyǎn*** *te-jee beeao-yan)* which is considered an art form.

If you are invited to someone's house, arrive on time and bring a gift. Perfume, make-up and red wine have become particularly popular gifts in recent years.

The basics

ballet 芭蕾 ***bāléi*** *ba-lay*
band 乐队 ***yuèduì*** *yway-dway*
bar 酒吧 ***jiǔbā*** *jyo-ba*
cinema 电影院 ***diànyǐngyuàn*** *dyen-ying-ywan*
circus 马戏表演 ***mǎxì biǎoyǎn*** *ma-shee beeao-yan*
classical music 古典音乐 ***gǔdiǎn yīnyuè*** *goo-dyen yin-yway*
club 夜总会 ***yèzǒnghuì*** *yay-zong-hway*
concert 音乐会 ***yīnyuèhuì*** *yin-yway-hway*

GOING OUT

dubbed film	配音电影 ***pèiyīn diànyǐng*** *pay-yin dyen-ying*
festival	联欢节 ***liánhuānjié*** *lyen-hwan-jyay*
film	电影 ***diànyǐng*** *dyen-ying*
folk music	民间音乐 ***mínjiān yīnyuè*** *min-jyen yin-yway*
group	乐队 ***yuèduì*** *yway-dway*
jazz	爵士乐 ***juéshìyuè*** *jway-sheu-yway*
modern dance	现代舞 ***xiàndàiwǔ*** *shyen-dy-woo*
musical	音乐剧 ***yīnyuèjù*** *yin-yway-joo*
party	晚会 ***wǎnhuì*** *wan-hway*
play	剧 ***jù*** *joo*
pop music	流行音乐 ***liúxíng yīnyuè*** *lyo-shing yin-yway*
rock music	摇滚乐 ***yáogǔnyuè*** *yao-goon-yway*
show	演出 ***yǎnchū*** *yan-choo*
subtitled film	原声加字幕 ***yuánshēng jiā zìmù*** *ywan-shung jya zeu-moo*
theatre	剧院 ***jùyuàn*** *joo-jywan*
ticket	票 ***piào*** *peeao*
to book	预订 ***yùdìng*** *yoo-ding*
to go out	到外边去 ***dào wàibiān qù*** *dao wy-byen choo*

SUGGESTIONS AND INVITATIONS

Expressing yourself

where can we go?
我们到哪儿去呢?
wǒmen dào nǎr qù ne?
wo-meun dao nar choo ne?

shall we go for a drink?
我们去喝酒，好吗?
wǒmen qù hē jiǔ, hǎo ma?
wo-meun choo he jyo, hao ma?

do you have plans?
你有计划吗?
nǐ yǒu jìhuà ma?
nee yoe jee-hwa ma?

what do you want to do?
你想做什么呢?
nǐ xiǎng zuò shénme ne?
nee shyang zwoe sheun-me ne?

what are you doing tonight?
今天晚上你做什么?
jīntiān wǎnshang nǐ zuò shénme?
jin-tyen wan-shang nee zwoe sheun-me?

would you like to go to …?
你想去 … 吗?
nǐ xiǎng qù … ma?
nee shyang choo … ma?

we were thinking of going to …
我们打算去 …
wǒmen dǎsuàn qù …
wo-meun da-swan choo …

I can't today, but maybe some other time
今天不行，也许其他时间可以
jīntiān bùxíng, yěxǔ qítā shíjiān kěyǐ
jin-tyen boo-shing, yay-shoo chee-ta sheu-jyen ke-yee

I'm not sure I can make it
我不知道能不能去
wǒ bù zhīdào néng bu néng qù
wo boo jeu-dao nung boo nung choo

I'd love to …
我非常想 …
wǒ fēicháng xiǎng …
wo fay-chang shyang …

ARRANGING TO MEET

Expressing yourself

what time shall we meet?
我们什么时间见？
wǒmen shénme shíjiān jiàn?
wo-meun sheun-me sheu-jyen jyen?

where shall we meet?
我们在哪儿见？
wǒmen zài nǎr jiàn?
wo-meun zy nar jyen?

would it be possible to meet a bit later?
晚一点儿见，可以吗？
wǎn yīdiǎnr jiàn, kěyǐ ma?
wan ee-dyar jyen, ke-yee ma?

I have to meet … at nine
我九点钟得见 …
wǒ jiǔ diǎn zhōng děi jiàn …
wo jyo dyen jong day jyen …

I don't know where it is but I'll find it on the map
我不知道在哪儿，但是我可以查地图找到
wǒ bù zhīdào zài nǎr, dànshì wǒ kěyǐ chá dìtú zhǎodào
wo boo jeu-dao zy nar, dan-sheu wo ke-yee cha dee-too jao-dao

see you tomorrow night
明天晚上见
míngtiān wǎnshang jiàn
ming-tyen wan-shang jyen

I'll meet you later, I have to stop by the hotel first
一会儿见，我得先去饭店
yīhuìr jiàn, wǒ děi xiān qù fàndiàn
ee-hwayr jyen, wo day shyen choo fan-dyen

I'll call/text you if there's a change of plan
如果有变化，我会给你打电话/发手机短信
rúguǒ yǒu biànhuà, wǒ huì gěi nǐ dǎ diànhuà/fā shǒujī duǎnxìn
joo-gwoe yoe byen-hwa, wo hway gay nee da dyen-hwa/fa shoe-jee dwan-shin

are you going to eat beforehand?
你先吃点儿东西吗?
nǐ xiān chī diǎnr dōngxi ma?
nee shyen cheu dyar dong-shee ma?

sorry I'm late
对不起，我来晚了
duìbuqǐ, wǒ lái wǎn le
dway-boo-chee, wo ly wan le

Understanding

你觉得可以吗?
nǐ juéde kěyǐ ma?
nee jway-de ke-yee ma?
is that OK with you?

我们在那儿见
wǒmen zài nàr jiàn
wo-meun zy nar jyen
I'll meet you there

我八点左右来接你
wǒ bā diǎn zuǒyòu lái jiē nǐ
wo ba dyen zwoe-yoe ly jyay nee
I'll come and pick you up about 8

我们可以在 … 外边见
wǒmen kěyǐ zài … wàibiān jiàn
wo-meun ke-yee zy…wy-byen jyen
we can meet outside …

我给你留下电话号码，明天你可以给我打电话
wǒ gěi nǐ liúxià diànhuà hàomǎ, míngtiān nǐ kěyǐ gěi wǒ dǎ diànhuà
wo gay nee lyo-shya dyen-hwa hao-ma, ming-tyen nee ke-yee gay wo da dyen-hwa
I'll give you my number and you can call me tomorrow

Some informal expressions

喝一杯 **hē yī bēi** *he ee bay* to have a drink
吃点儿东西 **chī diǎnr dōngxi** *cheu dyanr dong-shee* to have a bite to eat

FILMS, SHOWS AND CONCERTS

Expressing yourself

is there a guide to what's on?
有没有节目简介?
yǒu méi yǒu jiémù jiǎnjiè?
yoe may yoe jyay-moo jyen-jyay?

two tickets, please
请给我两张票
qǐng gěi wǒ liǎng zhāng piào
ching gay wo lyang jang peeao

I've seen the trailer
我看了电影预告
wǒ kàn le diànyǐng yùgào
wo kan le dyen-ying yoo-gao

I'd like to go and see a show
我想去看演出
wǒ xiǎng qù kàn yǎnchū
wo shyang choo kan yan-choo

I'd like three tickets for ...
我要三张 … 的票
wǒ yào sān zhāng ... de piào
wo yao san jang .... de peeao

it's called ...
叫做 …
jiào zuò ...
jeeao zwoe ...

what time does it start?
什么时间开始?
shénme shíjiān kāishǐ?
sheun-me sheu-jyen ky-sheu?

how long is it on for?
演出多长时间?
yǎnchū duō cháng shíjiān?
yan-choo dwoe chang sheu-jyen?

I'll find out whether there are still tickets available
我去看看是不是还有票
wǒ qù kànkan shì bu shì hái yǒu piào
wo choo kan-kan sheu boo sheu hy yoe peeao

do we need to book in advance?
我们得预先订票吗？
wǒmen děi yùxiān dìng piào ma?
wo-meun day yoo-shyen ding peeao ma?

are there tickets for another day?
有其他天的票吗？
yǒu qítā tiān de piào ma?
yoe chee-ta tyen de peeao ma?

I'd like to go to a bar with live music
我想到有现场音乐的酒吧去
wǒ xiǎng dào yǒu xiànchǎng yīnyuè de jiǔbā qù
wo shyang dao yoe shyen-chang yin-yway de jyo-ba choo

are there any free concerts?
有免费音乐会吗？
yǒu miǎnfèi yīnyuèhuì ma?
yoe myen-fay yin-yway-hway ma?

what sort of music is it?
这是什么音乐？
zhè shì shénme yīnyuè?
je sheu shen-me yin-yway?

Understanding

艺术电影院 *yìshù diànyǐngyuàn*	arthouse cinema
电影巨片 *diànyǐng jùpiān*	blockbuster
已预订 *yǐ yùdìng*	bookings
售票处 *shòupiàochù*	box office
日场 *rìchǎng*	matinée
位置不好的座位 *wèizhi bù hǎo de zuòwèi*	restricted view
从 … 起普遍上映 *cóng … qǐ pǔbiàn shàngyìng*	on general release from …

是露天音乐会
shì lùtiān yīnyuèhuì
sheu loo-tyen yin-yway-hway
it's an open-air concert

对它的评论很好
duì tā de pínglùn hěn hǎo
dway ta de ping-loon heun hao
it's had very good reviews

下星期上映
xià xīngqī shàngyìng
shya shing-chee shang-ying
it comes out next week

晚上八点在首都剧场上映
wǎnshang bā diǎn zài shǒudū jùchǎng shàngyìng
wan-shang ba dyen zy shoe-doo joo-chang shang-ying
it's on at 8pm at the Capital Theatre

那场电影票已售完
nà chǎng diànyǐng piào yǐ shòuwán
na chang dyen-ying peeao ee shoe-wan
that showing's sold out

… 以前的票都预订完了
… yǐqián de piào dōu yùdìng wán le
… ee-chyen de peeao doe yoo-ding wan le
it's all booked up until …

不用预先订票
bú yòng yùxiān dìng piào
boo yong yoo-shyen ding peeao
there's no need to book in advance

这个剧一共一个半小时，包括中间休息
zhè ge jù yīgòng yī ge bàn xiǎoshí, bāokuò zhōngjiān xiūxi
je ge joo ee-gong ee ge ban sheeao-sheu, bao-kwoe jong-jyen shyo-shee
the play lasts an hour and a half, including the interval

请您关掉手机
qǐng nín guāndiào shǒujī
ching nin gwan-deeow shoe-jee
please turn off your mobile phones

PARTIES AND CLUBS

Expressing yourself

I'm having a little leaving party tonight
今天晚上我要开一个小型告别晚会
jīntiān wǎnshang wǒ yào kāi yī ge xiǎoxíng gàobié wǎnhuì
jin-tyen wan-shang wo yao ky ee ge sheeao-shing gao-byay wan-hway

should I bring something to drink?
我带点酒，好不好？
wǒ dài diǎnr jiǔ, hǎo bu hǎo?
wo dy dyar jyo, hao boo hao?

we could go to a club afterwards
结束以后我们可以到夜总会去
jiéshù yǐhòu wǒmen kěyǐ dào yèzǒnghuì qù
jyay-shoo ee-hoe wo-meun ke-yee dao yay-zong-hway choo

do you have to pay to get in?
入场要买票吗？
rùchǎng yào mǎi piào ma?
joo-chang yao my peeao ma?

I have to meet someone inside
我得在里边见一个人
wǒ děi zài lǐbiān jiàn yī ge rén
wo day zy lee-byen jyen ee gee jeun

will you let me back in when I come back?
我回来的时候，可以再进入吗？
wǒ huílái de shíhou, kěyǐ zài jìnrù ma?
wo hway-ly de sheu-hoe, ke-yee zy jin-joo ma?

the DJ's really cool
音乐主持人真酷
yīnyuè zhǔchírén zhēn kù
yin-yway joo-cheu-jeun jeun koo

do you come here often?
你常来这儿吗？
nǐ cháng lái zhèr ma?
nee chang ly jer ma?

can I buy you a drink?
我请你喝酒，好不好？
wǒ qǐng nǐ hē jiǔ, hǎo bu hǎo?
wo ching nee he jyo, hao boo hao?

thanks, but I'm with my boyfriend
谢谢你，不过，我是和我男朋友一起来的
xièxie nĭ, búguò, wŏ shì hé wŏ nán péngyou yīqĭ lái de
shyay-shyay nee, boo-gwoe, wo sheu he wo nan pung-yoe ee-chee ly de

no thanks, I don't smoke
不用了，谢谢，我不会抽烟
bú yòng le, xièxie, wŏ bú huì chōuyān
boo yong le, shyay-shyay, wo boo hway choe-yan

Understanding

免费饮料***miănfèi yĭnliào*** free drink
衣帽间***yīmàojiān*** cloakroom
午夜后收费一百元人民币***wŭyè hòu shōu fèi yībăi yuán rénmínbì*** ¥100 after midnight

王兰芳那儿正开晚会
Wáng Lánfāng nàr zhèng kāi wănhuì
wang lan-fang nar jung ky wan-hway
there's a party at Wang Lanfang's place

你想跳舞吗?
nĭ xiăng tiàowŭ ma?
nee shyang teeao-woo ma?
do you want to dance?

我请你喝酒，好不好?
wŏ qĭng nĭ hē jiŭ, hăo bu hăo?
wo ching nee he jyo, hao boo hao?
can I buy you a drink?

你有火吗?
nĭ yŏu huŏ ma?
nee yoe hwoe ma?
have you got a light?

你有香烟吗?
nĭ yŏu xiāngyān ma?
nee yoe shyang-yan ma?
have you got a cigarette?

我们能再见面吗?
wŏmen néng zài jiànmiàn ma?
wo-meun nung zy jyen-myen ma?
can we see each other again?

我送你回家，好不好?
wŏ sòng nĭ huí jiā, hăo bu hăo?
wo song nee hway jya, hao boo hao?
can I see you home?

TOURISM AND SIGHTSEEING

The CITS (China International Travel Service中国国际旅行社 ***zhōngguó guojì lǚxí ngshè***) tourist information offices are open from 8am to 6pm with some closing for an hour for lunch. They should be able to provide you with information leaflets and a map of the town, and some have English-speaking guides and interpreters. You can also reserve train, plane and boat tickets, hotel rooms and theatre tickets. Sometimes agencies such as CITS may hold tickets for rail journeys, operas, acrobatics performances and concerts even when such tickets are sold out at stations and venues, but prices will be high. Every town has a tourist information office (旅游信息中心 ***lǚyóu xìnxī zhōngxīn*** *lu-yoe shin-shee jong-shin*) and you will be able to find at least one person who speaks English.

Museums are generally open from 9am to 4pm and closed on Mondays. Some tourist attractions stay open until 9pm in summer. Acrobatics performances are popular throughout China, and almost every city has its own troupe of performers.

The basics

ancient 古老 ***gǔlǎo*** *goo-lao*
antique 古董 ***gǔdǒng*** *goo-dong*
area 地方 ***dìfang*** *dee-fang*
castle 城堡 ***chéngbǎo*** *chung-bao*
cathedral 大教堂 ***dà jiàotáng*** *da jeeao-tang*
century 世纪 ***shìjì*** *sheu-jee*
church 教堂 ***jiàotáng*** *jeeao-tang*
exhibition 展览 ***zhǎnlǎn*** *jan-lan*
gallery 画廊 ***huàláng*** *hwa-lang*
modern art 现代美术 ***xiàndài měishù*** *shyen-dy may-shoo*
mosque 清真寺 ***qīngzhēnsì*** *ching-jeun-seu*
museum 博物馆 ***bówùguǎn*** *bo-woo-gwan*

painting	绘画作品 ***huìhuà zuòpǐn*** *hway-hwa zwoe-pin*
park	公园 ***gōngyuán*** *gong-ywan*
ruins	遗迹 ***yíjì*** *ee-jee*
sculpture	雕塑 ***diāosù*** *deeao-soo*
statue	塑像 ***sùxiàng*** *soo-shyang*
street map	街道地图 ***jiēdào dìtú*** *jyay-dao dee-too*
synagogue	犹太教堂 ***yóutài jiàotáng*** *yoe-ty jeeao-tang*
tour guide	导游 ***dǎoyóu*** *dao-yoe*
tourist	旅游者 ***lǚyóuzhě*** *lu-yoe-je*
tourist information centre	旅游信息中心 ***lǚyóu xìnxī zhōngxīn*** *lu-yoe shin-shee jong-shin*
town centre	市中心 ***shì zhōngxīn*** *sheu jong-shin*

Expressing yourself

I'd like some information on …
我想要一些关于 … 的信息材料
wǒ xiǎng yào yīxiē guānyú … de xìnxī cáiliào
wo shyang yao ee-shyay gwan-yoo … de shin-shee tsy-leeao

can you tell me where the tourist information centre is?
您可以告诉我旅游信息中心在哪儿吗?
nín kěyǐ gàosu wǒ lǚyóu xìnxī zhōngxīn zài nǎr ma?
nin ke-yee gao-soo wo lu-yoe shin-shee jong-shin zy nar ma?

do you have a street map of the town?
有城市街道地图吗?
yǒu chéngshì jiēdào dìtú ma?
yoe chung-sheu jyay-dao dee-too ma?

I was told there's an old mosque you can visit
我听说有一个古老的清真寺可以参观
wǒ tīngshuō yǒu yī ge gǔlǎo de qīngzhēnsì kěyǐ cānguān
wo ting-shwoe yoe ee ge goo-lao de ching-jeun-seu ke-yee tsan-gwan

can you show me where it is on the map?
您在地图上给我指出来，好吗?
nín zài dìtú shàng gěi wǒ zhǐchūlái, hǎo ma?
nin zy dee-too shang gay wo jeu-choo-ly, hao ma?

how do you get there?
怎么去那儿?
zěnme qù nàr?
zeun-me choo nar?

when was it built?
它是什么时候修的?
tā shì shénme shíhòu xiū de?
ta sheu sheun-me sheu-hoe shyo de?

is it free?
是不是免票?
shì bu shì miǎnpiào?
sheu boo sheu myen-peeao?

Understanding

免票 *miǎnpiào*	admission free
关门 *guānmén*	closed
战争 *zhànzhēng*	war
侵略 *qīnlüè*	invasion
开门 *kāimén*	open
修复 *xiūfù*	renovation
重建工作 *chóngjiàn gōngzuò*	restoration work
老城 *lǎochéng*	old town
导游参观 *dǎoyóu cānguān*	guided tour
您在这儿 *nín zài zhèr*	you are here *(on a map)*

到了那儿您还得打听
dào le nàr nín hái děi dǎting
dao le nar nin hy day da-ting
you'll have to ask when you get there

下一个导游参观两点开始
xià yī ge dǎoyóu cānguān liǎng diǎn kāishǐ
shya ee ge dao-yoe tsan-gwan lyang dyen ky-sheu
the next guided tour starts at 2 o'clock

MUSEUMS, EXHIBITIONS AND MONUMENTS

Expressing yourself

I've heard there's a very good ... exhibition on at the moment
我听说正在举行一个非常好的 … 展览
wǒ tīngshuō zhèng zài jǔxíng yī ge fēicháng hǎo de … zhǎnlǎn
wo ting-shwoe jung zy joo-shing ee ge fay-chang hao de … jan-lan

how much is it to get in?
门票多少钱?
ménpiào duōshǎo qián?
meun-peeao dwoe-shao chyen?

is this ticket valid for the exhibition as well?
这张票也可以参观展览吗?
zhè zhāng piào yě kěyǐ cānguān zhǎnlǎn ma?
je jang peeao yay ke-yee tsan-gwan jan-lan ma?

are there any discounts for young people?
有年轻人优惠票吗?
yǒu niánqīng rén yōuhuì piào ma?
yoe nyen-ching jeun yoe-hway peeao ma?

is it open on Mondays?
星期一开门吗?
xīngqīyī kāimén ma?
shing-chee-yee ky-meun ma?

two concessions and one full price, please
请给我两张优惠票，一张全价票
qǐng gěi wǒ liǎng zhāng yōuhuì piào, yī zhāng quánjià piào
ching gay wo lyang jang yoe-hway peeao, ee jang chwan-jya peeao

I have a student card
我有学生证
wǒ yǒu xuéshēngzhèng
wo yoe shway-shung-jung

Understanding

录音讲解 *lùyīn jiǎngjiě* audioguide
禁止使用闪光灯 *jìnzhǐ shǐyòng shǎnguāngdēng* no flash photography
禁止照相 *jìnzhǐ zhàoxiàng* no photography
长期展览 *chángqī zhǎnlǎn* permanent exhibition
请勿触摸 *qǐngwù chùmō* please do not touch
请安静 *qǐng ānjìng* silence, please
短期展览 *duǎnqī zhǎnlǎn* temporary exhibition
这个方向 *zhège fāngxiàng* this way
售票处 *shòupiàochù* ticket office

博物馆门票是 …
bówùguǎn ménpiào shì …
bo-woo-gwan meun-peeao sheu …
admission to the museum costs …

这张票也可以参观展览
zhè zhāng piào yě kěyǐ cānguān zhǎnlǎn
je jang peeao yay ke-yee tsan-gwan jan-lan
this ticket also allows you access to the exhibition

您带学生证了吗?
nín dài xuéshēngzhèng le ma?
nin dy shway-shung-jung le ma?
do you have your student card?

GIVING YOUR IMPRESSIONS

Expressing yourself

it's beautiful
真漂亮
zhēn piàoliang
jeun peeao-lyang

it was beautiful
真漂亮
zhēn piàoliang
jen peeao-lyang

it's fantastic
真了不起
zhēn liǎobuqǐ
jeun leeao-boo-chee

it was fantastic
真了不起
zhēn liǎobuqǐ
jeun leeao-boo-chee

I really enjoyed it
我觉得非常有意思
wǒ juéde fēicháng yǒu yìsi
wo jway-de fay-chang yoe yee-seu

I didn't like it that much
我并不那么喜欢
wǒ bìng bú nàme xǐhuan
wo bing boo na-me shee-hwan

it was a bit boring
没什么意思
méi shénme yìsi
may sheun-me yee-seu

it's expensive for what it is
就这个来说，票价贵了
jiù zhè ge lái shuō, piàojià guì le
jyo je ge ly shwoe, peeao-jya gway le

I'm not really a fan of modern art
我对现代美术并不喜欢
wǒ duì xiàndài měishù bìng bù xǐhuan
wo dway shyen-dy may-shoo bing boo shee-hwan

it's very touristy
旅游者太多，太热闹
lǚyóuzhě tài duō, tài rènao
lu-yoe-je ty dwoe, ty je-nao

it was really crowded
太拥挤了
tài yōngjǐ le
ty yong-jee le

we didn't go in the end, the queue was too long
我们后来没去，排队的人太多
wǒmen hòulái méiqù, páiduì de rén tài duō
wo-meun hoe-ly may choo, py-dway de jeun ty dwoe

we didn't have time to see everything
我们没时间把所有的东西都看了
wǒmen méi shíjiān bǎ suǒyǒu de dōngxī dōu kàn le
wo-meun may sheu-jyen ba swoe-yoe de dong-shee doe kan le

Understanding

著名 *zhùmíng* — famous
风景如画 *fēngjǐngrúhuà* — picturesque
传统 *chuántǒng* — traditional
典型 *diǎnxíng* — typical

你一定得去看看 …
nǐ yīdìng děi qù kànkan …
nee ee-ding day choo kan-kan …
you really must go and see …

我推荐你到 … 去
wǒ tuījiàn nǐ dào … qù
wo tway-jyen nee dao … choo
I recommend going to …

能看到全城的美丽景色
néng kàn dào quán chéng de měilì jǐng sè
nung kan dao chwan chung de may-lee jing-se
there's a wonderful view over the whole city

那儿变得有点儿太热闹了
nàr biànde yǒudiǎnr tài rènao le
nar byen-de yoe-dyar ty je-nao le
it's become a bit too touristy

海岸全被毁了
hǎi'àn quán bèi huǐ le
hy-an chwan bay hway le
the coast has been completely ruined

SPORTS AND GAMES

Although football, bowling and pool have all taken off in recent years, the most popular sports in China are basketball, badminton, volleyball and table-tennis. Table-tennis (乒乓球 *pīngpāngqiú ping-pang-chyo)* is played all over China – schools and universities have tables, as do some hotels.

Traditional Chinese sports include martial arts, wrestling and qigong. The main function of Chinese martial arts is to improve one's health and increase one's strength, and people can be seen practising in every public space.

Kite-flying is a very popular pastime and people do this in all the main squares, where al fresco ballroom dancing is also popular.

You can find out about walks and hiking in the area you are visiting at the local tourist information office, or at the reception desk of your hotel. Paths in popular tourist areas tend to be lined with souvenir vendors, photographers, and there is often an entrance fee.

In winter, both downhill and cross-country skiing are possible in the northernmost province 黑龙江 ***Hēilóngjiāng*** (*hay-long-jyang)*, and the sport is becoming increasingly popular, but be warned that temperatures can be extreme (as low as -30°C). You can also ice-skate on Beijing's lakes during the winter months.

Traditional board games include chess (象棋***xiàngqí*** *shyang-chee*) and go (围棋***wéiqí*** *way-chee*). The Chinese also enjoy playing cards and other games such as mahjong (麻将 ***májiàng*** *ma-jyang*).

The basics

badminton 羽毛球 ***yǔmáoqiú*** *yoo-mao-chyo*
ball 球 ***qiú*** *chyo*
basketball 篮球 ***lánqiú*** *lan-chyo*
board game 棋类 ***qílèi*** *chee-lay*
bowling 保龄球 ***bǎolíngqiú*** *bao-ling-chyo*
cards 牌 ***pái*** *py*

chess 棋 *qí* *chee*
cross-country skiing 越野滑雪 ***yuèyě huáxuě*** *yway-yay hwa-shway*
cycling 自行车赛 ***zìxíngchē sài*** *zeu-shing-che sy*
downhill skiing 下降滑雪 ***xiàjiàng huáxuě*** *shya-jyang hwa-shway*
football 足球 ***zúqiú*** *zoo-chyo*
hiking path 远足道 ***yuǎnzúdào*** *ywan-zoo-dao*
match 比赛 ***bǐsài*** *bee-sy*
mountain biking 自行车登山 ***zìxíngchē dēngshān*** *zeu-shing-che dung-shan*
play 玩儿 ***wánr*** *wanr*
pool *(game)* 落袋台球 ***luòdài táiqiú*** *lwoe-dy ty-chyo*
rugby 橄榄球 ***gǎnlǎnqiú*** *gan-lan-chyo*
ski 滑雪 ***huáxuě*** *hwa-shway*
snowboarding 滑雪板运动 ***huáxuěbǎn yùndòng*** *hwa-shway-ban yoon-dong*
sport 体育 ***tǐyù*** *tee-yoo*
surfing 冲浪 ***chōnglàng*** *chong-lang*
swimming 游泳 ***yóuyǒng*** *yoe-yong*
swimming pool 游泳池 ***yóuyǒngchí*** *yoe-yong-cheu*
table football 台上足球 ***táishàng zúqiú*** *ty-shang zoo-chyo*
tennis 网球 ***wǎngqiú*** *wang-chyo*
trip 旅行 ***lǚxíng*** *lu-shing*
to go hiking 去远足 ***qù yuǎnzú*** *choo ywan-zoo*
to have a game of cards 打一局（牌） ***dǎ yī jú pái*** *da ee joo py*

Expressing yourself

I'd like to hire … for an hour
我想租 … ，租一个小时
wǒ xiǎng zū …, zū yī ge xiǎoshí
wo shyang zoo … zoo ee ge sheeao-sheu

are there … lessons available?
有没有 … 课?
yǒu méi yǒu … kè?
yoe may yoe …ke?

how much is it per person per hour?
一个人一小时多少钱?
yī ge rén yī xiǎoshí duōshǎo qián?
ee ge jeun ee sheeao-sheu dwoe-shao chyen?

I've done it once or twice, a long time ago
很久以前做过一、两次
hěn jiǔ yǐqián zuò guo yī, liǎng cì
heun jyo ee-chyen zwoe gwoe ee, lyang tseu

I'm exhausted!
我累极了!
wǒ lèi jí le!
wo lay jee le!

I'd like to go and watch a football match
我想去看足球赛
wǒ xiǎng qù kàn zúqiú sài
wo shyang choo kan zoo-chyo sy

we played ...
我们玩儿过 …
wǒmen wánr guo ...
wo-meun wanr gwoe ...

Understanding

… 出租 *chūzū* … for hire

你以前玩儿过吗? 你是完全的初学者?
nǐ yǐqián wánr guo ma? nǐ shì wánquán de chūxuézhě?
nee ee-chyen wanr gwoe ma? nee sheu wan-chwan de choo-shway-je?
do you have any experience, or are you a complete beginner?

押金是 …
yājīn shì ...
ya-jin sheu ...
there is a deposit of ...

必须得买保险, 保险金是 …
bìxū děi mǎi bǎoxiǎn, bǎoxiǎnjīn shì ...
bee-shoo day my bao-shyen, bao-shyen-jin sheu ...
insurance is compulsory and costs ...

HIKING

Expressing yourself

are there any hiking paths around here?
这一带有远足道吗?
zhè yīdài yǒu yuǎnzúdào ma?
je ee-dy yoe ywan-zoo-dao ma?

can you recommend any good walks in the area?
您能给我推荐这个地方好的步行道吗?
nín néng gěi wǒ tuījiàn zhè ge dìfang hǎo de bùxíngdào ma?
nin nung gay wo tway-jyen je ge dee-fang hao de boo-shing-dao ma?

I've heard there's a nice walk by the lake
听说湖边有一条很好的步行道
tīngshuō húbiān yǒu yī tiáo hěn hǎo de bùxíngdào
ting-shwoe hoo-byen yoe ee teeao heun hao de boo-shing-dao

we're looking for a short walk somewhere round here
我们在找这儿附近的一条短步行道
wǒmen zài zhǎo zhèr fùjìn de yī tiáo duǎn bùxíngdào
wo-meun zy jao jer foo-jin de ee teeao dwan boo-shing-dao

can I hire hiking boots?
我可以租远足靴吗?
wǒ kěyǐ zū yuǎnzúxuē ma?
wo ke-yee zoo ywan-zoo-shway ma?

is it very steep?
很陡吗?
hěn dǒu ma?
heun doe ma?

is the path waymarked?
远足道有路标吗?
yuǎnzúdào yǒu lùbiāo ma?
ywan-zoo-dao yoe loo-beeao ma?

how long does the hike take?
这趟远足多长时间?
zhè tàng yuǎnzú duō cháng shíjiān?
je tang ywan-zoo dwoe chang sheu-jyen?

where's the start of the path?
远足道的起点在哪儿?
yuǎnzúdào de qǐdiǎn zài nǎr?
ywan-zoo-dao de chee-dyen zy nar?

is it a circular path?
是环形的吗?
shì huánxíng de ma?
sheu hwan-shing de ma?

Understanding

远足三小时左右，包括休息时间
yuǎnzú sān xiǎoshí zuǒyòu, bāokuò xiūxi shíjiān
ywan-zoo san sheeao-sheu zwoe-yoe, bao-kwoe shyo-shee sheu-jyen
it's about three hours' walk including rest stops

带防雨衣和旅行鞋
dài fángyǔyī hé lǚxíngxié
dy fang-yoo-yee he lu-shing-shyay
bring a waterproof jacket and some walking shoes

SKIING AND SNOWBOARDING

Expressing yourself

I'd like to hire skis, poles and boots
我想租滑雪板、滑雪杖和靴子
wǒ xiǎng zū huáxuěbǎn, huáxuězhàng hé xuēzi
wo shyang zoo hwa-shway-ban, hwa-shway-jang he shway-zeu

I'd like to hire a snowboard
我想租一个雪板
wǒ xiǎng zū yī ge xuěbǎn
wo shyang zoo ee ge shway-ban

they're too big/small
太大了/太小了
tài dà le/tài xiǎo le
ty da le/ty sheeao le

a day pass
当天有效票
dàngtiān yǒuxiào piào
dang-tyen yoe-sheeao peeao

I'm a complete beginner
我是完全的初学者
wǒ shì wánquán de chūxuézhě
wo sheu wan-chwan de choo-shway-je

Understanding

升降机 *shēngjiàngjī* chair lift
升降机票 *shēngjiàng jī piào* lift pass
滑雪升降机 *huáxuě shēngjiàngjī* ski lift

OTHER SPORTS

Expressing yourself

where can we hire bikes?
在哪儿租自行车?
zài nǎr zū zìxíngchē?
zy nar zoo zeu-shing-che?

are there any cycle paths?
有自行车道吗?
yǒu zìxíngchēdào ma?
yoe zeu-shing-che-dao ma?

does anyone have a football?
谁有足球?
shéi yǒu zúqiú?
shay yoe zoo-chyo?

which team do you support?
你支持哪个队?
nǐ zhīchí nǎ ge duì?
nee jeu-cheu na ge dway?

I support ...
我支持 …
wǒ zhīchí …
wo jeu-cheu …

is there an open-air swimming pool?
有露天游泳池吗?
yǒu lùtiān yóuyǒngchí ma?
yoe lu-tyen yoe-yong-cheu ma?

I'd like to hire a pair of skates for an hour
我想租一双冰鞋，租一个小时
wǒ xiǎng zū yī shuāng bīngxié, zū yī ge xiǎoshí
wo shyang zoo ee shwang bing-shyay, zoo ee ge sheeao-sheu

are there tai chi lessons available?
有没有太极课?
yǒu méi yǒu tàijí kè?
yoe may yoe ty-jee ke?

is there a golf course?
这儿有高尔夫球场吗?
zhèr yǒu gāo'ěrfū qiúchǎng ma?
jer yoe gao-er-foo chyo-chang ma?

where can we buy a kite?
哪儿卖风筝?
nǎr mài fēngzheng?
nar my fung-jung?

do you have a basketball team?
你们有篮球队吗?
nǐmen yǒu lánqiúduì ma?
nee-meun yoe lan-chyo-dway ma?

Understanding

离车站不远有一个公共网球场
lí chēzhàn bú yuǎn yǒu yī ge gōnggòng wǎngqiúchǎng
lee che-jan boo ywan yoe ee ge gong-gong wang-chyo-chang
there's a public tennis court not far from the station

这个网球场有人占了
zhè ge wǎngqiúchǎng yǒu rén zhàn le
je ge wang-chyo-chang yoe jeun jan le
the tennis court's occupied

这是你第一次骑马吗?
zhè shì nǐ dì yī cì qí mǎ ma?
je sheu nee dee ee tseu chee ma ma?
is this the first time you've been horse-riding?

你会游泳吗?
nǐ huì yóuyǒng ma?
nee hway yoe-yong ma?
can you swim?

你打篮球吗?
nǐ dǎ lánqiú ma?
nee da lan-chyo ma?
do you play basketball?

INDOOR GAMES

Expressing yourself

shall we have a game of cards?
我们打一局牌，好吗？
wǒmen dǎ yī jú pái, hǎoma?
wo-meun da ee joo py, hao ma?

does anyone know any good card games?
有人会好玩儿的牌游戏吗？
yǒu rén huì hǎowánr de pái yóuxì ma?
yoe jeun hway hao-wanr de py yoe-shee ma?

is anyone up for a game of chess?
有人愿意玩儿象棋吗？
yǒu rén yuànyì wánr xiàngqí ma?
yoe jeun ywan-ee wanr shyang-chee ma?

it's your turn
该你了
gāi nǐ le
gy nee le

Understanding

你会下棋吗？
nǐ huì xià qí ma?
nee hway shya chee ma?
do you know how to play chess?

有没有一盒扑克牌？
yǒu méi yǒu yī hé pūkèpái?
yoe may yoe ee he poo-ke-py?
do you have a pack of cards?

Some informal expressions

我累极了 ***wǒ lèi jí le*** wo lay jee le I'm absolutely knackered
他把我彻底打垮了 ***tā bǎ wǒ chèdǐ dǎkuǎ le*** ta ba wo che-dee da-kwa le he totally thrashed me

SHOPPING

小卖部 ***xiǎomàibù*** *sheeao-my-boo* are small local shops selling food and other basics which open early (around 7am) and stay open until between 10pm and midnight. They used to be cheaper than big shops, but this is less the case today.

Department stores (百货商场 ***bǎihuò shāngchǎng*** *by-hwoe shang-chang*) have fewer staff than western stores and opening hours vary (generally opening around 8am and closing between 7 and 10pm). They can be found in all big cities and sell modern consumer goods at relatively low prices. They accept credit cards.

Hotel shops sell various items like camera film, silk goods and foreign magazines, but they are expensive.

If you explore the small side streets, you will find stalls selling all kinds of goods. Haggling (讨价还价 ***tǎojiàhuánjià*** *tao-jya-hwan-jya*) is all part of the experience – it's not only the custom, but is essential if you want to pay anywhere near the real price. Do not attempt to haggle just for the sake of argument – it is considered very rude to refuse to buy something once the vendor has agreed to your price. Payment is always in cash.

Copies of works of art are sold everywhere – some museum shops sell them at highly inflated prices. Tourist areas are full of shops selling traditional Chinese handicrafts made of jade, pearl, lacquerware, silk, pottery and china.

Some informal expressions

真是敲竹杠 ***zhēn shì qiāo zhúgàng!*** *jeun sheu cheeao joo-gang!* that's a rip-off!

我一分钱也没有了 ***wǒ yī fēn qián yě méi yǒu le*** *wo ee feun chyen yay may yoe le* I'm skint

实在太贵了 ***shízài tài guì le*** *sheu-zy ty gway le* it costs an arm and a leg

真划算 ***zhēn huásuàn*** *jeun hwa-swan* it's a real bargain

Understanding

bakery	面包店 ***miànbāo diàn*** *myen-bao dyen*
butcher's	肉店 ***ròu diàn*** *joe dyen*
cash desk	收款台 ***shōukuǎntái*** *shoe-kwan-ty*
cheap	便宜 ***piányi*** *pyen-yee*
checkout	付款处 ***fùkuǎnchù*** *foo-kwan-choo*
clothes	衣服 ***yīfu*** *ee-foo*
cost	花费 ***huāfèi*** *hwa-fay*
department store	百货商店 ***bǎihuò shāngdiàn*** *by-hwoe shang-dyen*
expensive	贵 ***guì*** *gway*
gram	克 ***kè*** *ke*
greengrocer's	蔬菜水果店 ***shūcài shuǐguǒ diàn*** *shoo-tsy shway-gwoe dyen*
hypermarket	超大型自选商场 ***chāo dàxíng zìxuǎn shāngchǎng*** *chao da-shing zeu-shwan shang-chang*
kilo	公斤 ***gōngjīn*** *gong-jin*
present	礼物 ***lǐwù*** *lee-woo*
price	价格 ***jiàgé*** *jya-ge*
receipt	收据 ***shōujù*** *shoe-joo*
refund	退款 ***tuìkuǎn*** *tway-kwan*
sales	大减价 ***dàjiǎnjià*** *da-jyen-jya*
sales assistant	售货员 ***shòuhuòyuán*** *shoe-hwoe-ywan*
shop	商店 ***shāngdiàn*** *shang-dyen*
shopping centre	购物中心 ***gòuwù zhōngxīn*** *goe-woo jong-shin*
souvenir	纪念品 ***jìniànpǐn*** *jee-nyen-pin*
supermarket	超市 ***chāoshì*** *chao-sheu*
to buy	买 ***mǎi*** *my*
to pay	付款 ***fùkuǎn*** *foo-kwan*
to sell	卖 ***mài*** *my*

Expressing yourself

is there a supermarket near here?
这儿附近有超市吗?
zhèr fùjìn yǒu chāoshì ma?
jer foo-jin yoe chao-sheu ma?

where can I buy cigarettes?
哪儿卖香烟?
nǎr mài xiāngyān?
nar my shyang-yan?

I'd like ...
我想买 …
wǒ xiǎng mǎi ...
wo shyang my ...

I'm looking for ...
我想买 …
wǒ xiǎng mǎi ...
wo shyang my ...

do you sell ...?
你们卖不卖 … ?
nǐmen mài bu mài ...?
nee-meun my boo my ...?

can you order it for me?
您能为我进货吗?
nín néng wèi wǒ jìnhuò ma?
nin nung way wo jin-hwoe ma?

do you know where I might find some ...?
您知道哪儿能买到 … 吗?
nín zhīdao nǎr néng mǎidào ... ma?
nin jeu-dao nar nung my-dao ... ma?

how much is this?
多少钱?
duōshǎo qián?
dwoe-shao chyen?

I'll take it
好，我要了
hǎo, wǒ yào le
hao, wo yao le

I haven't got much money
我身上没带很多钱
wǒ shēn shang méi dài hěn duō qián
wo sheun shang may dy heun dwoe chyen

I haven't got enough money
我身上没带足够的钱
wǒ shēn shang méi dài zúgòu de qián
wo sheun shang may dy zoo-gwoe de chyen

that's everything, thanks
这是我要的所有的东西，谢谢
zhè shì wǒ yào de suǒyǒu de dōngxi, xièxie
je sheu wo yao de swoe-yoe de dong-shee, shyay-shyay

can I have a plastic bag?
我可以要一个（塑料）袋吗?
wǒ kěyǐ yào yī ge sùliào dài ma?
wo ke-yee yao ee ge soo-leeao dy ma?

I think you've made a mistake with my change
我觉得您找我的钱不对
wǒ juéde nín zhǎo wǒ de qián bú duì
wo jway-de nin jao wo de chyen boo dway

Understanding

…到…开门 ***… dào … kāimén*** — open from … to …
星期天/一点到三点关门 ***xīngqītiān/yī diǎn dào sān diǎn guānmén*** — closed Sundays/1pm to 3pm
特价优惠 ***tèjià yōuhuì*** — special offer
大减价 ***dàjiǎnjià*** — sales

还要其他的东西吗?
hái yào qítā de dōngxi ma?
hy yao chee-ta de dong-shee ma?
will there be anything else?

您要袋子吗?
nín yào dàizi ma?
nin yao dy-zeu ma?
would you like a bag?

PAYING

Expressing yourself

where do I pay?
在哪儿付款?
zài nǎr fùkuǎn?
zy nar foo-kwan?

how much do I owe you?
我应该给您多少钱?
wǒ yīnggāi gěi nín duōshǎo qián?
wo ying-gy gay nin dwoe-shao chyen?

could you write it down for me, please?
请给我写下来，好吗?
qǐng gěi wǒ xiě xiàlái, hǎo ma?
ching gay wo shyay shya-ly, hao ma?

can I pay by credit card?
我可以用信用卡付款吗?
wǒ kěyǐ yòng xìnyòngkǎ fùkuǎn ma?
wo ke-yee yong shin-yong-ka foo-kwan ma?

I'll pay in cash
我付现金
wǒ fù xiànjīn
wo foo shyen-jin

can I have a receipt?
您可以给我收据吗?
nín kěyǐ gěi wǒ shōujù ma?
nin ke-yee gay wo shoe-joo ma?

I'm sorry, I haven't got any change
对不起, 我身上没带零钱
duìbuqǐ, wǒ shēn shang méi dài língqián
dway-boo-chee, wo sheun shang may dy ling-chyen

Understanding

在收款台付款
zài shōukuǎntái fùkuǎn
zy shoe-kwan-ty foo-kwan
pay at the cash desk

您怎么付款?
nín zěnme fùkuǎn?
nin zeun-me foo-kwan?
how would you like to pay?

您有小点儿的钞票吗?
nín yǒu xiǎo diǎnr de chāopiào ma?
nin yoe sheeao dyar de chao-peeao ma?
do you have anything smaller?

您有身份证明吗?
nín yǒu shēnfèn zhèngmíng ma?
nin yoe sheun-feun jung-ming ma?
have you got any ID?

请在这儿签字
qǐng zài zhèr qiānzì
ching zy jer chyen-zeu
could you sign here, please?

FOOD

Expressing yourself

where can I buy food around here?
这一带什么地方能买到食品?
zhè yīdài shénme dìfang néng mǎidào shípǐn?
je ee-dy sheun-me dee-fang nung my-dao sheu-pin?

is there a market?
有市场吗?
yǒu shìchăng ma?
yoe sheu-chang ma?

is there a bakery around here?
这一带有面包店吗?
zhè yīdài yǒu miànbāo diàn ma?
je ee-dy yoe myen-bao dyen ma?

I'd like five Guangdong sausages
我想买五片广东香肠
wǒ xiăng măi wǔ guăngdōng xiāngcháng
wo shyang my woo gwang-dong shyang-chang

I'd like a box of tofu
我想买一盒豆腐
wǒ xiăng măi yī hé dòufu
wo shyang my ee he doe-foo

it's for four people
够四个人吃的
gòu sì ge rén chī de
goe seu ge jeun cheu de

about 300 grams
三百克左右
sānbăi kè zuǒyòu
san-by ke zwoe-yoe

a kilo of apples, please
请给我一公斤苹果
qĭng gĕi wǒ yī gōngjīn píngguǒ
ching gay wo ee gong-jin ping-gwoe

a bit less/more
再少一点儿/再多一点儿
zài shăo yīdiănr/zài duō yīdiănr
zy shao ee-dyar/zy dwoe ee-dyar

can I taste it?
可以尝一下吗?
kĕyĭ cháng yīxià ma?
ke-yee chang ee-shya ma?

does it travel well?
这个长途运输会变质吗?
zhè ge chángtú yùnshū huì biànzhì ma?
je ge chang-too yoon-shoo hway byen-jeu ma?

Understanding

在…之前消费 *zài…zhī qián xiāofèi* best before …
熟食品店 *shúshípĭn diàn* delicatessen
自制的 *zìzhì de* homemade
地方特产 *dìfāng tèchăn* local specialities
有机绿色 *yǒujī lǜsè* organic

每天一点以前都有市场
mĕitiān yī diăn yĭqián dōu yǒu shìchăng
may-tyen ee dyen ee-chyen doe yoe sheu-chang
there's a market every day until 1pm

在路口那儿有一个食品杂货店关门晚
zài lùkǒu nàr yǒu yī ge shípǐn záhuò diàn guānmén wǎn
zy loo-koe nar yoe ee ge sheu-pin za-hwoe dyen gwan-meun wan
there's a grocer's just on the corner that's open late

CLOTHES

Expressing yourself

I'm looking for the menswear section
我在找男装部
wǒ zài zhǎo nánzhuāng bù
wo zy jao nan-jwang boo

no thanks, I'm just looking
不用了，谢谢，我只是看看
bú yòng le, xièxie, wǒ zhǐ shì kànkan
boo yong le, shyay-shyay, wo jeu sheu kan-kan

can I try it on?
可以试一下吗？
kěyǐ shì yīxià ma?
ke-yee sheu ee-shya ma?

I'd like to try the one in the window
我想试一下橱窗里的那件
wǒ xiǎng shì yīxià chúchuāng lǐ de nà jiàn
wo shyang sheu ee-shya choo-chwang lee de na jyen

I take a size 39 (*in shoes*)
我穿三十九号鞋
wǒ chuān sānshíjiǔ hào xié
wo chwan san-sheu-jyo hao shyay

it doesn't fit
它不合适
tā bù héshì
ta boo he-sheu

where are the changing rooms?
试衣间在哪儿？
shìyījiān zài nǎr?
sheu-ee-jyen zy nar?

it's too big/small
太大/太小
tài dà/tài xiǎo
ty da/ty sheeao

SHOPPING

do you have it in another colour?
这件衣服有其他颜色的吗?
zhè jiàn yīfu yǒu qítā yánsè de ma?
je jyen ee-foo yoe chee-ta yan-se de ma?

do you have it in a smaller/bigger size?
有小一号/大一号的吗?
yǒu xiǎo yī hào/dà yī hào de ma?
yoe sheeao ee hao/da ee hao de ma?

do you have them in red?
有红色的吗?
yǒu hóngsè de ma?
yoe hong-se de ma?

yes, that's fine, I'll take them
很好，我要了
hěn hǎo, wǒ yào le
heun hao, wo yao le

no, I don't like it
不好，我不喜欢
bù hǎo, wǒ bù xǐhuan
boo hao, wo boo shee-hwan

I'll think about it
我再考虑一下
wǒ zài kǎolǜ yīxià
wo zy kao-lu ee-shya

I'd like to return this, it doesn't fit
我想退货，号码不合适
wǒ xiǎng tuìhuò, hàomǎ bù héshì
wo shyang tway-hwoe, hao-ma boo he-sheu

this ... has a hole in it, can I get a refund?
这 … 有个小洞，可以给我退款吗?
zhè ... yǒu ge xiǎo dòng, kěyǐ gěi wǒ tuìkuǎn ma?
je ... yoe ge sheeao dong, ke-yee gay wo tway-kwan ma?

Understanding

试衣间 *shìyījiān* — changing rooms
童装 *tóngzhuāng* — children's clothes
女装 *nǚzhuāng* — ladieswear
女式内衣 *nǚshì nèiyī* — lingerie
男装 *nánzhuāng* — menswear
星期天开门 *xīngqītiān kāimén* — open Sunday
减价商品不退货 *jiǎnjià shāngpǐn bú tuìhuò* — sale items cannot be returned

您好，买点儿什么？
nín hǎo, mǎi diǎnr shénme?
nin hao, my dianr sheun-me?
hello, can I help you?

那个号码没有了
nà ge hàomǎ méi yǒu le
na ge hao-ma may yoe le
we don't have any left in that size

非常合适
fēicháng héshì
fay-chang he-sheu
it's a good fit

如果不合适，您可以退货
rúguǒ bù héshì, nín kěyǐ tuìhuò
joo-gwoe boo he-sheu, nin ke-yee tway-hwoe
you can bring it back if it doesn't fit

我们只有蓝的和黑的
wǒmen zhǐ yǒu lán de hé hēi de
wo-meun zheu yoe lan de he hay de
we only have it in blue or black

很适合您穿
hěn shìhé nín chuān
heun sheu-he nin chwan
it suits you

SOUVENIRS AND PRESENTS

Expressing yourself

I'm looking for a present to take home
我想买一个礼物带回家
wǒ xiǎng mǎi yī ge lǐwù dài huí jiā
wo shyang my ee ge lee-woo dy hway jya

I'd like something that's easy to transport
我想买一个容易携带的东西
wǒ xiǎng mǎi yī ge róngyì xiédài de dōngxi
wo shyang my ee ge jong-ee shyay-dy de dong-shee

it's for a little girl of four
是给一个四岁小女孩买的
shì gěi yī ge sì suì xiǎo nǚhái mǎi de
sheu gay ee ge seu sway sheeao nu-hy my de

could you gift-wrap it for me?
请您把它礼品包装，可以吗？
qǐng nín bǎ tā lǐpǐn bāozhuāng, kěyǐ ma?
ching nin ba ta lee-pin bao-jwang, ke-yee ma?

Understanding

木头的/银的/金的/纯毛的 ***mùtou de/yín de/jīn de/chún máo de***	made of wood/silver/gold/wool
手工制造 ***shǒugōng zhìzào***	handmade
传统产品 ***chuántǒng chǎnpǐn***	traditionally made product

您想花多少钱？
nín xiǎng huā duōshǎo qián?
nin shyang hwa dwoe-shao chyen?
how much do you want to spend?

是作礼物吗？
shí zuò lǐwù ma?
sheu zwoe lee-woo ma?
is it for a present?

是这个地区的代表产品
shì zhè ge dìqū de dàibiǎo chǎnpǐn
sheu je ge dee-choo de dy-beeao chan-pin
it's typical of the region

PHOTOS

It is far cheaper to buy camera films and have photos developed in China than at home. You can have photos developed in specialist shops (冲印社 *chōngyìnshè chong-yin-she*) or in some chain stores (particularly the Japanese ones).

The basics

black and white 黑白 *hēibái hay-by*
camera 照相机 *zhàoxiàngjī jao-shyang-jee*
colour 彩色 *cǎisè tsy-se*
copy 印照片 *yìn zhàopiàn yin jao-pyen*
digital camera 数码相机 *shùmǎ xiàngjī shoo-ma shyang-jee*
disposable camera 一次性相机 *yīcì xìng xiàngjī ee-tseu shing shyang-jee*
exposure 曝光 *bàoguāng bao-gwang*
film 胶卷 *jiāojuǎn jeeow-jwan*
flash 闪光灯 *shǎnguāngdēng shan-gwang-dung*
glossy 光面 *guāngmiàn gwang-myen*
matte 磨砂面 *móshāmiàn mo-sha-myen*
memory card 内存卡 *nèicúnkǎ nay-tsoon-ka*
negative 底片 *dǐpiàn dee-pyen*
passport photo 护照照片 *hùzhào zhàopiàn hoo-jao jao-pyen*
photo booth 自动照相亭 *zìdòng zhàoxiàngtíng zeu-dong jao-shyang-ting*
reprint 再次印 *zài cì yìn zy tseu yin*
slide 幻灯片 *huàndēngpiàn hwan-dung-pyen*
to get photos developed 冲印照片 *chōngyìn zhàopiàn chong-yin jao-pyen*
to take a photo/ photos 照相 *zhàoxiàng jao-shyang*

Expressing yourself

could you take a photo of us, please?
请您给我们照张相，好吗？
qǐng nín gěi wǒmen zhào zhāng xiàng, hǎo ma?
ching nin gay wo-meun jao jang shyang, hao ma?

you just have to press this button
只要按一下这个按钮就行了
zhǐ yào àn yíxià zhè ge ànniǔ jiù xíng le
jeu yao an ee-shya je ge an-nyo jyo shing le

I'd like a 200 ASA colour film
我要一卷200 ASA彩色胶卷
wǒ yào yījuǎn èrbǎi ASA cǎisè jiāojuǎn
wo yao ee jwan er-by ASA tsy-se jeeao-jwan

do you have black and white films?
你们有黑白胶卷吗？
nǐmen yǒu hēibái jiāojuǎn ma?
nee-meun yoe hay-by jeeao-jwan ma?

how much is it to develop a film of 36 photos?
冲印一卷三十六张的胶卷多少钱？
chōngyìn yī juǎn sānshíliù zhāng de jiāojuǎn duōshǎo qián?
chong-yin ee jwan san-sheu-lyo jang de jeeao-jwan dwoe-shao chyen?

I'd like to have this film developed
我要冲印这个胶卷
wǒ yào chōngyìn zhè ge jiāojuǎn
wo yao chong-yin je ge jeeao-jwan

I'd like extra copies of some of the photos
我要加印其中一些照片
wǒ yào jiā yìn qízhōng yīxiē zhàopiàn
wo yao jya yin chee-jong ee-shyay jao-pyen

three copies of this one and two of this one
这个三张，这个两张
zhè ge sān zhāng, zhè ge liǎng zhāng
je ge san jang, je ge lyang jang

can I print my digital photos here?
这儿印数码照片吗？
zhèr yìn shùmǎ zhàopiàn ma?
jer yin shoo-ma jao-pyen ma?

can you put these photos on a CD for me?
您能把这些照片给我输入光盘吗？
nín néng bǎ zhè xiē zhàopiàn gěi wǒ shūrù guāngpán ma?
nin nung ba je shyay jao-pyen gay wo shoo-joo gwang-pan ma?

I've come to pick up my photos
我来取照片
wǒ lái qǔ zhàopiàn
wo ly choo jao-pyen

I've got a problem with my camera
我的照相机出问题了
wǒ de zhàoxiàngjī chū wèntí le
wo de jao-shyang-jee choo weun-tee le

I don't know what it is
我不知道怎么了
wǒ bù zhīdao zěnme le
wo boo jeu-dao zeun-me le

the flash doesn't work
闪光灯不亮
shǎnguāngdēng bú liàng
shan-gwang-dung boo lyang

Understanding

快捷服务 *kuàijié fúwù*	express service
照片输入光盘 *zhàopiàn shūrù guāngpán*	photos on CD
一小时冲印 *yīxiǎoshí chōngyìn*	photos developed in one hour
标准尺寸 *biāozhǔn chǐcùn*	standard format

可能电池用完了
kěnéng diànchí yòng wán le
ke-nung dyen-cheu yong wan le
maybe the battery's dead

我们有一台印数码照片的机器
wǒmen yǒu yī tái yìn shùmǎ zhàopiàn de jīqì
wo-meun yoe ee ty yin shoo-ma jao-pyen de jee-chee
we have a machine for printing digital photos

请告诉我名字，好吗？
qǐng gàosu wǒ míngzi, hǎo ma?
ching gao-soo wo ming-zeu, hao ma?
what's the name, please?

您什么时候要？
nín shénme shíhou yào?
nin sheun-me sheu-hoe yao?
when do you want them for?

我们有一小时快捷服务
wǒmen yǒu yīxiǎoshí kuàijié fúwù
wo-meun yoe ee-sheeow-sheu kwhy-jyay foo-woo
we can develop them in an hour

您的照片星期四中午来取
nín de zhàopiàn xīngqīsì zhōngwǔ lái qǔ
nin de jao-pyen shing-chee-seu jong-woo ly chu
your photos will be ready on Thursday at noon

BANKS

The currency of the People's Republic of China is the 人民币 *rénmínbì (jeun-min-bee)*, literally the "people's currency", abbreviated as *RMB*. The basic unit of the *RMB* is the 元 *yuán ywan*, colloquially known as 块 *kuài kwhy*. One-tenth of a *yuán* is called a 角 *jiǎo jeeao* or 毛 *máo mao*, and one-hundredth of a *yuán* a 分 *fēn feun*.

Notes: *100 yuán, 50 yuán, 10 yuán, 5 yuán, 2 yuán, 1 yuán, 5 jiǎo, 2 jiǎo, 1 jiǎo*

Coins: *1 yuan, 5 jiǎo, 1 jiǎo, 5 fēn, 2 fēn, 1 fēn*

You can change foreign currency and travellers' cheques at the border, in international airports, major branches of the Bank of China, tourist hotels and department stores. Don't forget to take your passport with you. The official exchange rate applies almost everywhere. Bureaux de change and banks are open from 9am to 4pm. There is a better rate for changing travellers' cheques than cash, and no commission is charged.

At the moment, most cash dispensers only take Chinese cards, except in Hong Kong, Beijing and Shanghai where international bank cards can be used. You can withdraw money using your Visa® or MasterCard® (with an extra 4% commission fee) but only at the main branch of the Bank of China (中国银行 *zhōngguó yínháng jong-gwoe yin-hang*) in big cities.

You can pay by credit card in medium- to high-quality hotels (3 stars and over), in large shops in big cities, in many tourist shops and in the tax-free areas of international airports.

The basics

bank 银行 *yínháng yin-hang*
bank account 银行账户 *yínháng zhànghù yin-hang jang-hoo*
banknote 钞票 *chāopiào chao-peeao*
bureau de change 外汇兑换处 *wàihuì duìhuànchù wy-hway dway-hwan-choo*

cashpoint	自动取款机 ***zìdòng qǔkuǎnjī*** *zeu-dong choo-kwan-jee*
change	零钱 ***língqián*** *ling-chyen*
cheque	支票 ***zhīpiào*** *zheu-peeao*
coin	硬币 ***yìngbì*** *ying-bee*
commission	手续费 ***shǒuxùfèi*** *shoe-shoo-fay*
credit card	信用卡 ***xìnyòngkǎ*** *shin-yong-ka*
PIN (number)	个人密码 ***gèrén mìmǎ*** *ge-jeun mee-ma*
Travellers Cheques®	旅行支票 ***lǚxíng zhīpiào*** *lu-shing jeu-peeao*
withdrawal	取款 ***qǔkuǎn*** *choo-kwan*
to change	换钱 ***huàn qián*** *hwan chyen*
to withdraw	取款 ***qǔkuǎn*** *choo-kwan*
to transfer	转帐 ***zhuǎnzhàng*** *jwan-jang*

Expressing yourself

where I can get some money changed?
在哪儿换钱?
zài nǎr huàn qián?
zy nar hwan chyen?

are banks open on Saturdays?
银行星期六开门吗?
yínháng xīngqīliù kāimén ma?
yin-hang shing-chee-lyo ky-meun ma?

I'm looking for a cashpoint
我在找自动取款机
wǒ zài zhǎo zìdòng qǔkuǎnjī
wo zy jao zeu-dong choo-kwan-jee

I'd like to change £100
我想换一百英镑
wǒ xiǎng huàn yībǎi yīngbàng
wo shyang hwan ee-by ying-bang

what commission do you charge?
手续费多少钱?
shǒuxùfèi duōshǎo qián?
shoe-shoo-fay dwoe-shao-chyen?

I'd like to transfer some money
我想转帐一些钱
wǒ xiǎng zhuǎnzhàng yīxiē qián
wo shyang jwan-jang ee-shyay chyen

I'd like to report the loss of my credit card
我要报告我的信用卡丢了
wǒ yào bàogào wǒ de xìnyòngkǎ diū le
woe yao bao-gao wo de shin-yong-ka dyo le

the cashpoint has swallowed my card
自动取款机把我的卡吞了
zìdòng qǔkuǎnjī bǎ wǒ de kǎ tūn le
zeu-dong choo-kwan-jee ba wo de ka toon le

Understanding

请插卡
qǐng chā kǎ
ching cha ka
please insert your card

请输入密码
qǐng shūrù mìmǎ
ching shoo-joo mee-ma
please enter your PIN number

请选择取款金额
qǐng xuǎnzé qǔ kuǎn jīn'é
ching shwan-ze choo kwan jin'e
please select amount for withdrawal

取款附带收据
qǔkuǎn fùdài shōujù
choo-kwan foo-dy shoe-joo
withdrawal with receipt

取款不带收据
qǔkuǎn bú dài shōujù
choo-kwan boo dy shoe-joo
withdrawal without receipt

请选择金额
qǐng xuǎnzé jīn'é
ching shwan-ze jin'e
please select the amount you require

机器故障，暂停服务
jīqì gùzhàng, zàntíng fúwù
jee-chee goo-jang, zan-ting foo-woo
out of service

POST OFFICES

The Chinese postal service is good, and provides quality domestic and international service. There are post offices in all cities and towns, easily recognizable by their eye-catching green logos. Most are open from 8am to 6pm Monday to Saturday, and on Sundays in some big cities. Postboxes are also green: those marked 内部 ***nèi bù*** *nay-boo* are for items being sent within China, and those marked 外部 ***wài bù*** *wy-boo* are for international mail.

Stamps are only sold at post offices and in large international hotels. Some hotels also have facilities for posting letters and parcels.

Items posted in China generally take five to ten days to reach Europe. Note that while most of the international courier services also operate widely in China, if you want to send books or magazines, they must be sent from an authorized post office.

The basics

airmail 航空邮件 ***hángkōng yóujiàn*** *hang-kong yoe-jyen*
envelope 信封 ***xìnfēng*** *shin-fung*
letter 信 ***xìn*** *shin*
mail 邮件 ***yóujiàn*** *yoe-jyen*
parcel 包裹 ***bāoguǒ*** *bao-gwoe*
post 邮件 ***yóujiàn*** *yoe-jyen*
postbox 邮筒 ***yóutǒng*** *yoe-tong*
postcard 明信片 ***míngxìnpiàn*** *ming-shin-pyen*
postcode 邮政编码 ***yóuzhèng biānmǎ*** *yoe-jung byen-ma*
post office 邮局 ***yóujú*** *yoe-joo*
stamp 邮票 ***yóupiào*** *yoe-peeao*
to post 寄 ***jì*** *jee*
to send 寄 ***jì*** *jee*
to write 写 ***xiě*** *shyay*

Expressing yourself

is there a post office around here?
这一带有邮局吗?
zhè yīdài yǒu yóujú ma?
je ee-dy yoe yoe-joo ma?

is there a postbox near here?
这儿附近有邮筒吗?
zhèr fùjìn yǒu yóutǒng ma?
jer foo-jin yoe yoe-tong ma?

is the post office open on Saturdays?
邮局星期六开门吗?
yóujú xīngqīliù kāimén ma?
yoe-joo shin-chee-lyo ky-meun ma?

what time does the post office close?
邮局几点关门?
yóujú jǐ diǎn guānmén?
yoe-joo jee dyen gwan-meun?

do you sell stamps?
你们卖邮票吗?
nǐmen mài yóupiào ma?
ni-meun my yoe-peeao ma?

I'd like ... stamps for the UK, please
我要 … 张到英国的邮票
wǒ yào ... zhāng dào yīngguó de yóupiào
wo yao...jang dao ying-gwoe de yoe-peeao

how long will it take to arrive?
多长时间能到?
duō cháng shíjiān néng dào?
dwoe chang sheu-jyen nung dao?

where can I buy envelopes?
哪儿卖信封?
nǎr mài xìnfēng?
nar my shin-fung?

Understanding

第一次开箱取信 *dì yī cì kāi xiāng qǔ xìn*	first collection
易碎 *yìsuì*	fragile
轻拿轻放 *qīng ná qīng fàng*	handle with care
最后一次开箱取信 *zuìhòu yī cì kāi xiāng qǔ xìn*	last collection
寄件人 *jìjiànrén*	sender

三到五天到达
sān dào wǔ tiān dàodá
san dao woo tyen dao-da
it'll take between 3 and 5 days

Making sense of addresses

On Chinese envelopes, for letters being sent within China, the address should be written in the middle of the envelope, with the name of the addressee underneath. The sender's name and address are often put on the bottom of the envelope. Postcodes are important, and envelopes are printed with spaces at the top for the postcode of the person to whom the letter is addressed.

When you address an envelope to be sent abroad, you can write the name and address as normal. It's best to put the name of the country in Chinese, though, to speed up delivery (英国 ***yīngguó*** *ying-gwoe* for the UK, 美国 ***měiguó*** *may-gwoe* for the US, 爱尔兰 ***ài'ěrlán*** *ay-er-lan* for Ireland).

INTERNET CAFÉS AND E-MAIL

Use of the Internet and e-mail is widespread, and there are Internet cafés in all large towns and cities. Hotels often have a business centre with computer facilities, and Internet cafés are usually open from 8am to 10pm.

The typing system commonly used in mainland China is based on 拼音 (*pīnyīn pin-yin*) which adopts the Latin alphabet to transcribe Chinese sounds. The international QWERTY keyboard is used, so visitors do not need a special keyboard to type in English.

The basics

e-mail 电子邮件 ***diànzǐ yóujiàn*** *dyen-zeu yoe-jyen*
e-mail address 电子邮箱地址 ***diànzǐ yóuxiāng dìzhǐ*** *dyen-zeu yoe-shyang dee-jeu*
Internet café 网吧 ***wǎngbā*** *wang-ba*
key 键 ***jiàn*** *jyen*
keyboard 键盘 ***jiànpán*** *jyen-pan*
to copy 复制 ***fùzhì*** *foo-jeu*
to cut 剪 ***jiǎn*** *jyen*
to delete 删除 ***shānchú*** *shan-choo*
to download 下载 ***xiàzǎi*** *shya-zy*
to e-mail somebody 给某人发电子邮件 ***gěi mǒurén fā diànzǐ yóujiàn*** *gay moe-jeun fa dyen-zeu yoe-jyen*
to paste 粘贴 ***zhāntiē*** *jan-tyay*
to receive 接收 ***jiēshōu*** *jyay-shoe*
to save 存 ***cún*** *tsoon*
to send an e-mail 发电子邮件 ***fā diànzǐ yóujiàn*** *fa dyen-zeu yoe-jyen*

Expressing yourself

is there an Internet café near here?
这儿附近有网吧吗?
zhèr fùjìn yǒu wǎngbā ma?
jer foo-jin yoe wang-ba ma?

do you have an e-mail address?
你有电子邮箱地址吗?
nǐ yǒu diànzǐ yóuxiāng dìzhǐ ma?
nee yoe dyen-zeu yoe-shyang dee-jeu ma?

how do I get online?
怎么上网?
zěnme shàng wǎng?
zeun-me shang wang?

I'd just like to check my e-mails
我只是想查一下电子邮件
wǒ zhǐshì xiǎng chá yīxià diànzǐ yóujiàn
wo jeu-sheu shyang cha ee-shya dyen-zeu yoe-jyen

would you mind helping me, I'm not sure what to do
帮个忙，好吗？我不清楚怎么做
bāng ge máng, hǎo ma? wǒ bù qīngchu zěnme zuò
bang ge mang, hao ma? wo boo ching-choo zeun-me zwoe

I can't find the at sign on this keyboard
这个键盘找不到 at-sign
zhè ge jiànpán zhǎo bu dào at-sign
je ge jyen-pan jao-boo dao at sign

it's not working
它不工作
tā bù gōngzuò
ta boo gong-zwoe

there's something wrong with the computer, it's frozen
这个电脑出毛病了，死机了
zhè ge diànnǎo chū máobing le, sǐ jī le
je ge dyen-nao choo mao-bing le, seu jee le

how much will it be for half an hour?
半小时多少钱?
bàn xiǎoshí duōshǎo qián?
ban sheeao-sheu dwoe-shao chyen?

when do I pay?
什么时候付费?
shénme shíhou fùfèi?
sheun-me sheu-hoe foo-fay?

Understanding

收件箱	*shōu jiàn xiāng*	inbox
发件箱	*fā jiàn xiāng*	outbox

你得等二十分钟左右
nǐ děi děng èrshí fēnzhōng zuǒyòu
nee day dung er-sheu feun-jong zwoe-yoe
you'll have to wait for 20 minutes or so

如果不清楚怎么做，就来问
rúguǒ bù qīngchu zěnme zuò, jiù lái wèn
joo-gwoe boo ching-choo zeun-me zwoe, jyo ly weun
just ask if you're not sure what to do

输入这个密码登录
shūrù zhè ge mìmǎ dēnglù
shoo-joo je ge mee-ma dung-loo
just enter this password to log on

TELEPHONE

There is an extensive mobile phone network in China, but, as when travelling anywhere, it is wise to find out beforehand the cost of using your mobile, and to ensure that any international bar has been removed. Operators in China charge for outgoing and incoming calls. If you are going to be working in China, or need to use a mobile frequently, it would be more economical to buy either a SIM card, costing about 100 RMB, or even a second phone once you arrive in China. Prepaid phone cards (with bilingual prompt) are also very useful, and are available from hotels, news-stands, post offices and stores, and in airports. Signs over shop doorways and in windows indicate where you can find payphones in shops, and they can also be found in hotel lobbies and in most post offices. Local calls are very cheap, though note that you pay even if you don't get through.

To call the UK from China, dial 00 44 followed by the phone number, including the area code but omitting the initial zero. The international dialling code for Ireland is 00 353, and for the US and Canada it is 001.

To call China from abroad, dial 00 86 followed by the area code (10 for Beijing, 21 for Shanghai, 871 for Kunming, 25 for Nanjing, 20 for Guangzhou) followed by the phone number.

Phone numbers are read out one digit at a time.

The basics

answering machine 电话留言机 *diànhuà liúyánjī* *dyen-hwa lyo-yan-jee*
call 电话 *diànhuà* *dyen-hwa*
directory enquiries 查询台 *cháxúntái* *cha-shoon-ty*
hello 喂 *wéi* *way*
international call 国际长途电话 *guójì chángtú diànhuà* *gwoe-jee chang-too dyen-hwa*
local call 本地电话 *běndì diànhuà* *beun-dee dyen-hwa*
message 留言 *liúyán* *lyo-yan*
mobile 手机 *shǒujī* *shoe-jee*

national call	国内电话 ***guónèi diànhuà*** *gwoe-nay dyen-hwa*
phone	电话 ***diànhuà*** *dyen-hwa*
phone book	电话簿 ***diànhuàbù*** *dyen-hwa-boo*
phone box	电话亭 ***diànhuàtíng*** *dyen-hwa-ting*
phone call	电话 ***diànhuà*** *dyen-hwa*
phone number	电话号码 ***diànhuà hàomă*** *dyen-hwa hao-ma*
phonecard	电话卡 ***diànhuàkă*** *dyen-hwa-ka*
ringtone	电话铃 ***diànhuàlíng*** *dyen-hwa-ling*
telephone	电话 ***diànhuà*** *dyen-hwa*
top-up card	手机充值卡 ***shŏujī chōngzhíkă*** *shoe-jee chong-jeu-ka*
Yellow Pages ®	黄页电话簿 ***huángyè diànhuàbù*** *hwang-yay dyen-hwa-boo*
to call	打电话 ***dă diànhuà*** *da dyen-hwa*

Expressing yourself

where can I buy a phonecard?
哪儿卖电话卡?
năr mài diànhuàkă?
nar my dyen-hwa-ka?

a …-yuan top-up card, please
我要一张 … 元的手机充值卡
wŏ yào yī zhāng … yuán de shŏujī chōngzhíkă
wo yao ee jang …ywan de shoe-jee chong-jeu-ka

I'd like to make a reverse-charge call
我想打一个对方付费电话
wŏ xiăng dă yī ge duìfāng fùfèi diànhuà
wo shyang da ee ge dway-fang foo-fay dyen-hwa

is there a phone box near here, please?
请问，这儿附近有电话亭吗?
qĭng wèn, zhèr fùjìn yŏu diànhuàtíng ma?
ching weun, jer foo-jin yoe dyen-hwa-ting ma?

can I plug my phone in here to recharge it?
我可以把手机插在这儿充电吗?
wŏ kěyĭ bă shŏujī chā zài zhèr chōngdiàn ma?
wo ke-yee ba shoe-jee cha zy jer chong-dyen ma?

do you have a mobile number?
你有手机号码吗?
nǐ yǒu shǒujī hàomǎ ma?
nee yoe shoe-jee hao-ma ma?

where can I contact you?
我在哪儿跟你联系?
wǒ zài nǎr gēn nǐ liánxi?
wo zy nar gen nee lyen-shee?

did you get my message?
你得到我的留言了吗?
nǐ dédào wǒ de liúyán le ma?
nee de-dao wo de lyo-yan le ma?

Understanding

您拨的号码是空号
nín bō de hàomǎ shì kōnghào
nin bo de hao-ma sheu kong-hao
the number you have dialled has not been recognized

请按井字键
qǐng àn jǐng zì jiàn
ching an jing zeu jyen
please press the hash key

MAKING A CALL

Expressing yourself

hello, this is David Brown (speaking)
喂，这是大卫．布朗在说话
wéi, zhè shì Dàwèi-Bùlǎng zài shuōhuà
way, je sheu Da-way Boo-lang zy shwoe-hwa

hello, could I speak to ..., please?
喂，我可以跟 … 说话吗?
wéi, wǒ kěyǐ gēn ... shuōhuà ma?
way, wo ke-yee gen ... shwoe-hwa ma?

hello, is that Ding Libo?
喂，是丁立波吗
wéi, shì Dīng Lìbō ma?
way, sheu ding lee-bo ma?

do you speak English?
您说英语吗？
nín shuō yīngyǔ ma?
nin shwoe ying-yoo ma?

could you speak more slowly, please?
请您说慢点儿，好吗？
qǐng nín shuō màn diǎnr, hǎo ma?
ching nin shwoe man dyar, hao ma?

I can't hear you, could you speak up, please?
我听不清楚，请您大声点儿，好吗？
wǒ tīng bù qīngchu, qǐng nín dàshēng diǎnr, hǎo ma?
wo ting boo ching-choo, ching nin da-shung dyar, hao ma?

could you tell him/her I called?
您告诉他/她，我给他/她打电话了，好吗？
nín gàosu tā/tā, wǒ gěi tā/tā dǎ diànhuà le, hǎo ma?
nin gao-soo ta/ta, wo gay ta/ta da dyen-hwa le, hao ma?

could you ask him/her to call me back?
您告诉他/她，给我回电话，好吗？
nín gàosu tā/tā, gěi wǒ huí diànhuà, hǎo ma?
nin gao-soo ta/ta, gay wo hway dyen-hwa, hao ma?

I'll call back later
我等会儿再给他/她打电话
wǒ děng huìr zài gěi tā/tā dǎ diànhuà
wo dung hwayr zy gay ta/ta da dyen-hwa

my name is ... and my number is ...
我叫 …，我的电话号码是 …
wǒ jiào ..., wǒ de diànhuà hàomǎ shì ...
wo jeeao ... wo de dyen-hwa hao-ma sheu ...

do you know when he/she might be available?
您知道什么时候能跟他/她说话吗？
nín zhīdao shénme shíhou néng gēn tā/tā shuōhuà ma?
nin jeu-dao sheun-me sheu-hoe nung geun ta/ta shwoe-hwa ma?

thank you, goodbye
谢谢，再见
xièxie, zàijiàn
shyay-shyay, zy-jyen

Understanding

您是谁?
nín shì shéi?
nin sheu shay?
who's calling?

他/她现在没在这儿
tā/tā xiànzài méi zài zhèr
ta/ta shyen-zy may zy jer
he's/she's not here at the moment

我告诉他/她您来电话了
wǒ gàosu tā/tā nín lái diànhuà le
wo gao-soo ta/ta nin ly dyen-hwa le
I'll tell him/her you called

请稍等
qǐng shāo děng
ching shao dung
hold on

您打错号码了
nín dǎ cuò hàomǎ le
nin da tswoe hao-ma le
you've got the wrong number

您留言，好吗?
nín liúyán, hǎo ma?
nin lyo-yan, hao ma?
do you want to leave a message?

我请他/她给您回电话
wǒ qǐng tā/tā gěi nín huí diànhuà
wo ching ta/ta gay nin hway dyen-hwa
I'll ask him/her to call you back

我把电话给他/她
wǒ bǎ diànhuà gěi tā/tā
wo ba dyen-hwa gay ta/ta
I'll just hand you over to him/her

PROBLEMS

Expressing yourself

I don't know the code
我不知道地区号码
wǒ bù zhīdào dìqū hàomǎ
wo boo jeu-dao dee-choo hao-ma

there's no reply
没人接
méi rén jiē
may jeun jyay

it's engaged
占线
zhàn xiàn
jan-shyen

I couldn't get through
打不通
dǎ bù tōng
da boo tong

I don't have much credit left on my phone
我卡上剩下的时间不多了
wǒ kǎ shang shèngxià de shíjiān bù duō le
wo ka shang shung-shya de sheu-jyen boo dwoe le

we're about to get cut off
马上就要断电话了
mǎshàng jiù yào duàn diànhuà le
ma-shang jyo yao dwan dyen-hwa le

the reception's really bad
我这儿听不清楚
wǒ zhèr tīng bù qīngchu
wo jer ting boo ching-choo

I can't get a signal
没有信号
méi yǒu xìnhào
may yoe shin-hao

Understanding

我几乎听不见
wǒ jīhū tīng bú jiàn
wo jee-hoo ting boo jyen
I can hardly hear you

这条线不好
zhè tiáo xiàn bù hǎo
je teeao shyen boo hao
it's a bad line

Common abbreviations

办 = 单位电话号码 *dānwèi diànhuà hàomǎ* work number
宅 = 住宅电话号码 *zhùzhái diànhuà hàomǎ* home number
手机 = 手机号码 *shǒujī hàomǎ* mobile number

HEALTH

Most Chinese hospitals have a section reserved for foreigners. Doctors are usually very well-trained and speak some English (at least medical English).

Every hospital and health centre has a Western medicine section (西医 *xīyī shee-yee*) and a Chinese medicine section (中医 ***zhōngyī*** *jong-yee*). Unless you specifically ask for a Chinese traditional medical treatment, you will automatically be sent to the Western section. Hospitals have their own pharmacies.

In some hospitals you can get prescriptions in English, but this is quite rare. Ask before you leave. Many big cities have private hospitals with international doctors, but consultation fees tend to be very high.

First-aid equipment is available in most supermarkets and in pharmacies (药店 ***yàodiàn*** *yao-dyen*), which are open from 9am to 10pm every day (including Sundays).

Make sure you take out appropriate health insurance for China before you set off. Check that you are covered for ambulance costs and emergency repatriation.

The basics

allergy 过敏 ***guòmǐn*** *gwoe-min*
ambulance 救护车 ***jiùhùchē*** *jyo-hoo-che*
aspirin 阿斯匹林 ***āsīpīlín*** *a-seu-pee-lin*
blood 血 ***xuè*** *shway*
broken 碎了 ***suì le*** *sway le*
casualty (department) 急诊部 ***jízhěnbù*** *jee-jeun-boo*
chemist's 药房 ***yàofáng*** *yao-fang*
condom 避孕套 ***bìyùntào*** *bee-yoon-tao*
dentist 牙医 ***yáyī*** *ya-yee*
diarrhoea 拉肚子 ***lādùzi*** *la-doo-zeu*
doctor 医生 ***yīshēng*** *ee-shung*
food poisoning 食物中毒 ***shíwù zhòngdú*** *sheu-woo jong-doo*

GP	家庭医生 ***jiātíng yīshēng*** *jya-ting ee-shung*
gynaecologist	妇科医生 ***fùkē yīshēng*** *foo-ke ee-shung*
hospital	医院 ***yīyuàn*** *ee-ywan*
infection	感染 ***gănrăn*** *gan-jan*
medicine	药 ***yào*** *yao*
painkiller	止疼药 ***zhĭténgyào*** *jeu-tung-yao*
periods	月经 ***yuèjīng*** *yway-jing*
plaster	橡皮膏 ***xiàngpígāo*** *shyang-pee-gao*
rash	红疹 ***hóngzhěn*** *hong-jeun*
spot	疱疹 ***pàozhěn*** *pao-jeun*
sunburn	晒伤 ***shàishāng*** *shy-shang*
surgical spirit	消毒酒精 ***xiāodú jiŭjīng*** *sheeao-doo jyo-jing*
tablet	药片 ***yàopiàn*** *yao-pyen*
temperature	发烧 ***fāshāo*** *fa-shao*
to vomit	呕吐 ***ŏutù*** *oe-too*
vaccination	打预防针 ***dă yùfángzhēn*** *da yoo-fang-jeun*
x-ray	X-光检查 ***X-guāng jiănchá*** *X-gwang jyen-cha*
to disinfect	消毒 ***xiāodú*** *sheeao-doo*
to faint	晕倒了 ***yūndăo le*** *yoon-dao le*

Expressing yourself

does anyone have an aspirin/a tampon/a plaster, by any chance?
哪位正好有阿斯匹林/月经棉条/橡皮膏
nă wèi zhènghăo yŏu āsīpīlín/yuèjīng miántiáo/xiàngpígāo?
na way jung-hao yoe a-seu-pee-lin/yway-jing myen-teeao/shyang-pee-gao?

I need to see a doctor
我得看医生
wŏ děi kàn yīshēng
wo day kan ee-shung

where can I find a doctor?
哪儿有医生?
năr yŏu yīshēng?
nar yoe ee-shung?

I'd like to make an appointment for today
我想预约今天
wŏ xiăng yùyuē jīntiān
wo shyang yoo-yway jin-tyen

as soon as possible
越快越好
yuè kuài yuè hǎo
yway kwhy yway hao

no, it doesn't matter
不要紧
bú yàojǐn
boo yao-jin

can you send an ambulance to …
能派救护车到 … 吗?
néng pài jiùhùchē dào … ma?
nung py jyo-hoo-che dao … ma?

I've broken my glasses
我的眼镜碎了
wǒ de yǎnjìng suì le
wo de yan-jing sway le

I've lost a contact lens
我丢了一片隐形眼镜
wǒ diū le yī piàn yǐnxíng yǎnjìng
wo dyo le ee pyen yin-shing yan-jing

Understanding

诊所 *zhěnsuǒ*	doctor's surgery
处方 *chǔfāng*	prescription
急诊部 *jízhěnbù*	casualty department

星期四以前没有预约了
xīngqīsì yǐqián méi yǒu yùyuē le
shing-chee-seu ee-chyen may yoe yoo-yway le
there are no available appointments until Thursday

星期五两点, 可以吗?
xīngqīwǔ liǎngdiǎn, kěyǐ ma?
shing-chee-woo lyang-dyen, ke-yee ma?
is Friday at 2pm OK?

AT THE DOCTOR'S OR THE HOSPITAL

Expressing yourself

I have an appointment with Dr …
我预约了 … 医生
wǒ yùyuē le … yīshēng
wo yoo-yway-le ….ee-shung

I don't feel very well
我觉得不舒服
wǒ juéde bù shūfu
wo jway-de boo shoo-foo

I don't know what it is
我不知道是怎么了
wǒ bù zhīdào shì zěnme le
wo boo jeu-dao sheu zeun-me le

I've got a headache
我头疼
wǒ tóu téng
wo toe tung

I feel very weak
我觉得浑身无力
wǒ juéde húnshēn wúlì
wo jway-de hoon-sheun woo-lee

I've been bitten/stung by …
我被 … 咬了/叮了
wǒ bèi … yǎo le/dīng le
wo bay… yao le/ding le

I've got a sore throat
我嗓子疼
wǒ sǎngzi téng
wo sang-zeu tung

I've got toothache/stomachache
我牙疼/肚子疼
wǒ yá téng/dùzi téng
wo ya tung/doo-zeu tung

my back hurts
我后背疼
wǒ hòubèi téng
wo hoe-bay tung

it hurts here
这儿疼
zhèr téng
jer tung

it's got worse
越来越利害
yuè lái yuè lìhai
yway ly yway lee-hy

it hurts
疼
téng
tung

I feel sick
我想吐
wǒ xiǎng tù
wo shyang too

it's been three days
已经三天了
yǐjīng sān tiān le
ee-jing san tyen le

it started last night
是昨天夜里开始的
shì zuótiān yèlǐ kāishǐ de
sheu zwoe-tyen yay-lee ky-sheu de

it's never happened to me before
我以前从来没有过这种情况
wǒ yǐqián cónglái méi yǒu guo zhè zhǒng qíngkuàng
wo ee-chyen tsong-ly may yoe gwoe je jong ching-kwang

I've got a temperature
我发烧了
wǒ fāshāo le
wo fa-shao le

I have a heart condition
我有心脏病
wǒ yǒu xīnzàngbìng
wo yoe shin-zang-bing

I have asthma
我有哮喘病
wǒ yǒu xiàochuǎnbìng
wo yoe sheeao-chwan-bing

it itches
痒
yǎng
yang

I've been on antibiotics for a week and I'm not getting any better
我吃了一个星期的抗生素了，可是一点儿不见好
wǒ chī le yī ge xīngqī de kàngshēngsù le, kěshì yīdiǎnr bú jiàn hǎo
wo cheu le ee ge shing-chee de kang-shung-soo le, ke-sheu ee-dyar boo jyen hao

I'm on the pill/the minipill
我在服避孕药/微型避孕药
wǒ zài fú bìyùnyào/wēixíng bìyùnyào
wo zy foo bee-yoon-yao/way-shing bee-yoon-yao

I'm ... months pregnant
我怀孕 … 个月了
wǒ huáiyùn … ge yuè le
wo hwhy-yoon … ge yway le

I've twisted my ankle
我脚脖子扭伤了
wǒ jiǎobózi niǔshāng le
wo jeeao-bo-zeu nyo-shang le

I've had a blackout
我晕倒了
wǒ yūndǎo le
wo yoon-dao le

is it serious?
严重吗?
yánzhòng ma?
yan-jong ma?

I'm allergic to penicillin
我对盘尼西林过敏
wǒ duì pánníxīlín guòmǐn
wo dway pan-nee-shee-lin gwoe-min

I fell and hurt my back
我摔了，伤了后背
wǒ shuāi le, shāng le hòubèi
wo shwhy le, shang le hoe-bay

I've lost a filling
我补的牙掉了一个
wǒ bǔ de yá diào le yī ge
wo boo de ya deeow le ee ge

is it contagious?
传染吗?
chuánrǎn ma?
chwan-jan ma?

how is he/she?
他/她怎么样了？
tā/tā zěnmeyàng le?
ta/ta zeun-me-yang le?

how much do I owe you?
我付多少钱？
wǒ fù duōshǎo qián?
wo foo dwoe-shao chyen?

can I have a receipt so I can get the money refunded?
可以给我收据吗？这样我可以报销
kěyǐ gěi wǒ shōujù ma? zhèyàng wǒ kěyǐ bàoxiāo?
ke-yee gay wo shoe-joo ma? je-yang wo ke-yee bao-sheeao?

Understanding

请在候诊室坐下等候
qǐng zài hòuzhěnshì zuòxià děnghòu
ching zy hoe-jeun-sheu zwoe-shya dung-hoe
if you'd like to take a seat in the waiting room

哪儿不舒服？
nǎr bù shūfu?
nar boo shoo-foo?
where does it hurt?

请躺下
qǐng tǎngxià
ching tang-shya
lie down, please

深呼吸
shēn hūxī
sheun hoo-shee
take a deep breath

我按这儿时，疼吗？
wǒ àn zhèr shí, téng ma?
wo an jer sheu, tung ma?
does it hurt when I press here?

你打 … 预防针了吗？
nǐ dǎ … yùfángzhēn le ma?
nee da … yoo-fang-jeun le ma?
have you been vaccinated against …?

你对 … 过敏吗？
nǐ duì … guòmǐn ma?
nee dway … gwoe-min ma?
are you allergic to …?

你在服其他的药吗？
nǐ zài fú qítā de yào ma?
nee zy foo chee-ta de yao ma?
are you taking any other medication?

我给你开个处方
wǒ gěi nǐ kāi ge chǔfāng
wo gay nee ky ge choo-fang
I'm going to write you a prescription

过几天就会好了
guò jǐ tiān jiù huì hǎo le
gwoe jee tyen jyo hway hao le
it should clear up in a few days

你需要手术
nǐ xūyào shǒushù
nee shoo-yao shoe-shoo
you're going to need an operation

很快会好的
hěn kuài huì hǎo de
hen kwhy hway hao de
it should heal quickly

一星期后来见我
yī xīngqī hòu lái jiàn wǒ
ee shing-chee hoe ly jyen wo
come back and see me in a week

AT THE CHEMIST'S

Expressing yourself

I'd like a box of plasters, please
请给我一盒橡皮膏，好吗？
qǐng gěi wǒ yī hé xiàngpígāo, hǎo ma?
ching gay wo ee he shyang-pee-gao, hao ma?

could I have something for a bad cold?
请给我一些重感冒药，好吗？
qǐng gěi wǒ yīxiē zhòng gǎnmào yào, hǎo ma?
ching gay wo ee-shyay jong gan-mao yao, hao ma?

I need something for a cough
我需要咳嗽药
wǒ xūyào késouyào
wo shoo-yao ke-soe-yao

I'm allergic to aspirin
我对阿斯匹林过敏
wǒ duì āsīpīlín guòmǐn
wo dway a-seu-pee-lin gwoe-min

I need the morning-after pill
我需要清晨服避孕药
wǒ xūyào qīngchén fú bìyùnyào
wo shoo-yao ching-cheun foo bee-yoon-yao

I'd like a bottle of solution for soft contact lenses
请给我一瓶软隐型眼镜清洗药水
qǐng gěi wǒ yī píng ruǎn yǐnxíng yǎnjìng qīngxǐ yàoshuǐ
ching gay wo ee ping jwan yin-shing yan-jing ching-shee yao-shway

Understanding

涂药 *tú yào*	to apply
处方药 *chǔfāng yào*	available on prescription only
胶囊 *jiāonáng*	capsule
禁忌症 *jìnjìzhèng*	contra-indications
药膏 *yàogāo*	cream
软膏 *ruǎngāo*	ointment
可能的副作用 *kěnéng de fùzuòyòng*	possible side effects
药粉 *yàofěn*	powder
栓剂 *shuānjì*	suppositories
糖浆 *tángjiāng*	syrup
药片 *yàopiàn*	tablet
每日三次，饭前服 *měi rì sān cì, fàn qián fú*	take three times a day before meals

Some informal expressions

我觉得不舒服 *wǒ juéde bù shūfu* *wo jway-de boo shoo-foo*
I feel really rough

感冒很难受 *gǎnmào hěn nánshòu* *gan-mao heun nan-shoe*
to have a stinking cold

HEALTH

PROBLEMS AND EMERGENCIES

Emergency numbers are *110* for police, *119* for the fire brigade and *120* for an ambulance.

Watch out for pickpockets in big cities, particularly at rail and bus stations, as well as on buses and long train journeys.

Hotels are usually quite safe. There is a security guard for each floor who is in charge of all the keys. All hotels have safe deposit boxes. Be careful, though, if you are staying in a dormitory.

It is essential to take out a good travel insurance policy before your trip. If you have something stolen, go straight to the nearest public safety office (公安局 *gōng'ānjú* *gong-an-joo*) to report it. You will have to fill in a form reporting the loss, and will need this document when you claim for the stolen goods on your insurance.

The basics

accident	事故 *shìgù* *sheu-goo*
ambulance	救护车 *jiùhùchē* *jyo-hoo-che*
broken	骨折 *gǔzhé* *goo-je*
coastguard	海岸救生队 *hǎi'àn jiùshēngduì* *hy-an jyo-shung-dway*
disabled	残疾人 *cánjírén* *tsan-jee-jeun*
doctor	医生 *yīshēng* *ee-shung*
emergency	紧急情况 *jǐnjí qíngkuàng* *jin-jee ching-kwang*
fire brigade	消防队 *xiāofángduì* *sheeao-fang-dway*
fire	着火 *zháohuǒ* *jao-hwoe*
hospital	医院 *yīyuàn* *ee-ywan*
ill	病了 *bìng le* *bing le*

injured 受伤 ***shòushāng*** *shoe-shang*
late 晚了 ***wǎn le*** *wan le*
police 警察 ***jǐngchá*** *jing-cha*

Expressing yourself

can you help me?
帮个忙，好吗？
bāng ge máng, hǎo ma?
bang ge mang, hao ma?

help!
救命！
jiù mìng!
jyo ming!

fire!
着火了！
zháohuǒ le!
jao-hwoe le!

be careful!
小心！
xiǎoxīn!
sheeao-shin!

it's an emergency!
紧急情况！
jǐnjí qíngkuàng!
jin-jee ching-kwang!

there's been an accident
出事故了
chū shìgù le
choo sheu-goo le

could I borrow your phone, please?
我可以借您的电话用一下吗？
wǒ kěyǐ jiè nín de diànhuà yòng yīxià ma?
wo ke-yee jyay nin de dyen-hwa yong ee-shya ma?

does anyone here speak English?
这儿有人说英语吗？
zhèr yǒu rén shuō yīngyǔ ma?
jer yoe jeun shwoe ying-yoo ma?

I need to contact the British consulate
我要跟英国领事馆联系
wǒ yào gēn yīngguó lǐngshìguǎn liánxì
wo yao geun ying-gwoe ling-sheu-gwan lyen-shee

where's the nearest police station?
最近的警察局在哪儿？
zuì jìn de jǐngchájú zài nǎr?
zway jin de jing-cha-joo zy nar?

what do I have to do?
我该怎么办呢?
wǒ gāi zěnme bàn ne?
wo gy zeun-me ban ne?

I've lost …
我丢了 …
wǒ diū le …
wo dyo le …

my passport/credit card has been stolen
我的护照/信用卡被偷了
wǒ de hùzhào/xìnyòngkǎ bèi tōu le
wo de hoo-jao/shin-yong-ka bay toe le

my bag's been snatched
我的包被抢走了
wǒ de bāo bèi qiǎngzǒu le
wo de bao bay chyang-zoe le

I've been attacked
我受到了攻击
wǒ shòudào le gōngjī
wo shoe-dao le gong-jee

my son/daughter is missing
我儿子/女儿丢了
wǒ érzi/nǚ'ér diū le
wo er-zeu/nu-er dyo le

my car's been towed away
我的车被拖走了
wǒ de chē bèi tuōzǒu le
wo de che bay twoe-zoe le

I've broken down
我的车抛锚了
wǒ de chē pāomáo le
wo de che pao-mao le

my car's been broken into
我的车被盗了
wǒ de chē bèi dào le
wo de che bay dao le

there's a man following me
有个男人在尾随我
yǒu ge nánrén zài wěisuí wǒ
yoe ge nan-jeun zy way-sway wo

is there disabled access?
有残疾人通道吗?
yǒu cánjírén tōngdào ma?
yoe tsan-jee-jeun tong-dao ma?

can you keep an eye on my things for a minute?
你给我看一会儿东西，好吗?
nǐ gěi wǒ kān yīhuìr dōngxi, hǎo ma?
nee gay wo kan ee-hwayr dong-shee, hao ma?

he's drowning, get help!
他要淹死了，快找人救!
tā yào yānsǐ le, kuài zhǎo rén jiù!
ta yao yan-seu le, kwhy jao jeun jyo!

Understanding

小心狗 *xiǎoxīn gǒu*	beware of the dog
车辆急修服务 *chēliàng jíxiū fúwù*	breakdown service
紧急出口 *jǐnjí chúkǒu*	emergency exit
失物招领 *shīwù zhāolǐng*	lost property
登山遇险营救 *dēngshān yùxiǎn yíngjiù*	mountain rescue
出故障了 *chū gùzhàng le*	out of order
警察局紧急情况救援 *jǐngchájú jǐnjí qíngkuàng jiùyuán*	police emergency services

POLICE

Expressing yourself

I want to report something stolen
我要报告我丢东西了
wǒ yào bàogào wǒ diū dōngxi le
wo yao bao-gao wo dyo dong-shee le

I need a document from the police for my insurance company
我需要警察局给我的保险公司开一份证明文件
wǒ xūyào jǐngchájú gěi wǒ de bǎoxiǎn gōngsī kāi yī fèn zhèngmíng wénjiàn
wo shoo-yao jing-cha-joo gay wo de bao-shyen gong-seu ky ee feun jung-ming weun-jyen

Understanding

Filling in forms

姓 *xìng*	surname
名 *míng*	first name
地址 *dìzhǐ*	address
邮政编码 *yóuzhèng biānmǎ*	postcode
国家 *guójiā*	country
国籍 *guójí*	nationality
出生日期 *chūshēng rìqī*	date of birth

出生地点 ***chūshēng dìdiǎn***	place of birth
年龄 ***niánlíng***	age
性别 ***xìngbié***	sex
停留时间 ***tíngliú shíjiān***	duration of stay
到达 ***dàodá rìqī***	arrival date
离开日期 ***líkāi rìqī***	departure date
职业 ***zhíyè***	occupation
护照号码 ***hùzhào hàomǎ***	passport number

这个物品需要交关税
zhè ge wùpǐn xūyào jiāo guānshuì
je ge woo-pin shu-yao jeeao gwan-shway
there's customs duty to pay on this item

请你打开这个包
qǐng nǐ dǎkāi zhè ge bāo
ching nee da-ky je ge bao
would you open this bag, please?

丢什么了?
diū shénme le
dyo sheun-me le
what's missing?

什么时候发生的?
shénme shíhou fāshēng de?
sheun-me sheu-hoe fa-shung de?
when did this happen?

你住在什么地方?
nǐ zhù zài shénme dìfang?
nee joo zy sheun-me dee-fang?
where are you staying?

你可以描述一下他/她/它吗?
nǐ kěyǐ miáoshù yīxià tā ma?
nee ke-yee meeao-shoo ee-shya ta ma?
can you describe him/her/it?

请在这儿签字
qǐng zài zhèr qiānzì
ching zy jer chyen-zeu
would you sign here, please?

请你填一下这张表
qǐng nǐ tián yīxià zhè zhāng biǎo
ching nee tyen ee-shya je jang beeao
would you fill in this form, please?

Some informal expressions

监狱 ***jiānyù*** *jyen-yoo* slammer, nick
被警察抓走了 ***bèi jǐngchá zhuā zǒu le*** *bay jing-cha jwa zoe le* to get nicked
东西被偷了 ***dōngxi bèi tōu le*** *dong-shee bay toe le* to get something nicked

TIME AND DATE

The Chinese official calendar has been for 50 years the Gregorian, or Western, calendar. This is universally used in China, so poses no difficulties for travellers. However, as in many other parts of the world, the "old" traditional lunar calendar, closely linked to the agricultural year, has a strong influence on seasons and festivals. The best known example is probably the movable date of Chinese New Year.

When visiting historical sites and museums, dates will be given as in the official calendar, but it may be helpful to have an overview of China's past, and this is often expressed in terms of emperors' reigns and dynasties, such as the 汉 **Hàn** *Han*, 唐 **Táng** *Tang*, 宋 **Sòng** *Song* and 明 **Míng** *Ming* dynasties.

The most famous Chinese emperors are probably 秦始皇 **Qín Shǐ Huáng** *chin shen hwang*, the emperor who unified China in 221BC, taking the country out of the "Warring States Period" (475–221BC) and 唐太宗 **Táng Tàizōng** *tang ty zong*, who ruled for 23 years from AD 627–50. The Tang dynasty continued until AD 907.

The basics

after 以后 **yǐhòu** *ee-hoe*
already 已经 **yǐjīng** *ee-jing*
always 总是 **zǒngshì** *zong-sheu*
at lunchtime 在午饭的时候 **zài wǔfàn de shíhou** *zy woo-fan de sheu-hoe*
at the beginning/end of 在 … 开始时/结束时 **zài … kāishǐ shí/jiéshù shí** *zy … ky-sheu sheu/jyay-shoo sheu*
at the moment 现在 **xiànzài** *shyen-zy*
before 以前 **yǐqián** *ee-chyen*
between … and … 在 … 之间 **… zài … zhījiān …** *zy … jeu-jyen …*
day 天 **tiān** *tyen*
during 在 … 期间/中 **zài … qījiān/zhōng** *zy … chee-jyen/jong*

early	早 ***zǎo*** *zao*
evening	晚上 ***wǎnshang*** *wan-shang*
for a long time	很长时间 ***hěn cháng shíjiān*** *heun chang sheu-jyen*
from … to …	从…到… ***cóng … dào …*** *tsong …dao …*
from time to time	有时 ***yǒushí*** *yoe-sheu*
in a little while	过一会儿 ***guò yīhuìr*** *gwoe ee-hwayr*
in the evening	在晚上 ***zài wǎnshang*** *zy wan-shang*
in the middle of	在…中 ***zài … zhōng*** *zy… jong*
last	最后 ***zuìhòu*** *zway-hoe*
late	晚 ***wǎn*** *wan*
midday	中午 ***zhōngwǔ*** *jong-woo*
midnight	午夜 ***wǔyè*** *woo-yay*
morning	早上 ***zǎoshang*** *zao-shang*
month	月 ***yuè*** *yway*
never	从来没 ***cónglái méi*** *tsong-ly may*
next	下个 ***xià ge*** *shya ge*
night	夜里 ***yè lǐ*** *yay lee*
not yet	还没有 ***hái méi yǒu*** *hy may yoe*
now	现在 ***xiànzài*** *shyen-zy*
occasionally	偶而 ***ǒu'ěr*** *oe-er*
often	常常 ***chángcháng*** *chang-chang*
rarely	很少 ***hěn shǎo*** *heun shao*
recently	最近 ***zuìjìn*** *zway-jin*
since	从…以来 ***cōng … yǐlái*** *tsong … ee-ly*
sometimes	有时候 ***yǒushíhou*** *yoe sheu-hoe*
soon	很快/不久 ***hěn kuài/bùjiǔ*** *heun kwhy/boo-jyo*
still	仍然 ***réngrán*** *jung-jan*
straightaway	马上 ***mǎshàng*** *ma-shang*
until	到…为止 ***dào … wéizhǐ*** *dao … wei-jeu*
week	星期/周 ***xīngqī/zhōu*** *shing-chee/joe*
weekend	周末 ***zhōumò*** *joe-mo*
year	年 ***nián*** *nyen*

Expressing yourself

see you soon!
再见!
zàijiàn!
zy-jyen!

see you on Monday!
星期一见!
xīngqīyī jiàn!
shing-chee-yee jyen!

sorry I'm late
对不起，我来晚了
duìbuqǐ, wǒ lái wǎn le
dway-boo-chee, wo ly wan le

I haven't had time to …
我还没时间 …
wǒ hái méi shíjiān …
wo hy may sheu-jyen …

I'm in a rush
我正忙着呢
wǒ zhèng mángzhe ne
wo jung mang-je ne

just a minute, please
请等一会儿
qǐng děng yīhuìr
ching dung ee-hwayr

I had a late night
我昨天晚上睡得很晚
wǒ zuótiān wǎnshang shuì de hén wǎn
wo zwoe-tyen wan-shang shway de heun wan

I waited ages
我等了很长时间
wǒ děng le hěn cháng shíjiān
wo dung le heun chang sheu-jyen

see you later!
回头见!
huítóu jiàn!
hway-toe jyen!

have a good weekend!
祝你周末愉快!
zhù nǐ zhōumò yúkuài!
joo nee joe-mo yoo-kwy!

I haven't been there yet
我还没去过那儿呢
wǒ hái méi qù guo nàr ne
wo hy may choo gwoe nar ne

I've got plenty of time
我有足够的时间
wǒ yǒu zúgòu de shíjiān
wo yoe zoo-gwoe de sheu-jyen

hurry up!
快!
kuài!
kwy!

I got up very early
我起床很早
wǒ qǐchuáng hěn zǎo
wo chee-chwang heun zao

I have to get up very early tomorrow to catch my plane
明天我得早起赶飞机
míngtiān wǒ děi zǎo qǐ gǎn fēijī
ming-tyen wo day zao chee gan fay-jee

we only have four days left
我们只剩下四天了
wǒmen zhǐ shèngxià sì tiān le
wo-meun jeu shung-shya seu tyen le

THE DATE

How to express the date

The date is always given in the order year (年 *nián* *nyen*), month (月 *yuè* *yway*), day (日 *rì* *jeu*).

2 January 1634:	***1634 年 1 月 2 日 yī liù sān sì nián yī yuè èr rì*** *ee lyo san seu nyen ee yway er jeu*
in June 1867	***1867 年 6月 yī bā liù qī nián liù yuè*** *ee ba lyo chee nyen lyo yway*
from 1904 to 1909	***从1904 年到 1909 年 cóng yī jiǔ líng sì nián dào yī jiǔ líng jiǔ nián*** *tsong ee jyo ling seu nyen dao ee jyo ling jyo nyen*

"Century" is translated as 世纪 ***shìjì*** *sheu-jee*.

early 17th century	***17 世纪初 shíqī shìjì chū*** *sheu-chee sheu-jee choo*
mid-17th century	***17 世纪中 shíqī shìjì zhōng*** *sheu-chee sheu-jee jong*
late 17th century	***17 世纪末 shíqī shìjì mò*** *sheu-chee sheu-jee mo*

The basics

... ago … 前 ... *qián* ... chyen
at the beginning/end of 在 … 开始时/结束时 *zài ... kāishǐ shí/jiéshù shí* zy ky-sheu sheu/jyay-shoo sheu
in the middle of 在 … 中 *zài ... zhōng* zy ... jong
in two days' time 两天后 *liǎng tiān hòu* lyang tyen hoe
last night 昨天夜里 *zuótiān yè lǐ* zwoe-tyen yay lee
the day after tomorrow 后天 *hòutiān* hoe-tyen
the day before yesterday 前天 *qiántiān* chyen-tyen
today 今天 *jīntiān* jin-tyen
tomorrow 明天 *míngtiān* ming-tyen
tomorrow morning/afternoon/evening 明天早上/下午/晚上 *míngtiān zǎoshang /xiàwǔ/wǎnshang* ming-tyen zao-shang/shya-woo/wan-shang
yesterday 昨天 *zuótiān* zwoe-tyen
yesterday morning/afternoon/evening 昨天早上/下午/晚上 *zuótiān zǎoshang/xiàwǔ/wǎnshang* zwoe-tyen zao-shang/shya-woo/wan-shang

Expressing yourself

I was born in 1975
我出生在 1975 年
wǒ chūshēng zài yī jiǔ qī wǔ nián
wo choo-shung zy ee jyo chee woo nyen

I came here a few years ago
我几年前来到这里
wǒ jǐ nián qián láidào zhèlǐ
wo jee nyen chyen ly-dao je-lee

I was here last year at the same time
去年的这个时候我在这里
qùnián de zhè ge shíhou wǒ zài zhèlǐ
choo-nyen de je ge sheu-hoe wo zy je-lee

what's the date today?
今天几号?
jīntiān jǐ hào?
jin-tyen jee hao?

it's the 1st of May
五月一号
wǔ yuè yī hào
woo yway ee hao

we're leaving tomorrow
我们明天走
wǒmen míngtiān zǒu
wo-meun ming-tyen zoe

what day is it today?
今天星期几?
jīntiān xīngqī jǐ?
jin-tyen shing-chee jee?

I'm staying until Sunday
我呆到星期天
wǒ dāi dào xīngqītiān
wo dy dao shing-chee-tyen

I already have plans for Tuesday
我星期二已经有计划了
wǒ xīngqī'èr yǐjīng yǒu jìhuà le
wo shing-chee-er ee-jing yoe jee-hwa le

Understanding

一次/两次 *yī cì/liǎng cì*	once/twice
一小时三次/一天三次 *yī xiǎoshí sān cì/yī tiān sān cì*	three times an hour/a day
每天 *měi tiān*	every day
每星期一 *měi xīngqīyī*	every Monday

它是十九世纪中修建的
tā shì shíjiǔ shìjì zhōng xiūjiàn de
ta sheu sheu-jyo sheu-jee jong shyo-jyen de
it was built in the mid-nineteenth century

这儿夏天很热闹
zhèr xiàtiān hěn rènao
jer shya-tyen heun je-nao
it gets very busy here in the summer

你们什么时候走?
nǐmen shénme shíhou zǒu?
nee-meun sheun-me sheu-hoe zoe?
when are you leaving?

你们呆多长时间?
nǐmen dāi duō cháng shíjiān?
nee-meun dy dwoe chang sheu-jyen?
how long are you staying?

THE TIME

Telling the time

"Hour" is translated as 点 **diǎn** (*dyen*) and "minute" as 分 **fēn** (*feun*). To say "four o'clock in the morning" you have to say "morning + four + hours": 早上四点 **zǎoshang sì diǎn** (*zao-shang seu dyen*).

Some informal expressions

两点整 ***liǎng diǎn zhěng*** *lyang-dyen jung*
at 2 o'clock on the dot
刚过八点 ***gāng guò bā diǎn*** *gang gwoe ba-dyen*
it's just gone 8 o'clock

The basics

early	早 ***zǎo*** *zao*
half an hour	半小时 ***bàn xiǎoshí*** *ban sheeao-sheu*
in the afternoon	在下午 ***zài xiàwǔ*** *zy shya-woo*
in the morning	在早上 ***zài zǎoshang*** *zy zao-shang*
late	晚点 ***wǎndiǎn*** *wan-dyen*
midday	中午 ***zhōngwǔ*** *jong-woo*
midnight	午夜 ***wǔyè*** *woo-yay*
on time	准时 ***zhǔnshí*** *joon-sheu*
quarter of an hour	一刻钟 ***yī kè zhōng*** *ee ke jong*
three quarters of an hour	三刻钟 ***sān kè zhōng*** *san ke jong*

Expressing yourself

what time is it?
几点了？
jǐ diǎn le?
jee dyen le?

excuse me, have you got the time, please?
请问，几点了？
qǐng wèn, jǐ diǎn le?
ching weun, jee dyen le?

it's exactly three o'clock
三点整
sān diǎn zhěng
san dyen jung

it's nearly one o'clock
快一点了
kuài yī diǎn le
kwhy ee dyen le

it's ten past one
一点十分
yī diǎn shí fēn
ee dyen sheu feun

it's a quarter past one
一点一刻
yī diǎn yī kè
ee dyen ee ke

it's a quarter to one
差一刻一点
chà yī kè yī diǎn
cha ee ke ee dyen

it's twenty past twelve
十二点二十
shí'èr diǎn èrshí
sheu-er dyen er-sheu

it's twenty to twelve
差二十十二点
chà èrshí shí'èr diǎn
cha er-sheu sheu-er dyen

it's half past one
一点半
yī diǎn bàn
ee dyen ban

I arrived at about two o'clock
我是两点左右到的
wǒ shì liǎng diǎn zuǒyòu dào de
wo sheu lyang dyen zwoe-yoe dao le

I set my alarm for nine
我把闹钟上到九点
wǒ bǎ nàozhōng shàng dào jiǔ diǎn
wo ba nao-jong shang dao jyo dyen

I waited twenty minutes
我等了二十分钟
wǒ děng le èrshí fēn zhōng
wo dung le er-sheu feun jong

the train was fifteen minutes late
火车晚点一刻钟
huǒchē wǎndiǎn yī kè zhōng
hwoe-che wan-dyen ee ke jong

I got home an hour ago
我是一小时以前到家的
wǒ shì yī xiǎoshí yǐqián dào jiā de
wo sheu ee sheeao-sheu ee-chyen dao jya de

shall we meet in half an hour?
我们半小时以后见，好吗？
wǒmen bàn xiǎoshí yǐhòu jiàn, hǎo ma?
wo-meun ban sheeao-sheu ee-hoe jyen, hao ma?

I'll be back in a quarter of an hour
我一刻钟以后回来
wǒ yī kè zhōng yǐhòu huílái
wo ee ke jong ee-hoe hway-ly

there's a three-hour time difference between … and …
在…和…之间时差是三小时
zài … hé … zhījiān shíchā shì sān xiǎoshí
zy … he … jeu-jyen sheu-cha sheu san sheeao-sheu

Understanding

正点和半点开出 ***zhèngdiǎn hé bàndiǎn kāichū*** departs on the hour and the half-hour

上午十点到下午四点开门 ***shàngwǔ shí diǎn dào xiàwǔ sì diǎn kāimén*** open from 10am to 4pm

每天晚上七点上演
měi tiān wǎnshang qī diǎn shàngyǎn
may tyen wan-shang chee dyen shang-yan
it's on every evening at seven

演出一个半小时左右
yǎnchū yī ge bàn xiǎoshí zuǒyòu
yan-choo ee ge ban sheeao-sheu zwoe-yoe
it lasts around an hour and a half

早上十点开门
zǎoshang shí diǎn kāimén
zao-shang sheu dyen ky-meun
it opens at ten in the morning

NUMBERS

The Chinese number system seems complicated, but is in fact very logical.

When nouns are numbered or pointed out as "this" or "that", they carry a classifier related to the class of the noun: 书 ***shū*** *shoo* (book), for example, carries the classifier 本 ***běn*** *ben*, meaning "volume": "this book" becomes 这本书 ***zhè běn shū*** *jeu beun shoo*. There are over 50 classifiers in common use in Chinese. However, the all-purpose classifier 个 ***gè*** ge (4th tone, but usually unstressed) can double for most of them. The structure is always number–classifier–noun.

The decimal point is called ***diǎn*** *dyen*: 1.2 = ***yī diǎn èr*** *ee dyen er*. The prefix 第 ***dì*** *dee* is used to form ordinal numbers (1st, 2nd, 3rd etc) ***dì sān*** *dee san* = the third.

Some numbers carry special connotations: the word for death 死 ***sǐ*** seu is pronounced similarly to the number 4 ***sì*** *seu* so 4 is not a popular number. However, the pronunciation of 8 ***bā*** *ba* in Cantonese, one of the major Chinese dialects, is almost the same as 发 ***fā*** *fa* which means "flourishing in business", thus signifying wealth or good luck! For this reason, the Beijing Olympics will begin at 8.08 on 8 August 2008.

In Chinese, the four figures making up the name of a year are read out as four separate numbers and 年 ***nián*** *nyen* (year) is put at the end. For example, 1975 年 is read ***yī jiǔ qī wǔ nián*** *(ee jyo chee woo nyen)*.

The names of the 12 months are produced by combining the cardinal numbers 1 to 12 with 月 ***yuè*** *yway* (month). For example, September, the ninth month, is 九月 ***jiǔyuè*** *jyo-yway*. Dates in the month are produced by combining the numbers 1 to 31 with 号 ***hào*** *hao* when speaking or 日 ***rì*** *jeu* when writing: for example, 12 October would be 十月十二号 ***shíyuè shí'èr hào*** *sheu-yway sheu-er hao*.

To express Monday to Saturday, the cardinal numbers from 1 to 6 follow 星期 ***xīngqī*** *shing-chee* week. The word for Sunday is 星期天 ***xīngqītiān*** *shing-chee-tyen* or 星期日 ***xīngqīrì*** *shing-chee-jeu*.

There are two words for 2: 二 ***èr*** *er* is used in counting and compound numbers while 两 ***liǎng*** *lyang* is used for two of the same thing (similar to "a couple of"). In double-digit numbers, units are added to the tens, so 12 is 十二 ***shí'èr*** *sheu-er* (10+2). To form multiples of 10, the multiplier precedes 十 ***shí*** *sheu* (ten), so that 20 is 二十 ***èrshí*** *er-sheu* (2x10); 22 is 二十二 ***èrshí'èr*** *er-sheu-er* (2x10+2).

0	零 ***líng*** *ling*
1	一 ***yī*** *ee*
2	二 ***èr*** *er*
3	三 ***sān*** *san*
4	四 ***sì*** *seu*
5	五 ***wǔ*** *woo*
6	六 ***liù*** *lyo*
7	七 ***qī*** *chee*
8	八 ***bā*** *ba*
9	九 ***jiǔ*** *jyo*
10	十 ***shí*** *sheu*
11	十一 ***shíyī*** *sheu-yee*
12	十二 ***shí'èr*** *sheu-er*
13	十三 ***shísān*** *sheu-san*
14	十四 ***shísì*** *sheu-seu*
15	十五 ***shíwǔ*** *sheu-woo*
16	十六 ***shíliù*** *sheu-lyo*
17	十七 ***shíqī*** *sheu-chee*
18	十八 ***shíbā*** *sheu-ba*
19	十九 ***shíjiǔ*** *sheu-jyo*
20	二十 ***èrshí*** *er-sheu*
21	二十一 ***èrshíyī*** *er-sheu-yee*
22	二十二 ***èrshí'èr*** *er-sheu-er*
30	三十 ***sānshí*** *san-sheu*
35	三十五 ***sānshíwǔ*** *san-sheu-woo*
40	四十 ***sìshí*** *seu-sheu*
50	五十 ***wǔshí*** *woo-sheu*
60	六十 ***liùshí*** *lyo-sheu*
70	七十 ***qīshí*** *chee-sheu*
80	八十 ***bāshí*** *ba-sheu*
90	九十 ***jiǔshí*** *jyo-sheu*

100	一百 ***yībăi*** ee-by
101	一百零一 ***yībăi líng yī*** ee-by ling ee
200	二百 ***èrbăi*** er-by
500	五百 ***wŭbăi*** woo-by
1000	一千 ***yīqiān*** ee-chyen
2000	两千 ***liăngqiān*** lyen-chyen
10000	一万 ***yīwàn*** ee-wan
1000000	一百万 ***yībăiwàn*** ee-by-wan
first	第一 ***dì yī*** dee-yee
second	第二 ***dì èr*** dee-er
third	第三 ***dì sān*** dee san
fourth	第四 ***dì sì*** dee seu
fifth	第五 ***dì wŭ*** dee woo
sixth	第六 ***dì liù*** dee lyo
seventh	第七 ***dì qī*** dee chee
eighth	第八 ***dì bā*** dee ba
ninth	第九 ***dì jiŭ*** dee jyo
tenth	第十 ***dì shí*** dee sheu
twentieth	第二十 ***dì èrshí*** dee er-sheu

20 plus 3 equals 23
二十加三等于二十三
èrshí jiā sān děngyú èrshísān
er-sheu jya san dung-yoo er-sheu-san

20 minus 3 equals 17
二十减三等于十七
èrshí jiăn sān děngyú shíqī
er-sheu jyen san dung-yoo sheu-chee

20 multiplied by 4 equals 80
二十乘以四等于八十
èrshí chéngyĭ sì děngyú bāshí
er-sheu chung-ee seu dung-yoo ba-sheu

20 divided by 4 equals 5
二十除以四等于五
èrshí chúyĭ sì děngyú wŭ
er-sheu choo-ee seu dung-yoo woo

DICTIONARY

ENGLISH-CHINESE DICTIONARY

A

a *see grammar*
able: to be able to 能 *néng* nung
about … 左右 … *zuŏyòu* … zwoe-yoe; **to be about to do** 要做 *yào zuò* yao zwoe
above 在 … 上方 *zài* … *shàngfāng* zy … shang-fang
abroad 在国外 *zài guówài* zy gwoe-way
accept 收 *shōu* shoe
access 通道 *tōngdào* tong-dao **135**
accident 事故 *shìgù* sheu-goo **39**, **134**
accommodation 住处 *zhùchù* joo-choo
across 穿过 *chuānguò* chwan-gwoe
adaptor 插座转换 *chāzuò zhuǎnhuàn* cha-zwoe jwan-hwan
address 地址 *dìzhǐ* dee-jeu
admission 门票 *ménpiào* meun-peeao
advance: in advance 预先 *yùxiān* yoo-shyen **77**
advice 意见 *yìjiàn* ee-jyen
advise 提出意见建议 *tíchū yìjiàn jiànyì* tee-choo ee-jyen jyen-yee
aeroplane 飞机 *fēijī* fay-jee
after 以后 *yǐhòu* ee-hoe
afternoon 下午 *xiàwǔ* shya-woo
after-sun (cream) 护肤霜 *hùfūshuāng* hoo-foo-shwang
again 再 *zài* zy
against 反对 *fǎnduì* fan-dway
age 年龄 *niánlíng* nyen-ling
air 空气 *kōngqì* kong-chee
air conditioning 空调 *kōngtiáo* kong-tyo
airline 航空公司 *hángkōng gōngsī* hang-kong gong-seu
airmail 航空邮件 *hángkōng yóujiàn* hang-kong yoe-jyen
airport 机场 *jīchǎng* jee-chang
alarm clock 闹钟 *nàozhōng* nao-jong
alcohol 白酒 *báijiǔ* by-jyo
alive 活 *huó* hwoe
all 所有的 *suǒyǒu de* swoe-yoe de; **all day** 一整天 *yī zhěng tiān* ee jung tyen; **all week** 一星期 … 都 *yī xīngqī* … *dōu* ee shing-chee doe; **all the better** 更好 *gèng hǎo* gung hao; **all the same** 一样 *yīyàng* ee-yang; **all the time** 一直 *yīzhí* ee-jeu
allergic 过敏 *guòmǐn* gwoe-min **58**, **129**, **131**
almost 几乎 *jīhū* jee-hoo
already 已经 *yǐjīng* ee-jing
also 也 *yě* yay
although 虽然 … 可是 *suīrán* … *kěshì* sway-jan … ke-sheu
always 总是 *zǒngshì* zong-sheu
ambulance 救护车 *jiùhùchē* jyo-hoo-che **127**
American (*n*) 美国人 *měiguórén* may-gwoe-jeun
American (*adj*) 美国的 *měiguó de* may-gwoe de
among 在 … 中 *zài* … *zhōng* zy … jong
anaesthetic 麻醉 *mázuì* ma-zway
and 和 *hé* he, 跟 *gēn* geun
animal 动物 *dòngwù* dong-woo
ankle 脚脖子 *jiǎobózi* jya-bao-zeu
anniversary 周年纪念日 *zhōunián jìniànrì* joe-nyen jee- nyen-jeu
another 另一个 *lìng yī ge* ling ee ge

answer *(n & v)* 回答 ***huídá*** *hway- da*
answering machine 电话留言机 ***diànhuà liúyánjī*** *dyen-hwa lyo-yan-jee*
ant 蚂蚁 ***mǎyǐ*** *ma-yee*
antibiotics 抗生素 ***kàngshēngsù*** *kang-shung-soo*
anybody, **anyone** 任何人 ***rènhé rén*** *jeun-he jeun*
anything 任何事物 ***rènhé shìwù*** *jeun-he sheu-woo*
anyway 无论如何 ***wúlùnrúhé*** *woo-loon-joo-he*
appendicitis 阑尾炎 ***lánwěiyán*** *lan-way-yan*
appointment 预约 ***yùyuē*** *yoo-yway*; **to make an appointment** 预约 ***yùyuē*** *yoo-yway* **126**; **to have an appointment with …** 预约了 … ***yùyuē le*** *… yoo-yway le …* **127**
April 四月 ***sìyuè*** *seu-yway*
area 地方 ***dìfang*** *dee-fang*; **in the area** 在这个地方 ***zài zhè ge dìfang*** *zy je ge dee-fang*
arm 胳膊 ***gēbo*** *ge-bo*
around 在 … 这儿附近 ***zài … zhèr fùjìn*** *zy … jer foo-jin*
arrange 安排 ***ānpái*** *an-py*; **to arrange to meet** 安排和 … 见面 ***ānpái hé … jiànmiàn*** *an-py he … jyen-myen*
arrival 到达 ***dàodá*** *dao-da*
arrive 到达 ***dàodá*** *dao-da*
art 美术 ***měishù*** *may-shoo*
artist 画家 ***huàjiā*** *hwa-jya*
as 像 … 一样 ***xiàng … yīyàng*** *shyang … ee-yang*; **as soon as possible** 越快越好 ***yuè kuài yuè hǎo*** *yway kwhy yway hao*; **as soon as …** 一 … 就 … ***yī … jiù …*** *ee … jyo …*; **as well as** 也 ***yě*** *yay*
ashtray 烟灰缸 ***yānhuīgāng*** *yan-hway-gang* **56**
ask *(request)* 请 ***qǐng*** *ching*; **to ask a question** 问问题 ***wèn wèntí*** *weun weun-tee*

aspirin 阿斯匹林 ***āsīpīlín*** *a-seu-pee-lin*
asthma 哮喘病 ***xiàochuǎnbìng*** *sheeao-chwan-bing*
at 在 ***zài*** *zy*
attack 攻击 ***gōngjī*** *gong-jee* **135**
August 八月 ***bāyuè*** *ba-yway*
autumn 秋天 ***qiūtiān*** *chyo-tyen*
available 可使用的 ***kě shǐyòng de*** *ke sheu-yong de*
away: 10 miles away 十英里以外 ***shí yīnglǐ yǐwài*** *sheu ying-lee ee-wy*

B

baby 婴儿 ***yīng'ér*** *ying-er*
baby's bottle 奶瓶 ***nǎipíng*** *ny-ping*
back 后背 ***hòubèi*** *hoe-bay*; **at the back of …** 在 … 后边 ***zai … hòubian*** *zy … hoe-byen*
backpack 背包 ***bēibāo*** *bay-bao*
bad 糟糕 ***zāogāo*** *zao-gao*; **it's not bad** 还行。 ***hái xíng*** *hy shing*
bag 包 ***bāo*** *bao*
baggage 行李 ***xíngli*** *shing-lee*
bake 烤 ***kǎo*** *kao*
baker's 面包店 ***miànbāodiàn*** *myen-bao-dyen*
balcony 阳台 ***yángtái*** *yang-ty*
bandage 绷带 ***bēngdài*** *bung-dy*
bank 银行 ***yínháng*** *yin-hang* **111**
banknote 钞票 ***chāopiào*** *chao-peeao*
bar 酒吧 ***jiǔbā*** *jyo-ba*
barbecue 烧烤 ***shāokǎo*** *shao-kao*
bath （洗）澡 ***(xǐ) zǎo*** *(shee) zao*; **to have a bath** 洗澡 ***xǐzǎo*** *shee-zao*
bathroom 洗澡间 ***xǐzǎojiān*** *shee-zao-jyen*
bath towel 浴巾 ***yùjīn*** *yoo-jin*
battery *(for appliance)* 电池 ***diànchí*** *dyen-cheu* **39**
be 是 ***shì*** *sheu*
beach 海滩 ***hǎitān*** *hy-tan*
beard 胡子 ***húzi*** *hoo-zeu*

beautiful 漂亮 ***piàoliang*** *peeao-lyang*; *(weather)* 晴朗 ***qínglǎng*** *ching-lang*
because 因为 ***yīnwèi*** *yin-way*; **because of** 由于 ***yóuyú*** *yoe-yoo*
bed 床 ***chuáng*** *chwang*
bee 蜜蜂 ***mìfēng*** *mee-fung*
before 以前 ***yǐqián*** *ee-chyen*
begin 开始 ***kāishǐ*** *ky-sheu*
beginning 开始 ***kāishǐ*** *ky-sheu*
behind 在 … 后边 ***zài … hòubian*** *zy … hoe-byen*
believe 相信 ***xiāngxìn*** *shyang-shin*
below 在 … 下边 ***zài … xiàbian*** *zy … shya-byen*
beside 在 … 旁边 ***zài … bángbiān*** *zy... bang-byen*
best 最好的 ***zuìhǎo de*** *zway-hao de*; **the best** 最好的 ***zuìhǎo de*** *zway-hao de*
better 更好 ***gènghǎo*** *gung-hao*; **to get better** 好起来 ***hǎo qǐlái*** *hao chee-ly*; **it's better to …** 最好是 … ***zuìhǎo shì*** … *jway-hao sheu* …
between 在 … 之间 ***zài … zhījiān*** *zy … jeu-jyen*
bicycle 自行车 ***zìxíngchē*** *zeu- shing-che* **38**
bicycle pump 自行车打气筒 ***zìxíngchē dǎqìtǒng*** *zeu-shing-che da-chee-tong*
big 大 ***dà*** *da*
bike 自行车 ***zìxíngchē*** *zeu-shing-che*
bill 账单 ***zhàngdān*** *jang-dan* **61**
bin 垃圾箱 ***lājīxiāng*** *la-jee-shyang*
binoculars 望远镜 ***wàngyuǎnjìng*** *wang-ywan-jing*
birthday 生日 ***shēngrì*** *shung-jeu*
bit 一点儿 ***yīdiǎnr*** *ee-dyar*
bite *(n & v)* 咬 ***yǎo*** *yao*
black 黑 ***hēi*** *hay*
blanket 毯子 ***tǎnzi*** *tan-zeu*
bleed 出血 ***chūxuè*** *choo-shway*
bless: bless you! 为你祝福 ***wèi nǐ zhùfú*** *way nee joo-foo*

blind 盲人 ***mángrén*** *mang-jeun*
blister 水疱 ***shuǐpào*** *shway-pao*
blood 血 ***xuè*** *shway*
blood pressure 血压 ***xuèyā*** *shway-ya*
blue 蓝色 ***lánsè*** *lan-se*
board *(for game)* 棋类 ***qílèi*** *chee-lay*
boarding 登机 ***dēngjī*** *dung-jee*
boat 船 ***chuán*** *chwan*
body 身体 ***shēntǐ*** *sheun-tee*
book *(n)* 书 ***shū*** *shoo*
book *(v)* 订 ***dìng*** *ding* **30**, **77**
bookshop 书店 ***shūdiàn*** *shoo-dyen*
boot 靴子 ***xuēzi*** *shway-zeu*; *(of car)* 汽车行李箱 ***qìchē xínglixiāng*** *chee-che shing-lee-shyang*
borrow 借 ***jiè*** *jyay*
both 两个都 ***liǎng ge dōu*** *lyang ge doe*; **both of us** 我们两个 ***wǒmen liǎng ge*** *wo-meun lyang ge*
bottle 瓶子 ***píngzi*** *ping-zeu*
bottle opener 开瓶器 ***kāipíngqì*** *ky-ping-chee*
bottom 底部 ***dǐbù*** *dee-boo*; **at the bottom** 在底部 ***zài dǐbù*** *zy dee-boo*; **at the bottom of** 在 … 的底部 ***zài … de dǐbù*** *zy … de dee-boo*
bowl 碗 ***wǎn*** *wan*
bra 胸罩 ***xiōngzhào*** *shyong-jao*
brake *(n)* 闸 ***zhá*** *ja*
brake *(v)* 刹车 ***shāchē*** *sha-che*
bread 面包 ***miànbāo*** *myen-bao*
break 摔碎 ***shuāi suì*** *shwhy sway*; **to break one's leg** 摔断了腿 ***shuāi duàn le tuǐ*** *shwhy dwan le tway*
break down 出故障 ***chū gùzhàng*** *choo goo-jang*
breakdown 故障 ***gùzhàng*** *goo-jang* **39**, **135**
breakdown service 车辆急修服务 ***chēliàng jí xiū fúwù*** *che-lyang jee shyo foo-woo*
breakfast 早餐 ***zǎocān*** *zao-tsan*; **to have breakfast** 吃早餐 ***chī zǎocān*** *cheu zao-tsan*

bridge 桥 *qiáo* *cheeao*
bring *(bring with)* 带来 *dàilái* *dy-ly*; *(bring to)* 拿 … 来 *ná … lái* *na … ly*
brochure 小册子 *xiǎocèzi* *shee-ao tse-zee*
broken *(object)* 碎了 *suì le* *sway le*; *(bone)* 骨折 *gǔzhé* *goo-je*
bronchitis 支气管炎 *zhīqìguǎnyán* *jeu-chee-gwan-yan*
brother 兄弟 *xiōngdì* *shiong-dee*; *(younger)* 弟弟 *dìdi* *dee-dee*; *(elder)* 哥哥 *gēge* *ge-ge*
brown 咖啡色 *kāfēisè* *ka-fay-se*
brush 刷子 *shuāzi* *shwa-zeu*
build 修建 *xiūjiàn* *shyo-jyen*
building 建筑物 *jiànzhùwù* *jyen-joo-woo*
bump *(v)* 撞 *zhuàng* *jwang*
bumper 汽车保险杠 *qìchē bǎoxiǎngàng* *chee-che bao-shyen-gang*
buoy 浮标 *fúbiāo* *foo-beeao*
burn *(n)* 晒伤 *shàishāng* *shy-shang*
burn *(v)* 燃烧 *ránshāo* *jan-shao*; **to burn oneself** 烫伤 *tàngshāng* *tang-shang*
burst *(adj & v)* 爆了 *bào le* *bao le*
bus 公共汽车 *gōnggòng qìchē* *gong-gong chee-che* **36**
bus route 公共汽车路线 *gōnggòng qìchē lùxiàn* *gong-gong chee-che loo-shyen*
bus station 公共汽车总站 *gōnggòng qìchē zǒngzhàn* *gong-gong chee-che zong-jan*
bus stop 汽车站 *qìchēzhàn* *chee-che-jan*
busy 热闹 *rènao* *je-nao*
but 可是 *kěshì* *ke-sheu*
butcher's 肉店 *ròudiàn* *joe-dyen*
buy 买 *mǎi* *my* **30**, **98**, **100**
by *(with place)* 在 … 旁边 *zài … pángbiān* *zy… pang-byen*; *(means)* 用 *yòng* *yong*; **by car** 坐车 *zuò chē* *zwoe che*
bye! 再见！ *zàijiàn!* *zy-jyen!*

C

café 咖啡厅 *kāfēitīng* *ka-fay-ting*
call *(n)* 电话 *diànhuà* *dyen-hwa*
call *(v)* 打电话 *dǎ diànhuà* *da dyen-hwa* **122**; **I am called John** 我叫约翰 *wǒ jiào yuēhàn* *wo jeeow yway-han*
call back 回电话 *huí diànhuà* *hway dyen-hwa* **122**
camera 照相机 *zhàoxiàngjī* *jao-shyang-jee*
camper 野营者 *yěyíngzhě* *yay-ying-je*
camping 野营 *yěyíng* *yay-ying*; **to go camping** 去野营 *qù yěyíng* *choo yay-ying*
camping stove 野营炉 *yěyínglú* *yay-ying-loo*
campsite 野营地 *yěyíngdì* *yay- ying-dee* **51**
can *(n)* 罐头 *guàntou* *gwan-toe*
can *(v)* 能 *néng* *nung*; **I can't** 我不能 *wǒ bù néng* *wo boo nung*
cancel 取消 *qǔxiāo* *choo-sheeao*
candle 蜡烛 *làzhú* *la-joo*
can opener 开罐器 *kāiguànqì* *ky-gwan-chee*
car 小汽车 *xiǎoqìchē* *sheeao- chee-che*
caravan 旅行房车 *lǚxíng fángchē* *lu-shing fang-che*
card 卡 *kǎ* *ka*
car park 停车场 *tíngchēchǎng* *ting-che-chang*
carry 携带 *xiédài* *shyay-dy*
case: in case of … 假如 … *jiǎrú …* *jya-joo …*
cash 现金 *xiànjīn* *shyen-jin*; **to pay cash** 付现金 *fù xiànjīn* *foo shyen-jin* **100**
cashpoint 自动取款机 *zìdòng qǔkuǎnjī* *zeu-dong choo-kwan-jee* **111**, **112**
catch 抓住 *zhuāzhù* *jwa-joo*
CD 光盘 *guāngpán* *gwang-pan*

cemetery 墓地 ***mùdì*** *moo-dee*
centimetre 厘米 ***límǐ*** *lee-mee*
centre 中心 ***zhōngxīn*** *jong-shin*
century 世纪 ***shìjì*** *sheu-jee*
chair 椅子 ***yǐzi*** *ee-zeu*
change *(n)* 找的钱 ***zhǎo de qián*** *jao de chyen; (money)* 找的钱 ***zhǎo de qián*** *jao-de-chyen* **99**, **100**
changing room 试衣间 ***shìyījiān*** *sheu-yee-jyen* **102**
channel 电视频道 ***diànshì píndào*** *dyen-sheu pin-dao*
charge *(n)* 费用 ***fèiyòng*** *fay-yong*
charge *(v)* 收费 ***shōu fèi*** *shoe-fay*
cheap 便宜 ***piányi*** *pyen-yee*
check 检查 ***jiǎnchá*** *jyen-cha*
check in 住进旅馆 ***zhùjìn lǚguǎn*** *joo-jin lu-gwan*
check-in 登机 ***dēngjī*** *dung-jee* **32**
checkout 付款处 ***fùkuǎnchù*** *foo-kwan-choo*
cheers! 干杯！ ***gānbēi!*** *gan-bay!*
chemist's 药房 ***yàofáng*** *yao-fang*
cheque 支票 ***zhīpiào*** *jeu-peeao*
chest 胸 ***xiōng*** *shyong*
child 孩子 ***háizi*** *hy-zeu*
chilly 冷飕飕 ***lěng sōusōu*** *lung soe-soe*
chin 下巴 ***xiàba*** *shya-ba*
chopsticks 筷子 ***kuàizi*** *kwhy-zeu*
cigar 雪茄 ***xuějiā*** *shway-jya*
cigarette 香烟 ***xiāngyān*** *shyang- yan*
cigarette paper 卷烟纸 ***juǎnyānzhǐ*** *jwan-yan-jeu*
cinema 电影院 ***diànyǐngyuàn*** *dyen-ying-ywan*
circus 马戏表演 ***mǎxì biǎoyǎn*** *ma-shee beeao-yan*
city 城市 ***chéngshì*** *chung-sheu*
clean *(adj)* 干净 ***gānjìng*** *gan-jing*
clean *(v)* 打扫 … 干净 ***dǎsǎo … gānjìng*** *da-sao … gan-jing*
climate 气候 ***qìhòu*** *chee-hoe*
climbing 登山 ***dēngshān*** *dung- shan*
cloakroom 衣帽间 ***yīmàojiān*** *ee-mao-jyen*
close *(v)* 关 ***guān*** *gwan*
closed 关门了 ***guānmén le*** *gwan-meun le*
closing time 关门时间 ***guānmén shíjiān*** *gwan-meun sheu-jyen*
clothes 衣服 ***yīfu*** *ee-foo*
clutch 汽车离合器 ***qìchē líhéqì*** *chee-che lee-he-chee*
coach 大巴士 ***dàbāshì*** *da-ba-sheu* **36**
coast 海岸 ***hǎi'àn*** *hy-an*
coat hanger 衣架 ***yījià*** *ee-jya*
cockroach 蟑螂 ***zhāngláng*** *jang-lang*
coffee 咖啡 ***kāfēi*** *ka-fay*
coil *(contraceptive)* 避孕环 ***bìyùnhuán*** *bee-yoon-hwan*
coin 硬币 ***yìngbì*** *ying-bee*
Coke® 可乐 ***kělè*** *ke-le*
cold: to have a cold 感冒了 ***gǎnmào le*** *gan-mao le*
cold *(adj)* 冷 ***lěng*** *lung*; **it's cold** 天很冷 ***tiān hěn lěng*** *tyen heun lung*; **I'm cold** 我觉得冷 ***wǒ juéde lěng*** *wo jway-de lung*
collection 收藏品 ***shōucángpǐn*** *shoe-tsang-pin*
colour 颜色 ***yánsè*** *yan-se; (film)* 彩色 ***cǎisè*** *tsy-se*
comb 梳子 ***shūzi*** *shoo-zeu*
come 来 ***lái*** *ly*
come back 回来 ***huílái*** *hway-ly*
come in 进来 ***jìnlái*** *jin-ly*
come out 出去 ***chūqù*** *choo-choo*
comfortable 舒服 ***shūfu*** *shoo-foo*
company 公司 ***gōngsī*** *gong-seu*
compartment *(in train)* 火车车厢 ***huǒchē chēxiāng*** *hwoe-che che-shyang*
complain 抱怨 ***bào yuàn*** *bao ywan*
comprehensive insurance 全包的保险 ***quán bāo de bǎoxiǎn*** *chwan bao de bao-shyen*
computer 电脑 ***diànnǎo*** *dyen-nao*
concert 音乐会 ***yīnyuèhuì*** *yin- yway-hway* **76**

concert hall 音乐厅 *yīnyuètīng* yin-yway-ting
concession (ticket) 减价票 *jiǎnjiàpiào* jyen-jya-peeao **30, 84**
condom 避孕套 *bìyùntào* bee-yoon-tao
confirm 确认 *quèrèn* chway-jeun
connection 中转 *zhōngzhuǎn* jong-jwan **33**
constipated 便秘 *biànmì* byen- mee
consulate 领事馆 *lǐngshìguǎn* ling-sheu-gwan **134**
contact (n) 联系 *liánxì* lyen-shee
contact (v) 和 … 联系 *hé … liánxì* he … lyen-shee **121**
contact lenses 隐形眼镜 *yǐnxíng yǎnjìng* yin-shing yan-jing
contagious 传染 *chuánrǎn* chwan-jan
contraceptive 避孕用品 *bìyùn yòngpǐn* bee-yoon yong-pin
cook (v) 做饭 *zuòfàn* zwoe-fan
cooked 熟的 *shú de* shoo de
cooking 烹调 *pēngtiáo* pung- teeao; **to do the cooking** 做饭 *zuòfàn* zwoe-fan
cool 凉快 *liángkuai* lyang-kwhy
corkscrew 瓶塞起子 *píngsāi qǐzi* ping-sy chee-zeu
correct 对 *duì* dway
cost (v) 花（钱） *huā (qián)* hua (chyen)
cotton 棉布 *miánbù* myen-boo
cotton bud 棉签 *miánqiān* myen-chyen
cotton wool 药棉 *yàomián* yao-myen
cough (n & v) 咳嗽 *késou* ke-soe; **to have a cough** 咳嗽 *késou* ke-soe
count 计算 *jìsuàn* jee-swan
country (nation) 国家 *guójiā* gwoe-jya; (countryside) 乡村 *xiāngcūn* shyang-tsoon
countryside 农村 *nóngcūn* nong-tsoon
course: of course 当然 *dāngrán* dang-jan
cover (n) 盖子 *gàizi* gy-zeu; (blanket) 床单 *chuángdān* chwang-dan
cover (v) 盖 *gài* gy
credit card 信用卡 *xìnyòngkǎ* shin-yong-ka **44, 61, 99, 112**
cross (n) 十字 *shízì* sheu-zeu
cross (v) 穿过 *chuānguò* chwan-gwoe
cry 哭 *kū* koo
cup 杯子 *bēizi* bay-zeu
currency 货币 *huòbì* hwoe-bee
customs 海关 *hǎiguān* hy-gwan
cut 切 *qiē* chyay; **to cut oneself** 切伤自己 *qiēshāng zìjǐ* chyay- shang zeu-jee
cycle path 自行车道 *zìxíngchēdào* zeu-shing-che-dao

D

damaged 毁坏 *huǐhuài* hway-hwhy
damp 潮湿 *cháoshī* chao-sheu
dance (n) 舞蹈 *wǔdǎo* woo-dao
dance (v) 跳舞 *tiàowǔ* teeao-woo
dangerous 危险 *wēixiǎn* way- shyen
dark 暗 *àn* an; **dark blue** 深蓝 *shēnlán* sheun-lan
date (n) 日期 *rìqī* jeu-chee; **out of date** 过时的 *guòshí de* gwoe- sheu de
date (from) 日期 *riìqī* jeu-chee
date of birth 出生日期 *chūshēng rìqī* choo-shung jeu-chee
daughter 女儿 *nǚ'ér* nu-er
day 天 *tiān* tyen; **the day after tomorrow** 后天 *hòutiān* hoe-tyen; **the day before yesterday** 前天 *qiántiān* chyen-tyen
dead (battery) 用完了 *yòng wán le* yong wan le
deaf 聋 *lóng* long
dear 昂贵 *ánggui* ang-gway
debit card 直接划账卡 *zhíjiē huàzhàngkǎ* jeu-jyay hwa-jang-ka
December 十二月 *shí'èryuè* sheu-er-yway

declare 申报 *shēnbào* sheun-bao
deep 深 *shēn* sheun
degree 度 *dù* doo
delay 推迟 *tuīchí* tway-cheu
delayed 晚点 *wǎndiǎn* wan-dyen
dentist 牙医 *yā yī* ya-ee
deodorant 除味剂 *chúwèijì* choo-way-jee
department 部 *bù* boo
department store 百货商店 *bǎihuò shāngdiàn* by-hwoe shang-dyen
departure 开出 *kāichū* ky-choo
depend: that depends on ... 视 ... 而定 *shì ... ér dìng* sheu ... er ding
deposit *(advance payment)* 预付款 *yùfùkuǎn* yoo-foo-kwan; *(security money)* 押金 *yājīn* ya-jin
dessert 甜食 *tiánshí* tyen-sheu **58**
develop: to get a film developed 冲印胶卷 *chōngyìn jiāojuǎn* chong-yin jeeao-jwan **107**
diabetes 糖尿病 *tángniàobìng* tang-neeow-bing
dialling code 地区号码 *dìqū hàomǎ* dee-choo hao-ma
diarrhoea: to have diarrhoea 拉肚子 *lādùzi* la-doo-zeu
die 死 *sǐ* seu
diesel 柴油 *cháiyóu* chy-yoe
diet 日常饮食 *rìcháng yǐnshí* jeu-chang yin-sheu
different from 和 ... 不同 *hé ... bù tóng* he ... boo tong
difficult 难 *nán* nan
digital camera 数码相机 *shùmǎ xiàngjī* shoo-ma shyang-jee
dinner 晚餐 *wǎncān* wan-tsan; **to have dinner** 吃晚餐 *chī wǎncān* cheu wan-tsan
direct 直接 *zhíjiē* jeu-jyay
direction 方向 *fāngxiàng* fang-shyang
directory 电话簿 *diànhuàbù* dyen-hwa-boo
directory enquiries 查询台 *cháxúntái* cha-shoon-ty
dirty 脏 *zāng* zang
disabled 残疾人 *cánjírén* tsan- jee-jeun **135**
disco 迪斯科 *dísīkē* dee-seu-ke
discount *(price cut)* 减价 *jiǎnjià* jyen-jya; *(special offer)* 优惠 *yōuhuì* yoe-hway **84**; **to give someone a discount** 给某人优惠 *gěi mǒurén yōuhuì* gay moe-jeun yoe-hway
dish 一盘菜 *yī pán cài* ee pan tsy
dishes 餐具 *cānjù* tsan-joo; **to do the dishes** 洗餐具 *xǐ cānjù* shee tsan-joo
dish towel 餐具毛巾 *cānjù máojīn* tsan-joo mao-jin
dishwasher 洗碗机 *xǐwǎnjī* shee-wan-jee
disinfect 消毒 *xiāodú* sheeao-doo
disposable 一次性使用的 *yīcìxìng shǐyòng de* ee-tseu-shing sheu-yong de
disturb 打扰 *dǎrǎo* da-jao; **do not disturb** 请勿打扰 *qǐng wù dǎrǎo* ching woo da-jao
dive 潜水 *qiánshuǐ* chyen-shway
diving: to go diving 去潜水 *qù qiánshuǐ* choo chyen-shway
do 做 *zuò* zwoe; **do you have a light?** 你有火吗？ *nǐ yǒu huǒ ma?* nee yoe hwoe ma?
doctor 医生 *yīshēng* ee-shung **126**
door 门 *mén* meun
door code 入门密码 *rùmén mìmǎ* joo-meun mee-ma
downstairs 楼下 *lóuxià* loe-shya
draught beer 散装啤酒 *sǎnzhuāng píjiǔ* san-jwang pee-jyo
dress: to get dressed 穿上衣服 *chuānshang yīfu* chwan-shang ee-foo
dressing 食物调料 *shíwù tiáoliào* sheu-woo teeao-leeao
drink *(n)* 饮料 *yǐnliào* yin-leeao; **to go for a drink** 去喝酒 *qù hē jiǔ* choo he jyo **55**, **73**

drink (v) 喝 *hē* he
drinking water 饮用水 *yǐnyòngshuǐ* yin-yong-shway
drive (n) **to go for a drive** 开车走一趟 *kāichē zǒu yī tàng* ky-che zoe ee tang
drive (v) 开车 *kāichē* ky-che
driving licence 驾驶执照 *jiàshǐ zhízhào* jya-sheu jeu-jao
drops 药水 *yàoshuǐ* yao-shway
drown 淹死 *yānsǐ* yan-seu
drugs 毒品 *dúpǐn* doo-pin
drunk 喝醉 *hēzuì* he-zway
dry (adj) 干的 *gān de* gan de
dry (v) 弄干 *nòng gān* nong gan
dry cleaner's 干洗店 *gānxǐdiàn* gan-shee-dyen
duck 鸭子 *yāzi* ya-zeu
during 在 … 期间 *zài … qījiān* zy … chee-jyen; **during the week** 在这个星期中 *zài zhè ge xīngqī zhōng* zy jeu ge shing-chee jong
dustbin 垃圾箱 *lājīxiāng* la-jee-shyang
duty chemist's 值班药房 *zhíbān yàofáng* jeu-ban yao-fang

E

each 每 *měi* may; **each one** 每个 *měi ge* may ge
ear 耳朵 *ěrduo* er-dwoe
early 早 *zǎo* zao
earplugs 耳塞 *ěrsāi* er-sy
earth 土 *tǔ* too; 地球 *dìqiú* dee- chyo
east 东 *dōng* dong; **in the east** 在东部 *zài dōngbù* zy dong-boo; **(to the) east of** 在 … 的东边 *zài … de dōngbian* zy … de dong-byen
easy 容易 *róngyì* jong-yee
eat 吃 *chī* cheu **55**
economy class 飞机经济舱 *fēijī jīngjìcāng* fay-jee jing-jee-tsang
Elastoplast® 橡皮膏 *xiàngpígāo* shyang-pee-gao
electric 电动 *diàndòng* dyen-dong
electricity 电 *diàn* dyen
electricity meter 电表 *diànbiǎo* dyen-beeao
electric shaver 电动剃须刀 *diàndòng tìxūdāo* dyen-dong tee-shoo-dao
e-mail 电子邮件 *diànzǐ yóujiàn* dyen-zeu yoe-jyen
e-mail address 电子邮箱地址 *diànzǐ yóuxiāng dìzhǐ* dyen-zeu yoe-shyang dee-jeu **24**, **117**
embassy 大使馆 *dàshǐguǎn* da-sheu-gwan
emergency 紧急情况 *jǐnjí qíngkuàng* jin-jee ching-kwang **134**; **in an emergency** 发生紧急情况的时候 *fāshēng jǐnjí qíngkuàng de shíhou* fa-shung jin-jee ching- kwang de sheu-hoe
emergency exit 紧急出口 *jǐnjí chūkǒu* jin-jee choo-koe
empty 空的 *kōng de* kong de
end 结束 *jiéshù* jyay-shoo; **at the end of …** 在 … 结束时 *zài … jiéshù shí* zy… jyay-shoo sheu; **at the end of the street** 在路的尽头 *zài lù de jìntóu* zy loo de jin-toe
engaged (telephone) 占线 *zhànxiàn* jan-shyen
engine 发动机 *fādòngjī* fa-dong-jee
England 英格兰 *yīnggélán* ying-ge-lan
English 英语 *yīngyǔ* ying-yoo; 英格兰人 *yīnggélán rén* ying-ge-lan-jeun
enjoy: enjoy your meal! 吃好! *chī hǎo!* cheu hao!; **to enjoy oneself** 玩儿得好 *wánr de hǎo* wanr de hao
enough 足够 *zúgòu* zoo-gwoe; **that's enough** 够了 *gòu le* goe le
entrance 入口 *rùkǒu* joo-koe
envelope 信封 *xìnfēng* shin-fung
epileptic 癫痫 *diānxián* dyen- shyen
equipment 设备 *shèbèi* she-bay
Europe 欧洲 *ōuzhōu* oe-joe
European 欧洲人 *ōuzhōurén* oe-joe-jeun

evening 晚上 *wǎnshang* wan-shang; **in the evening** 在晚上 *zài wǎnshang* zy wan-shang
every 每 *měi* may; **every day** 每天 *měi tiān* may tyen
everybody, **everyone** 每个人 *měi ge rén* may ge jeun
everywhere 到处 *dàochù* dao- choo
except 除 … 外 *chú … wài* choo … wy
exceptional 特别好 *tèbié hǎo* te-byay hao
excess 超重的部分 *chāozhòng de bùfen* chao-jong de boo-feun
exchange 兑换 *duìhuàn* dway- hwan
exchange rate 汇率 *huìlǜ* hway-lu
excuse (n) 借口 *jièkǒu* jyay-koe
excuse (v) **excuse me** 请原谅 *qǐng yuánliàng* ching ywan-lyang
exhausted 累极了 *lèi jí le* lay jee le
exhaust pipe 汽车排气管 *qìchē páiqìguǎn* chee-che py-chee-gwan
exhibition 展览 *zhǎnlǎn* jan-lan **84**
exit 出口 *chūkǒu* choo-koe
expensive 贵 *guì* gway
expiry date 过期日期 *guòqī rìqī* gwoe-chee jeu-chee
express 快 *kuài* kwhy
extra 额外的 *éwài de* e-wy de
eye 眼睛 *yǎnjing* yan-jing

F

face 脸 *liǎn* lyen
facecloth 脸巾 *liǎnjīn* lyen-jin
faint 晕倒了 *yūn dǎo le* yoon dao le
fair (n) 市场 *shìchǎng* sheu-chang
fall (v) 摔倒 *shuāidǎo* shwhy-dao; **to fall asleep** 睡了 *shuì le* shway le; **to fall ill** 病了 *bìng le* bing le
family 家 *jiā* jya
far 远 *yuǎn* ywan; **far from** 一点儿也不 *yīdiǎnr yě bù* ee-dyar yay boo
fare 车费 *chēfèi* che-fay
fast 快 *kuài* kwhy
fast-food restaurant 快餐店 *kuàicāndiàn* kwhy-tsan-dyen
fat 胖 *pàng* pang
father 父亲 *fùqin* foo-chin
favour 偏爱 *piān'ài* pyen-eye; **to do someone a favour** 帮某人忙 *bāng mǒurén máng* bang moe- jeun mang
favourite 特别喜爱的 *tèbié xǐ'ài de* te-byay shee-eye de
fax 传真 *chuánzhēn* chwan-jeun
February 二月 *èryuè* er-yway
feel 觉得 *juéde* jway-de; **to feel good** 觉得很好 *juéde hěn hǎo* jway-de heun hao; **to feel bad** 觉得不舒服 *juéde bù shūfu* jway-de boo shoo-foo **128**
feeling 感情 *gǎnqíng* gan-ching
ferry 渡船 *dùchuán* doo-chwan
festival 联欢节日 *liánhuānjié rì* lyen-hwan-jyay reu
fetch: to go and fetch someone 去叫某人 *qù jiào mǒurén* choo jeeao moe-jeun; **to go and fetch something** 去取某物 *qù qǔ mǒuwù* choo choo moe-woo
fever 发烧 *fāshāo* fa-shao; **to have a fever** 发烧了 *fāshāo le* fa-shao le
few 极少 *jí shǎo* jee shao
fiancé 未婚夫 *wèihūnfū* way-hoon-foo
fiancée 未婚妻 *wèihūnqī* way-hoon-chee
fight 打架 *dǎjià* da-jya
fill 装满 *zhuāng mǎn* jwang man
fill in, **fill out** 填表 *tiánbiǎo* tyen-beeao
fill up: to fill up with petrol 加满汽油 *jiā mǎn qìyóu* jya man chee-yoe
filling (in tooth) 补的牙 *bǔ de yá* boo de ya
film (for camera) 胶卷 *jiāojuǎn* jeeao-jwan **107**; (movie) 电影 *diànyǐng* dyen-ying
finally 最后 *zuìhòu* zway-hoe
find 找到 *zhǎodào* jao-dao
fine (n) 罚款 *fákuǎn* fa-kwan
fine (adj) 好的 *hǎo de* hao de; **I'm fine** 我很好 *wǒ hěn hǎo* wo heun hao

finger 手指 *shǒuzhǐ* shoe-jeu
finish 结束 *jiéshù* jyay-shoo
fire 火 *huǒ* hwoe; **fire!** 着火了！ *zháohuǒ le!* jao-hwoe le!
fire brigade 消防队 *xiāofángduì* sheeao-fang-dway
fireworks 烟花 *yānhuā* yan-hwa
first 第一 *dì yī* dee ee; **first (of all)** 首先 *shǒuxiān* shoe-shyen
first class 一等 *yīděng* ee-dung
first floor 一楼 *yī lóu* yi loe
first name 名字 *míngzi* ming-zeu
fish (n) 鱼 *yú* yoo
fishmonger's 鱼贩 *yúfàn* yoo-fan
fitting room 试衣间 *shìyījiān* sheu-yee-jyen
fizzy 汽水 *qìshuǐ* chee-shway
flash (on camera) 闪光灯 *shǎnguāngdēng* shan-gwang-dung
flask 热水瓶 *rèshuǐpíng* jeu-shway-ping
flat (adj) 平 *píng* ping; **flat tyre** 轮带瘪了 *lúndài biě le* loon-dy byay le
flat (n) 单元楼 *dānyuánlóu* dan-ywan-loe
flavour 味道 *wèidao* way-dao
flaw 毛病 *máobìng* mao-bing
flight 航班 *hángbān* hang-ban
flip-flops 平底人字拖鞋 *píngdǐ rénzì tuōxié* ping-dee jeun-zeu twoe-shyay
floor 地板 *dìbǎn* dee-ban; (storey) 楼层 *lóucéng* loe-tsung; **on the floor** 在地板上 *zài dìbǎn shang* zy dee-ban shang
flu 感冒 *gǎnmào* gan-mao
fly (n) 苍蝇 *cāngying* tsang-ying
fly (v) 飞 *fēi* fay
food 食物 *shíwù* sheu-woo **100**
food poisoning 食物中毒 *shíwù zhòngdú* sheu-woo jong-doo
foot 脚 *jiǎo* jeeao
for 为了 *wèi le* way le; **for me** 为了 (我) *wèi le (wǒ)* way le wo; **for an hour** 一小时 *yī xiǎoshí* ee sheeao-sheu
forbidden 禁止 *jìnzhǐ* jin-jeu
forecast 预报 *yùbào* yoo-bao
forehead 前额 *qián'é* chyen-e
foreign 外国的 *wàiguó de* wy- gwoe de
foreigner 外国人 *wàiguórén* wy-gwoe-jeun
forest 森林 *sēnlín* seun-lin
fork 叉子 *chāzi* cha-zeu
former 以前的 *yǐqián de* ee-chyen de
forward (adj) 位于前部的 *wèiyú qiánbù de* way-yoo chyen-boo de
fracture 骨折 *gǔzhé* goo-je
fragile 易碎 *yìsuì* ee-sway
free 免费 *miǎnfèi* myen-fay **83**
freezer 冷冻箱 *lěngdòngxiāng* lung-dong-shyang
Friday 星期五 *xīngqīwǔ* shing- chee-woo
fridge 冰箱 *bīngxiāng* bing-shyang
fried 油煎的 *yóujiān de* yoe-jyen de
friend 朋友 *péngyou* pung-yoe
from 从 *cóng* tsong; **from … to …** 从 …到 … *cóng … dào …* tsong … dao…
front 前部 *qiánbù* chyen-boo; **in front of …** 在 … 的前面 *zài … de qiánmiàn* zy … de chyen-myen
fry 油煎 *yóujiān* yoe-jyen
frying pan 煎锅 *jiānguō* jyen-gwoe
full 满了 *mǎn le* man le; **full of** 充满了 *chōngmǎn le* chong-man le
full board 全食宿 *quánshísù* chwan-sheu-soo
full fare, **full price** 全价票 *quánjiàpiào* chwan-jya-peeao **84**
fuse 保险丝 *bǎoxiǎnsī* bao-shyen-seu

gallery 画廊 *huàláng* hwa-lang
game 游戏 *yóuxì* yoe-shee **95**; **to have a game of cards** 打一局牌 *dǎ yī jú pái* da ee yoo py
garage (for repairs) 修车厂 *xiūchēchǎng* shyo-che-chang **38**

garden 花园 *huāyuán* *hwa-ywan*
gas 煤气灶 *méiqìzào* *may-chee- zao*
gas cylinder 煤气罐 *méiqìguàn* *mei-chee-gwan*
gastric flu 肠胃机能紊乱 *chángwèi jīnéng wěnluàn* *chang-way jee-nung weun-lwan*
gate 门 *mén* *meun*
gauze 薄纱布 *báoshābù* *bao- sha-boo*
gay 同性恋 *tóngxìngliàn* *tong- shing-lyen*
gearbox 变速箱 *biànsùxiāng* *byen-soo-shyang*
general 一般 *yībān* *ee-ban*
gents' (toilet) 男厕所 *náncèsuǒ* *nan-tseu-swoe*
Germany 德国 *déguó* *de-gwoe*
get 得到 *dédào* *de-dao*
get off (*transport*) 下 *xià* *shya* **36**
get up 起床 *qǐchuáng* *chee- chwang*
gift wrap 礼品包装 *lǐpǐn bāozhuāng* *lee-pin bao-jwang*
girl 女孩 *nǚhái* *nu-hy*
girlfriend 女朋友 *nǚpéngyou* *nu-pung-yoe*
give 给 *gěi* *gay*
give back 还给 *huángěi* *hwan-gay*
glass 玻璃杯 *bōlibēi* *bo-lee-bay*; **a glass of water** 一杯水 *yī bēi shuǐ* *ee bay shway*; **a glass of wine** *yī bēi jiǔ* *ee bay jyo*
glasses 眼镜 *yǎnjìng* *yan-jing*
gluten-free 不含面粉成分的 *bù hán miànfěn chéngfèn de* *boo han myen-feun chung-feun de*
go 去 *qù* *choo*, 到 … 去 *dào … qù* *dao … choo*; **to go to London** 到伦敦去 *dào lúndūn qù* *dao loon-doon choo*; **we're going home tomorrow** 我们明天回家 *wǒmen míngtiān huíjiā* *wo-meun ming-tyen hway-jya*
go away 离家外出 *líjiā wàichū* *lee-jya wy-choo*
go in 进去 *jìnqù* *jin-choo*
go out 出去 *chūqù* *choo-choo*
go with … (*complement*) 和 … 一起去 *hé … yīqǐ qù* *he … ee-chee choo*; (*accompany*) 跟 … 一起去 *gēn … yīqǐ qù* *geun … ee-chee chu*
good 好 *hǎo* *hao*; **good morning** 早上好 *zǎoshang hǎo* *zao-shang hao*; **good afternoon** 下午好 *xiàwǔ hǎo* *shya-woo hao*; **good evening** 晚上好 *wǎnshang hǎo* *wan-shang hao*
goodbye 再见 *zàijiàn* *zy-jyen*
goodnight 晚安 *wǎn'ān* *wan-an*
goods 货物 *huòwù* *hwoe-woo*
GP 家庭医生 *jiātíng yīshēng* *jya- ting ee-shung*
grams 克 *kè* *ke* **101**
grass 草地 *cǎodì* *tsao-dee*
great 好极了 *hǎo jí le* *hao jee le*
Great Britain 大不列颠 *dàbùlièdiān* *da-boo-lyay-dyen*
green 绿色 *lǜsè* *lu-se*
grey 灰色 *huīsè* *hway-se*
grocer's 食品杂货店 *shípǐn záhuòdiàn* *sheu-pin za-hwoe-dyen*
ground 地面 *dìmiàn* *dee-myen*; **on the ground** 在地上 *zài dì shang* *zy dee shang*
ground floor 一楼 *yī lóu* *ee loe*
grow 长 *zhǎng* *jang*
guarantee 保修单 *bǎoxiūdān* *bao-shyo-dan*
guest 客人 *kèrén* *ke-jeun*
guest house 宾馆 *bīnguǎn* *bin-gwan*
guide 导游 *dǎoyóu* *dao-yoe* **76**
guidebook 指南书 *zhǐnánshū* *jeu-nan-shoo*
guided tour 导游参观 *dǎoyóu cānguān* *dao-yoe tsan-gwan*
gynaecologist 妇科医生 *fùkē yīshēng* *foo-ke ee-shung*

H

hair 头发 *tóufa* *toe-fa*
hairdresser 美发师 *měifàshī* *mei-fa-sheu*

hairdrier 吹风机 *chuīfēngjī* *chway-fung-jee*
half 半 *bàn* *ban*; **half a litre** 半公升 *bàn gōngshēng* *ban gong-shung*; **half a kilo** 半公斤 *bàn gōngjīn* *ban gong-jin*; **half an hour** 半小时 *bàn xiǎoshí* *ban sheeao-sheu*
half-board 半食宿 *bànshísù* *ban-sheu-soo*
hand 手 *shǒu* *shoe*
handbag 女用手包 *nǚyòng shǒubāo* *nu-yong shoe-bao*
handbrake 手闸 *shǒuzhá* *shoe-ja*
handicapped 残疾人 *cánjírén* *tsan-jee-jeun*
handkerchief 手绢 *shǒujuàn* *shoe-jwan*
hand luggage 手提行李 *shǒutí xíngli* *shoe-tee shing-lee* **32**
hand-made 手工制造 *shǒugōng zhìzào* *shoe-gong jeu-zao*
hangover 酒后头疼 *jiǔ hòu tóu téng* *jyo hoe toe tung*
happen 发生 *fāshēng* *fa-shung*
happy 高兴 *gāoxìng* *gao-shing*
hard 困难 *kùnnan* *koon-nan*
hashish 大麻 *dàmá* *da-ma*
hat 帽子 *màozi* *mao-zeu*
hate 讨厌 *tǎoyàn* *tao-yan*
have 有 *yǒu* *yoe*
have to 得 *děi* *day*; **I have to go** 我得走了 *wǒ děi zǒu le* *wo day zoe le*
hay fever 花粉病 *huāfěnbìng* *hwa-feun-bing*
he 他 *tā* *ta*
head 头 *tóu* *toe*
headache: to have a headache 头疼 *tóu téng* *toe tung*
headlight 车前灯 *chēqiándēng* *che-chyen-dung*
health 健康 *jiànkāng* *jyen-kang*
hear 听到 *tīngdào* *ting-dao*
heart 心脏 *xīnzàng* *shin-zang*
heart attack 心脏病发作 *xīnzàngbìng fāzuò* *shin-zang-bing fa-zwoe*
heat 炎热 *yánrè* *yan-je*
heating 暖气 *nuǎnqì* *nwan-chee*
heavy 沉 *chén* *cheun*
hello 你好 *nǐ hǎo* *nee hao*; *(on telephone)* 喂 *wéi* *way*
helmet 头盔 *tóukuī* *toe-kway*
help *(n)* 帮忙 *bāngmáng* *bang- mang* **134**; **to call for help** 请人帮忙 *qǐng rén bāngmáng* *ching jeun bang-mang*; **help!** 救命! *jiùmìng!* *jyo-ming!*
help *(v)* 帮忙 *bāngmáng* *bang- mang*
her 她 *tā* *ta*
here 这儿 *zhèr* *jer*; **here is/are** 给你 *gěi nǐ* *gay nee*
hers 她的 *tā de* *ta de*
hi! 哎! *ài!* *eye!*
hi-fi 音响 *yīnxiǎng* *yin-shyang*
high 高 *gāo* *gao*
high blood pressure 高血压 *gāoxuèyā* *gao-shway-ya*
hiking 远足 *yuǎnzú* *ywan-zoo* **91**; **to go hiking** 去远足 *qù yuǎnzú* *choo ywan-zoo*
hill 小山 *xiǎoshān* *sheeao-shan*
him 他 *tā* *ta*
himself 他自己 *tā zìjǐ* *ta zeu-jee*
hip 臀部 *túnbù* *toon-boo*
hire *(n & v)* 租 *zū* *zoo* **38**, **89**, **92**, **93**
his 他的 *tā de* *ta de*
hitchhike 搭车 *dāchē* *da-che*
hitchhiking 搭车旅行 *dāchē lǚxíng* *da-che lu-shing*
hold 拿着 *názhe* *na-je*
hold on! *(on the phone)* 别挂电话! *bié guà diànhuà!* *byay gwa dyen-hwa!*
holiday(s) 假期 *jiàqī* *jya-chee*; **on holiday** 度假 *dùjià* *doo-jya* **22**
home 家 *jiā* *jya*; **at home** 在家 *zài jiā* *zy jya*; **to go home** 回家 *huí jiā* *hway jya*
homosexual 同性恋 *tóngxìngliàn* *tong-shing-lyen*
honest 诚实 *chéngshí* *chung-sheu*
honeymoon 蜜月 *mìyuè* *mee-yway*
Hong Kong 香港 *xiānggǎng* *shyang-gang*

horse 马 *mǎ* ma
hospital 医院 *yīyuàn* ee-ywan
hot 热 *rè* je; **it's hot** 天很热 *tiān hěn rè* tyen heun je; **hot drink** 热饮 *rèyǐn* je-yin
hotel 饭店 *fàndiàn* fan-dyen
hotplate 加热板 *jiārèbǎn* jya-je-ban
hour 小时 *xiǎoshí* sheeao-sheu; **an hour and a half** 一个半小时 *yī ge bàn xiǎoshí* ee ge ban sheeao-sheu
house 房子 *fángzi* fang-zeu
housework 家务 *jiāwù* jya-woo; **to do the housework** 做家务 *zuò jiāwù* zwoe jya-woo
how 怎么样 *zěnmeyàng* zeun-me-yang; **how are you?** 你好吗? *nǐ hǎo ma?* nee hao ma?
hunger 饥饿 *jī'è* jee-e
hungry: to be hungry 饿 *è* e
hurry: to be in a hurry 正忙着 *zhèng mángzhe* jung mang-je
hurry (up) 赶快 *gǎnkuài* gan-kwhy
hurt: it hurts 疼 *téng* tung **128**; **my head hurts** 我头疼 *wǒ tóu téng* wo toe tung
husband 丈夫 *zhàngfu* jang-foo

I

I 我 *wǒ* wo; **I'm English** 我是英格兰人 *wǒ shì yīnggélán rén* wo sheu ying-ge-lan jeun; **I'm 22 (years old)** 我二十二岁 *wǒ èrshí'èr suì* wo er-sheu-er sway
ice 冰 *bīng* bing
ice cube 冰块 *bīngkuài* bing-kwhy
identity card 身份证 *shēnfènzhèng* sheun-feun-jung
identity papers 身份证明文件 *shēnfèn zhèngmíng wénjiàn* sheun-feun jung-ming weun-jyen
if 如果 *rúguǒ* joo-gwoe
ill 病了 *bìng le* bing le
illness 病 *bìng* bing
important 重要 *zhòngyào* jong-yao
in 在 *zài* zy; **in England** 在英格兰 *zài yīnggélán* zy ying-ge-lan; **in 2006** 在二零零六年 *zài èr líng líng liù nián* zy er ling ling lyo nyen; **in English** 用英语 *yòng yīngyǔ* yong ying-yoo; **in the 19th century** 在十九世纪 *zài shíjiǔ shìjì* zy sheu-jyo sheu-jee; **in an hour** 一小时后 *yī xiǎoshí hòu* ee sheeao-sheu hoe
included 包括 *bāokuò* bao-kwoe **61**
independent 独立 *dúlì* doo-lee
indicator *(on car)* 汽车变向指示灯 *qìchē biànxiàng zhǐshìdēng* chee-che byen-shyang jeu-sheu-dung
infection 感染 *gǎnrǎn* gan-jan
information 信息 *xìnxī* shin-shee **82**
injection 打针 *dǎzhēn* da-jeun
injured 受伤 *shòushāng* shoe-shang
insect 昆虫 *kūnchóng* koon-chong
insecticide 杀虫剂 *shāchóngjì* sha-chong-jee
inside ... 在 ... 里 *zài ... lǐ* zy... lee
instead 代替 *dàitì* dy-tee; **instead of** 代替 *dàitì* dy-tee
insurance 保险 *bǎoxiǎn* bao-shyen **39**
international 国际 *guójì* gwoe-jee
international money order 国际汇票 *guójì huìpiào* gwoe-jee hway-peeao
Internet 互联网 *hùliánwǎng* hoo-lyen-wang
Internet café 网吧 *wǎngbā* wang-ba **117**
invite 邀请 *yāoqǐng* yao-ching
Ireland 爱尔兰 *ài'ěrlán* eye-er-lan
iron *(n)* 熨斗 *yùndǒu* yoon-doe
iron *(v)* 熨衣服 *yùnyīfu* yoon-yee-foo
island 岛 *dǎo* dao
it 它 *tā* ta; **it's beautiful** 真漂亮 *zhēn piàoliang* jeun peeao-lyang; **it's warm** *(weather)* 天很暖和 *tiān hěn nuǎnhuo* tyen heun nwan-hwoe
itchy: it's itchy 痒 *yǎng* yang
item 物品 *wùpǐn* woo-pin

J

jacket 上衣 *shàngyī* shang-yee
January 一月 *yīyuè* ee-yway
jetlag 时差反应 *shíchā fănyìng* sheu-cha fan-ying
jeweller's 珠宝店 *zhūbăodiàn* joo-bao-dyen
jewellery 珠宝首饰 *zhūbăo shŏushì* joo-bao shoe-sheu
job 工作 *gōngzuò* gong-zwoe
journey 旅行 *lǚxíng* lu-shing
jug 罐子 *guànzi* gwan-zeu
juice 汁 *zhī* jeu
July 七月 *qīyuè* chee-yway
jumper 套头毛衣 *tàotóu máoyī* tao-toe mao-yee
June 六月 *liùyuè* lyo-yway
just 就 *jiù* jyo; **just before** 就在…之前 *jiù zài… zhīqián* jyo zy … jeu-chyen; **just a little** 就一点儿 *jiù yīdiănr* jyo ee-dyar; **just one** 就一个 *jiù yī ge* jyo ee ge; **I've just arrived** 我刚到达 *wŏ gāng dàodá* wo gang dao-da; **just in case** 以防万一 *yĭfáng wànyī* ee-fang wan-yee

K

kayak 划艇 *huátĭng* hwa-ting
keep 保存 *băocún* bao-tsoon
key *(for door)* 钥匙 *yàoshi* yao-sheu **39**, **47**; *(on computer)* 键 *jiàn* jyen
kidney 肾 *shèn* sheun
kill 杀死 *shāsĭ* sha-seu
kilometre 公里 *gōnglĭ* gong-lee
kind: what kind of …? 哪种 … ? *nă zhŏng …?* na jong …?
kitchen 厨房 *chúfáng* choo-fang
knee 膝盖 *xīgài* shee-gy
knife 刀 *dāo* dao
knock down 车撞人 *chē zhuàng rén* che jwang jeun
know 知道 *zhīdao* jeu-dao; **I don't know** 我不知道 *wŏ bù zhīdào* wo boo jeu-dao

L

ladies' (toilet) 女厕所 *nǚcèsuŏ* nu-tse-swoe
lake 湖 *hú* hoo
lamp 灯 *dēng* dung
landmark 标志性建筑 *biāozhìxìng jiànzhù* beeao-jeu-shing jyen-joo
landscape 景色 *jĭngsè* jing-se
language 语言 *yŭyán* yoo-ywan
laptop 便携式电脑 *biànxiéshì diànnăo* byen-shyay-sheu dyen-nao
last *(adj)* 最后 *zuìhòu* zway-hoe; **last year** 去年 *qùnián* choo-nyen
last *(v)* 持续 *chíxù* cheu-shoo
late 晚 *wăn* wan; *(transport)* 晚点 *wăndiăn* wan-dyen
late-night opening 营业到深夜 *yíngyè dào shēnyè* ying-yay dao sheun-yay
laugh 大笑 *dàxiào* da-sheeao
launderette 自助洗衣店 *zìzhù xĭyīdiàn* zeu-joo shee-yee-dyen
lawyer 律师 *lǜshī* lu-sheu
leaflet 散页印刷品 *sănyè yìnshuāpĭn* san-yay yin-shwa-pin
leak 漏 *lòu* loe
learn 学 *xué* shway
least: the least 最少的 *zuì shăo de* zway shao de; **at least** 至少 *zhìshăo* jeu-shao
leave 离开 *líkāi* lee-ky; 走 *zŏu* zoe
left *(n) (direction)* 左边 *zuŏbiān* zwoe-byen; **to the left (of)** 在…的左边 *zài … de zuŏbian* zy … de zwoe-byen
left *(adj) (remaining)* 剩下 *shèngxià* shung-shya
left-luggage (office) 行李寄存处 *xíngli jìcúnchù* shing-lee jee-tsoon-choo
leg 腿 *tuĭ* tway
lend 借 *jiè* jyay
lens 镜片 *jìngpiàn* jing-pyen
lenses 镜片 *jìngpiàn* jing-pyen
less 更少的 *gèng shăo de* gung shao

de; **less than ...** 比 ... 少 *bǐ ... shǎo* bee ... shao
let 出租 *chūzū* choo-zoo
letter 信 *xìn* shin
letterbox 信箱 *xìnxiāng* shin-shyang
library 图书馆 *túshūguǎn* too-shoo-gwan
life 生活 *shēnghuó* shung-hwoe
lift (elevator) 电梯 *diàntī* dyen-tee
light (adj) 浅色 *qiǎnsè* chyen-se; **light blue** 浅蓝 *qiǎnlán* chyen-lan
light (n)灯 *dēng* dung; **do you have a light?** 你有火吗? *nǐ yǒu huǒ ma?* nee yoe hwoe ma?
light (v) 点燃 *diǎnrán* dyen-jan
light bulb 灯泡 *dēngpào* dung-pao
lighter 打火机 *dǎhuǒjī* da-hwoe-jee
lighthouse 灯塔 *dēngtǎ* dung-ta
like (adv)也就是说 *yě jiù shì shuō* yay jyo sheu shwoe
like (v) 喜欢 *xǐhuan* shee-hwan; **I'd like ...** 我想 ... *wǒ xiǎng* ... wo shyang ... **25**
line (phone line) 电话线 *diànhuàxiàn* dyen-hwa-shyen
lip 嘴唇 *zuǐchún* zway-choon
listen 听 *tīng* ting
listings magazine 影视娱乐预告期刊 *yǐngshì yúlè yúgào qīkān* ying-sheu yoo-le yoo-gao chee-kan
litre 公升 *gōngshēng* gong-shung
little (adj) 一点儿 *yīdiǎnr* ee-dyar
little: a little 有点儿 *yǒudiǎnr* yoe-dyar
live 活着 *huózhe* hwoe-je
liver 肝 *gān* gan
living room 起居室 *qǐjūshì* chee-joo-sheu
local time 本地时间 *běndì shíjiān* beun-dee sheu-jyen
lock 锁 *suǒ* swoe
long 长 *cháng* chang; **a long time** 很长时间 *hěn cháng shíjiān* heun chang sheu-jyen; **how long?** 多长时间? *duō cháng shíjiān?* dwoe chang sheu-jyen?
look 看 *kàn* kan; **to look tired** 看起来很累 *kànqǐlái hěn lèi* kan-chee-ly heun lay
look after照管 *zhàoguǎn* jao-gwan
look at 看 *kàn* kan
look for 找 *zhǎo* jao **18**, **98**
look like 看起来会 *kànqǐlái huì* kan-chee-ly hway
lorry 卡车 *kǎchē* ka-che
lose 丢了 *diū le* dyo le **39**, **135**; **to get lost** 迷路 *mílù* mee-loo; **to be lost** 丢了 *diū le* dyo le **18**
lot: a lot (of) 大量(的) *dàliàng (de)* da-lyang (de)
loud 大声 *dàshēng* da-shung
low 低 *dī* dee
low blood pressure 低血压 *dīxuèyā* dee-shway-ya
low-fat 低脂肪 *dīzhīfáng* dee-jeu-fang
luck 运气 *yùnqì* yoon-chee
lucky: to be lucky 幸运 *xìngyùn* shing-yoon
luggage 行李 *xíngli* shing-lee **33**
lukewarm 温 *wēn* weun
lunch 午餐 *wǔcān* woo-tsan; **to have lunch** 吃午餐 *chī wǔcān* cheu woo-tsan
lung 肺 *fèi* fay

M

magazine 杂志 *zázhì* za-jeu
maiden name 女人婚前姓 *nǚrén hūnqiánxìng* nu-jeun hoon-chyen-shing
mail 邮件 *yóujiàn* yoe-jyen
main 主要 *zhǔyào* joo-yao
main course 主菜 *zhǔcài* joo-tsy
make 做 *zuò* zwoe
man 男人 *nánrén* nan-jeun
manage 管理 *guǎnlǐ* gwan-lee; **to manage to do something** 设法完成某事 *shèfǎ wánchéng mǒushì* she-fa wan-chung moe-sheu

manager 经理 *jīnglǐ* jing-lee
many 很多 *hěn duō* heun dwoe; **how many?** 多少？*duōshǎo?* dwoe-shao?; **how many times?** 多少次？*duōshǎo cì?* dwoe-shao tseu?
map 地图 *dìtú* dee-too **18**, **35**, **75**, **82**
March 三月 *sānyuè* san-yway
market 市场 *shìchǎng* sheu-chang **101**
married 已婚 *yǐhūn* ee-hoon
match (for fire) 火柴 *huǒchái* hwoe-chy; (game) 比赛 *bǐsài* bee-sy
material 布料 *bùliào* boo-leeao
matter: it doesn't matter 没关系 *méi guānxi* may gwan-shee
mattress 床垫 *chuángdiàn* chwang-dyen
May 五月 *wǔyuè* woo-yway
maybe 也许 *yěxǔ* yay-shoo
me 我 *wǒ* wo; **me too** 我也是 *wǒ yě shì* wo yay sheu
meal 一顿饭 *yī dùn fàn* ee doon fan
mean: it means ... 它的意思是 … *tā de yìsi shì* ... ta de ee-seu sheu ...; **what does ... mean?** … 是什么意思？… *shì shénme yìsi?* ... sheu sheun-me ee-seu?
medicine 药 *yào* yao
medium 中号 *zhōnghào* jong-hao; (meat) 适中熟 *shìzhōng shú* sheu-jong shoo
meet 和 … 见面 *he* ... *jiànmian* he ... jyen-myen **74**
meeting 开会 *kāihuì* ky-hway
member 会员 *huìyuán* hway-ywan
menu 菜单 *càidān* tsy-dan
message 留言 *liúyán* lyo-yan **121**
meter 仪表 *yíbiǎo* ee-beeao
metre 米 *mǐ* mee
microwave 微波炉 *wēibōlú* way-bo-loo
midday 中午 *zhōngwǔ* jong-woo
middle 中间 *zhōngjiān* jong-jyen; **in the middle of ...** 在 … 中 *zài* ... *zhōng* zy ... jong
midnight 午夜 *wǔyè* woo-yay
might: it might rain 也许会下雨 *yěxǔhuì xiàyǔ* yay-shoo-hway shya-yoo
mind: I don't mind 我不介意 *wǒ bú jièyì* wo boo jyay-yee
mine 我的 *wǒ de* wo de
mineral water 矿泉水 *kuàngquánshuǐ* kwang-chwan-shway
minute 分钟 *fēn zhōng* feun jong; **at the last minute** 最后一分钟 *zuìhòu yī fēn zhōng* zway-hoe ee feun jong
mirror 镜子 *jìngzi* jing-zeu
Miss 小姐 *xiǎojie* sheeao-jyay
miss 误了 *wù le* woo le **33**, **36**; **we missed the train** 我们误了火车 *wòmen wù le huǒchē* wo-meun woo le hwoe-che; **there are two ... missing** 有两个 … 不见了 *yǒu liǎng ge* ... *bú jiàn le* yoe lyang ge ... boo jyen le
mistake 错 *cuò* tswoe; **to make a mistake** 出错 *chūcuò* choo-tswoe **99**
mobile (phone) 手机 *shǒujī* shoe-jee **121**
modern 现代 *xiàndài* shyen-dy
moment 一会儿 *yīhuìr* ee-hwayr; **at the moment** 现在 *xiànzài* shyen-zy
monastery 寺院 *sìyuàn* seu-ywan
Monday 星期一 *xīngqīyī* shing-chee-yee
money 钱 *qián* chyen **98**, **111**
month 月 *yuè* yway
monument 纪念碑 *jìniànbēi* jee-nyen-bay
moon 月亮 *yuèliang* yway-lyang
moped 机动脚踏车 *jīdòng jiǎotàchē* jee-dong jeeao-ta-che
more 更多 *gèng duō* gung dwoe; **more than ...** 比 … 多 *bǐ* ... *duō* bee ... dwoe; **much more, a lot more** 多很多 *duō hěn duō* dwoe heun dwoe; **there's no more ...** 没有 … 了 *méi yǒu* ... *le* may yoe ... le

morning 早上 *zǎoshang* *zao-shang*
morning-after pill 清晨服避孕药 *qīngchén fú bìyùnyào* *ching-cheun foo boo-yoon-yao* **131**
mosquito 蚊子 *wénzi* *weun-zeu*
most: the most 最 *zuì* *zway*; **most people** 大多数人 *dàduōshù rén* *da-dwoe-shoo jeun*
mother 母亲 *mǔqin* *moo-chin*
motorbike 摩托车 *mótuōchē* *mo-twoe-che*
motorway 高速公路 *gāosù gōnglù* *gao-soo gong-loo*
mountain 山 *shān* *shan*
mountain bike 登山车 *dēngshānchē* *dung-shan-che*
mouse 电脑鼠标 *diànnǎo shǔbiāo* *dyen-nao shoo-beeao*
mouth 嘴 *zuǐ* *zway*
movie 电影 *diànyǐng* *dyen-ying*
Mr 先生 *xiānsheng* *shyen-shung*
Mrs 太太 *tàitai* *ty-ty*
much: how much? 多少? *duōshǎo?* *dwoe-shao?*; **how much is it?**, **how much does it cost?** 多少钱? *duōshǎo qián?* *dwoe-shao chyen?*
muscle 肌肉 *jīròu* *jee-joe*
museum 博物馆 *bówùguǎn* *bo-woo-gwan*
music 音乐 *yīnyuè* *yin-yway*
must *(obligation)* 得 *děi* *day*; *(presumption)* 一定是 *yīdìng shì* *ee-ding sheu*; **it must be 5 o'clock** 一定是五点钟了 *yīdìng shì wǔ diǎn zhōng le* *ee-ding sheu woo dyen jong le*; **I must go** 我得走了 *wǒ děi zǒu le* *wo day zoe le*
my 我的 *wǒ de* *wo de*
myself 我自己 *wǒ zìjǐ* *wo zeu-jee*

N

nail *(on finger, toe)* 指甲 *zhījia* *jeu-jya*
naked 赤裸 *chìluǒ* *cheu-lwoe*
name 名字 *míngzi* *ming-zeu* **44**, **57**; **my name is …** 我叫 … *wǒ jiào* … *wo jeeao* … **20**
napkin 餐巾 *cānjīn* *tsan-jin*
nappy 尿布 *niàobù* *neeao-boo*
national holiday 国庆节 *guóqìngjié* *gwoe-ching-jyay*
nature 大自然 *dàzìrán* *da-zeu-jan*
near 附近 *fùjìn* *foo-jin*; **near the hotel** 在饭店附近 *zài fàndiàn fùjìn* *zy fan-dyen foo-jin*; **the nearest** 最近的 *zuì jìn de* *zway jin de*
necessary 有必要 *yǒubìyào* *yoe-bee-yao*
neck 脖子 *bózi* *bo-zeu*
need 需要 *xūyào* *shoo-yao*
neighbour 邻居 *línju* *lin-joo*
neither: neither do I 我也不 *wǒ yě bù* *wo yay boo*; **neither … nor …** 既不 … 也不 … *jì bù … yě bù …* *jee boo … yay boo …*
nervous 紧张 *jǐnzhāng* *jin-jang*
never 从来没 *cónglái méi* *tsong-ly may*
new 新 *xīn* *shin*
news 新闻 *xīnwén* *shin-weun*
newsagent 报刊店 *bàokāndiàn* *bao-kan-dyen*
newspaper 报 *bào* *bao*
newsstand 报摊 *bàotān* *bao-tan*
next 下(一) *xià (yī)* *shya (ee)*; **next Friday/next week/next year** 下星期五/下星期/明年 *xià xīngqīwǔ/xià xīngqī/míngnián* *shia shing-chee-woo/shia shing-chee/ming-nyen*
New Year 新年 *xīnnián* *shin-nyen*
nice 好心 *hǎoxīn* *hao-shin*
night 夜里 *yèlǐ* *yay-lee* **45**, **48**, **52**
nightclub 夜总会 *yèzǒnghuì* *yay-zong-hway*
no 不 *bù* *boo*; **no, thank you** 不用了，谢谢 *búyòng le, xièxie* *boo-yong le, shyay-shay*; **no idea** 不知道 *bù zhīdào* *boo jeu-dao*
nobody 没人 *méi rén* *may jeun*
noise 声音 *shēngyīn* *shung-yin*; **to make a noise** 发出声音 *fāchū*

shēngyīn *fa-choo shung-yin*
noisy 喧闹 ***xuānnào*** *shwan-nao*
non-drinking water 非饮用水 ***fēi yǐnyòngshuǐ*** *fay yin-yong-shway*
none 全无 ***quánwú*** *chwan-woo*
non-smoker 不抽烟的人 ***bù chōuyān de rén*** *boo choe-yan de jeun*
noon 正午 ***zhèngwǔ*** *jung-woo*
north 北 ***běi*** *bay*; **in the north** 在北部 ***zài běibù*** *zy bay-boo*; **(to the) north of** 在 … 的北边 ***zài … de běibian*** *zy … de bay-byen*
nose 鼻子 ***bízi*** *bee-zeu*
not 不 ***bù*** *boo*; **not yet** 还没有 ***hái méi yǒu*** *hy may yoe*; **not at all** 一点儿也不 ***yīdiǎnr yě bù*** *ee-dyar yay boo*
note 笔记 ***bǐjì*** *bee-jee*
notebook 笔记本 ***bǐjìběn*** *bee-jee-beun*
nothing 什么也没有 ***shénme yě méi yǒu*** *sheun-me yay may yoe*
novel 长篇小说 ***chángpiān xiǎoshuō*** *chang-pyen sheeao-shwoe*
November 十一月 ***shíyīyuè*** *sheu-ee-yway*
now 现在 ***xiànzài*** *shyen-zy*
nowadays 现代 ***xiàndài*** *shyen-dy*
nowhere 哪儿也没 ***nǎr yě méi*** *nar yay may*
number 号码 ***hàomǎ*** *hao-ma*
nurse 护士 ***hùshi*** *hoo-sheu*

O

obvious 明显 ***míngxiǎn*** *ming-shyen*
ocean 海洋 ***hǎiyáng*** *hy-yang*
o'clock: one o'clock 一点钟 ***yī diǎn zhōng*** *ee dyen jong*; **three o'clock** 三点钟 ***sān diǎn zhōng*** *san dyen jong*
October 十月 ***shíyuè*** *sheu-yway*
of 的 ***de*** *de*
offer 主动给 ***zhǔdòng gěi*** *joo-dong gay*
often 常常 ***chángcháng*** *chang-chang*
oil 油 ***yóu*** *yoe*
ointment 软膏 ***ruǎngāo*** *rwan-gao*
OK 行 ***xíng*** *shing*, 好 ***hǎo*** *hao*
old 老 ***lǎo*** *lao*, 旧 ***jiù*** *jyo*; **how old are you?** 你多大？ ***nǐ duō dà?*** *nee dwoe da*; **old people** 老年人 ***lǎoniánrén*** *lao-nyen-jeun*
old town 老城 ***lǎo chéng*** *lao chung*
on 在 ***…zài …*** *zy*; **it's on at …** 在 … 点演 ***zài … diǎn yǎn*** *zy … dyen yan*
once 一次 ***yī cì*** *ee tseu*; **once a day/an hour** 每天一次 ***měi tiān yī cì*** *may tyen ee tseu*; 小时一次 ***měi xiǎoshí yī cì*** *may sheeow-sheu ee tseu*
one 一 ***yī*** *ee*
only 仅有的 ***jǐnyǒu de*** *jin-yoe de*
open *(adj)* 开门 ***kāimén*** *ky-meun*
open *(v)* 开门 ***kāimén*** *ky-meun*
operate 动手术 ***dòng shǒushù*** *dong shoe-shoo*
operation: to have an operation 动手术 ***dòng shǒushù*** *dong shoe-shoo*
opinion 意见 ***yìjiàn*** *ee-jyen*; **in my opinion** 我觉得 ***wǒ juéde*** *wo jway-de*
opportunity 机会 ***jīhuì*** *jee-hway*
opposite *(n)* 相反 ***xiāngfǎn*** *shyang-fan*
opposite *(prep)* 对面 ***duìmiàn*** *dway-myen*
optician 眼镜店 ***yǎnjìngdiàn*** *yan-jing-dyen*
or 或者 ***huòzhě*** *hwoe-je*, 还是 ***háishì*** *hy-sheu*
orange 橙子 ***chéngzi*** *chung-zeu*
orchestra 管弦乐队 ***guǎnxián yuèduì*** *gwan-shyen yway-dway*
order *(n)* 点菜 ***diǎncài*** *dyen-tsy*; **out of order** 出故障了 ***chū gùzhàng le*** *choo goo-jang*
order *(v)*点菜 ***diǎncài*** *dyen-tsy* **58**, **59**
organic 有机绿色 ***yǒujīlǜsè*** *yoe-jee-lu-se*
organize 组织 ***zǔzhī*** *zoo-jeu*
other 其他 ***qítā*** *chee-ta*; **others** 其他的人 ***qítā de rén*** *chee-ta de jeun*, 其他的东西 ***qítā de dōngxi*** *chee-ta de dong-shee*

otherwise 不然的话 ***bùrándehuà*** *boo-ran-de-hua*
our 我们的 ***wǒmen de*** *wo-meun de*
ours 我们的 ***wǒmen de*** *wo-meun de*
outside 外面 ***wàimian*** *wy-myen*
outward journey 开出 ***kāichū*** *ky-choo*
oven 烤箱 ***kǎoxiāng*** *kai-shyang*
over: over there 在那儿 ***zài nàr*** *zy nar*
overdone 肉做老了 ***ròu zuò lǎo le*** *joe zwoe lao le*
overweight: my luggage is overweight 我的行李超重了 ***wǒ de xíngli chāozhòng le*** *wo de shing-lee chao-jong le*
owe 该钱 ***gāiqián*** *gy-chyen* **61**, **99**
own *(adj)* 自己的 ***zìjǐ de*** *zeu-jee*; **my own car** 我自己的车 ***wǒzìjǐ de chē*** *wo zeu-jee de che*
own *(v)* 拥有 ***yōngyǒu*** *yong-yoe*
owner 物主 ***wùzhǔ*** *woo-joo*

P

pack: to pack one's suitcase 打包装箱 ***dǎbāo*** *da-bao*
package holiday 包价旅游 ***bāojià lǚyóu*** *bao-jia lu-yoe*
packed 挤满了 ***jǐ mǎn le*** *jee man le*
packet 一包 ***yī bāo*** *ee bao*
painting 画儿 ***huàr*** *huar*
pair 一双 ***yī shuāng*** *ee shwang*; **a pair of pyjamas** 一套睡衣裤 ***yī tào shuìyīkù*** *ee taoshway-ee-koo*; **a pair of shorts** 一条短裤 ***yī tiáo duǎnkù*** *dwan-koo*
palace 宫殿 ***gōngdiàn*** *gong-dyen*
pants 裤子 ***kùzi*** *koo-zeu*
paper 纸 ***zhǐ*** *jeu*; **paper napkin** 纸餐巾 ***zhǐcānjīn*** *jeu-tsan-jin*; **paper tissue** 纸巾 ***zhǐjīn*** *jeu-jin*
parcel 包裹 ***bāoguǒ*** *bao-gwoe*
pardon? 请再说一遍，好吗？ ***qǐng zài shuō yī biàn, hǎo ma?*** *ching zy shwoe ee byen, hao ma?*
parents 父母 ***fùmǔ*** *foo-moo*
park *(n)* 公园 ***gōngyuán*** *gong-ywan*
park *(v)* 停车 ***tíngchē*** *ting-che*
parking space 停车位置 ***tíngchē wèizhi*** *ting-cheway-jeu*
part 部分 ***bùfen*** *boo-feun*; **to be a part of** 是 … 的一部分 ***shì … de yībùfen*** *sheu … de boo-feun*
party 晚会 ***wǎnhuì*** *wan-hway*
pass *(n)* 票 ***piào*** *peeow*
pass *(v)* 递给 ***dìgěi*** *dee-gay*
passenger 乘客 ***chéngkè*** *chung-ke*
passport 护照 ***hùzhào*** *hoo-jao*
past 过去 ***guòqù*** *gwoe-chu*; **a quarter past ten** 十点一刻 ***shí diǎn yī kè*** *sheu dyen yi keu*
path 小路 ***xiǎolù*** *sheeow-loo* **91**
patient 病人 ***bìngrén*** *bing-jeun*
pay 付款 ***fùkuǎn*** *foo-kwan* **99**, **100**
pedestrian 行人 ***xíngrén*** *shing-jeun*
pedestrianized street 步行街 ***bùxíngjiē*** *boo-shing-jyay*
pee 小便 ***xiǎobiàn*** *sheeow-byen*
peel 削皮 ***xiāopí*** *sheeow-pee*
pen 笔 ***bǐ*** *bee*
pencil 铅笔 ***qiānbǐ*** *chyen-bee*
people 人们 ***rénmen*** *jeun-meun* **56**
percent 百分之… ***bǎifénzhī …*** *by-feun-jeu*
perfect 好极了 ***hǎo jí le*** *hao jee le*
perfume 香水 ***xiāngshuǐ*** *shyang-shway*
perhaps 也许 ***yěxǔ*** *ye-shoo*
periods 月经 ***yuèjīng*** *yway-jing*
person 人 ***rén*** *jeun*
personal stereo 随身听 ***suíshēntīng*** *sway-sheun-ting*
petrol 汽油 ***qìyóu*** *chee-yoe*
petrol station 加油站 ***jiāyóuzhàn*** *jia-yoe-jan*
phone *(n)* 电话 ***diǎnhuà*** *dyen-hua* **134**
phone *(v)* 打电话 ***dǎ diànhuà*** *da dyen-hua*
phone box 电话亭 ***diànhuàtíng*** *dyen-hua-ting* **120**
phone call 电话 ***diànhuà*** *dyen-hua*;

ENG-CHI DICTIONARY

to make a phone call 打电话 ***dă diànhuà*** *da dyen-hua*
phonecard 电话卡 ***diànhuàkă*** *dyen-hua-ka* **120**
phone number 电话号码 ***diànhuà hàomă*** *dyen-hua hao-ma*
photo 照片 ***zhàopiàn*** *jao-pyen* **107**; **to take a photo of** 照 … ***zhào …*** *jao*; **to take someone's photo** 给某人照相 ***gěi mŏurén zhàoxiàng*** *gay moe-jeun jao-shyang*
picnic 野餐 ***yěcān*** *ye-tsan*; **to have a picnic** 野餐 ***yěcān*** *ye-tsan*
pie 西式馅饼 ***xīshì xiànbĭng*** *shee-sheu shyen-bing*
piece 片 ***piàn*** *pyen*; **a piece of** 一片 ***yī piàn*** *ee pyen*; **a piece of fruit** 一个水果 ***yī ge shuĭguŏ*** *ee ge shway-gwoe*
piles 痔疮 ***zhìchuāng*** *zheu-chwang*
pill 避孕药片 ***bìyùn yàopiàn*** *bee-yoon yao-pyen*; **to be on the pill** 服避孕药 ***fú bìyùnyào*** *foo bee-yoon-yao* **129**
pillow 枕头 ***zhěntou*** *jeun-toe*
pillowcase 枕套 ***zhěntào*** *jeun-tao*
PIN (number) 个人密码 ***gèrén mìmă*** *ge-jeun mee-ma*
pink 粉色 ***fěnsè*** *feun-seu*
pity: it's a pity 真遗憾 ***zhēn yíhàn*** *jeun ee-han*
place 地方 ***dìfang*** *dee-fang*
plan 计划 ***jìhuà*** *jee-hua*
plane 飞机 ***fēijī*** *fay-jee*
plant 植物 ***zhíwù*** *jeu-woo*
plaster (cast) 石膏 ***shígāo*** *sheu-gao*
plastic 塑料 ***sùliào*** *soo-leeow*
plastic bag 塑料袋 ***sùliàodài*** *soo-leeow-dy* **98**
plate 盘子 ***pánzi*** *pan-zeu*
platform 站台 ***zhàntái*** *jan-ty* **36**
play *(n)* 话剧 ***huàjù*** *hua-joo*
play *(v)* 玩儿 ***wánr*** *wanr*
please 请 ***qĭng*** *ching*
pleased 高兴 ***gāoxìng*** *gao-shing*; **pleased to meet you!** 很高兴认识您！ ***hěn gāoxìng rènshi nín!*** *heun gao-shing jeun-sheu nin!*
pleasure 乐趣 ***lèqù*** *le-chu*
plug 插头 ***chātóu*** *cha-toe*
plug in 插入插座 ***chārù chāzuò*** *cha-roo cha-zwoe*
plumber 管工 ***guăngōng*** *guan-gong*
point 指 ***zhĭ*** *jeu*
police 警察 ***jĭngchá*** *jing-cha*
policeman 警察 ***jĭngchá*** *jing-cha*
police station 警察局 ***jĭngchájú*** *jing-cha-ju* **134**
police woman 女警察 ***nǚ jĭngchá*** *nu jing-cha*
poor 穷 ***qióng*** *chyong*
port 港口 ***găngkŏu*** *gang-koe*
portrait 画像 ***huàxiàng*** *hua-shing*
possible 可能 ***kěnéng*** *ke-nung*
post 邮件 ***yóujiàn*** *yoe-jyen*
postbox 邮筒 ***yóutŏng*** *yoe-tong* **114**
postcard 明信片 ***míngxìnpiàn*** *ming-shin-pyen*
postcode 邮政编码 ***yóuzhèng biānmă*** *yoe-jung byen-ma*
poster 海报 ***hăibào*** *hy-bao*
poste restante 存局候领 ***cúnjú hòulĭng*** *tsoon-joo hoe-ling*
post office 邮局 ***yóujú*** *yoe-joo* **114**
pot 饭锅 ***fànguō*** *fan-gwoe*
pound (currency) 英镑 ***yīngbàng*** *ying-bang*
powder 粉 ***fěn*** *feun*
pram 婴儿车 ***yīng'érchē*** *ying-er-che*
prefer 更喜欢 ***gèng xĭhuan*** *gung shee-hwan*
pregnant 怀孕 ***huáiyùn*** *hwhy-yoon* **129**
prepare 准备 ***zhŭnbèi*** *joon-bay*
present *(n)* 礼物 ***lĭwù*** *lee-woo* **104**
press 新闻媒体 ***xīnwén méitĭ*** *shin-weun may-tee*
pressure 压力 ***yālì*** *ya-lee*
previous 以前的 ***yĭqián de*** *ee-chyen de*
price 价格 ***jiàgé*** *jya-ge*
private 私人的 ***sīrén de*** *seu-jeun de*
prize 奖 ***jiăng*** *jyang*

probably 也许 *yěxǔ* yay-shoo
problem 问题 *wèntí* weun-tee
procession 队列 *duìliè* dway-lyay
product 产品 *chǎnpǐn* chan-pin
profession 职业 *zhíyè* jeu-yay
programme 节目 *jiémù* jyay-moo
promise 许诺 *xǔnuò* shoo-nwoe
propose 提出建议 *tíchū jiànyì* tee-choo jyen-yee
protect 保护 *bǎohù* bao-hoo
public 公众 *gōngzhòng* gong-jong
public holiday 公众假日 *gōngzhòng jiàrì* gong-jong jya-jeu
pull 拉 *lā* la
purple 紫色 *zǐsè* zeu-se
purse 钱包 *qiánbāo* chyen-bao
push 推 *tuī* tway
pushchair 折叠婴儿推车 *zhé dié yīng ér tuī chē* je dyay ying er tway-che
put 放 *fàng* fang

Q

quality 质量 *zhìliàng* jeu-lyang; **of good quality** 质量好*zhìliàng hǎo* jeu-lyang hao; **of bad quality** 质量坏 *zhìliàng huài* jeu-lyang hwhy
quarter 四分之一 *sì fēn zhī yī* seu feun jeu ee; **a quarter of an hour** 一刻钟 *yīkè zhōng* ee-ke jong; **a quarter to ten** 差一刻十点 *chà yīkè shí diǎn* cha yee-ke sheu dyen
question 问题 *wèntí* weun-tee
queue (n & v) 排队 *páiduì* py-dway
quick 快 *kuài* kwhy
quickly 快 *kuài* kwhy
quiet 安静 *ānjìng* an-jing
quite 相当 *xiāngdāng* shyang-dang; **quite a lot of** 相当多 *xiāngdāng duō* shyang-dang dwoe

R

racket 球拍 *qiúpāi* chyo-py
radiator 暖气 *nuǎnqì* nwan-chee
radio 收音机 *shōuyīnjī* shoe-yin-jee
radio station 广播电台 *guǎngbō diàntái* gwang-bo dyen-ty
rain 雨 *yǔ* yoo
rain: it's raining下雨了 *xiàyǔ le* shya-yoo le
raincoat 雨衣 *yǔyī* yoo-yee
rape 强奸 *qiángjiān* chyang-jyen
rare 半熟 *bàn shóu* ban-shoe; (meat) 外焦里嫩 *wàijiāolǐnèn* wy-jeeao-lee-neun
rarely 很少 *hěn shǎo* heun shao
rather 相当 *xiāngdāng* shyang-dang
raw 生的 *shēng de* shung de
razor 剃须刀 *tìxūdāo* tee-shoo-dao
razor blade 刀片 *dāopiàn* dao-pyen
reach 到达 *dàodá* dao-da
read 读 *dú* doo
ready 准备好 *zhǔnbèi hǎo* joon-bay hao
reasonable 合理 *hélǐ* he-lee
receipt 收据 *shōujù* shoe-joo **100**, **130**
receive 收到 *shōudào* shoe-dao
reception 前台 *qiántái* chyen-ty; (on phone) 收听 *shōutīng* shoe-ting; **at reception** 在前台 *zài qiántái* zy chyen-ty **49**
receptionist 前台 *qiántái* chyen-ty
recognize 认出 *rènchū* jeun-choo
recommend 推荐 *tuījiàn* tway-jyen **46**, **55**
red 红色 *hóngsè* hong-se
red light 红灯 *hóngdēng* hong-dung
reduce 减价 *jiǎnjià* jyen-jya
reduction 减价 *jiǎnjià* jyen-jya
red wine 红葡萄酒 *hóng pútáojiǔ* hong poo-tao-jyo
refrigerator 冰箱 *bīngxiāng* bing-shyang
refund (n & v) 退款 *tuìkuǎn* tway-kwan **103**; **to get a refund** 退款 *tuìkuǎn* tway-kwan
refuse 拒绝 *jùjué* joo-jway
registered 已登记 *yǐ dēngjì* ee dung-jee
registration number 登记号码

dēngjì hàomă dung-jee hao-ma
remember 记得 *jìde* jee-de
remind 提醒 *tíxǐng* tee-shing
remove 去除 *qùchú* choo-choo
rent (n) 租金 *zūjīn* zoo-jin
rent (v) 租 *zū* zoo **50**
rental 租金收入 *zūjīn shōurù* zoo-jin shoe-joo
reopen 再开门 *zài kāimén* zy ky-meun
repair 修理 *xiūlǐ* shyo-lee **39**; **to get something repaired** 把某物送去修理 *bă mŏuwù sòngqù xiūlǐ* ba moe-woo song-choo shyo-lee
repeat 重复 *chóngfù* chong-foo **15**
reserve 订 *dìng* ding **45, 56, 57**
reserved 已预订 *yǐ yùdìng* ee yoo-ding
rest (n) **the rest** 其余的部分 *qíyú de bùfen* chee-yoo de boo-feun
rest (n & v) 休息 *xiūxi* shyo-shee
restaurant 餐馆 *cānguăn* tsan-gwan **55**
return 返回 *fănhuí* fan-hway
return ticket 往返票 *wăngfănpiào* wang-fan-peeao
reverse-charge call 对方付费电话 *duìfāng fùfèi diànhuà* dway-fang foo-fay dyen-hwa
reverse gear 倒车档 *dào chē dăng* dao che dang
rheumatism 风湿病 *fēngshībìng* fung-sheu-bing
rib 肋骨 *lèigŭ* lay-goo
right (n) 权利 *quánlì* chwan-lee; **to have the right to …** 有权利做 … *yŏu quánlì zuò …* yoe chwan-lee zwoe …; **to the right of …** 在 … 的右边 *zài … de yòubian* zy … de yoe-byen
right (adj) (correct) 对 *duì* dway
right (adv) **right away** 马上 *măshàng* ma-shang; **right beside …** 就在 … 旁边 *jiù zài … pángbiān* jyo zy … pang-byen
ring 电话铃 *diànhuàlíng* dyen-hwa-ling
ripe 成熟 *chéngshú* chung-shoo
rip-off 敲竹杠 *qiāo zhúgàng* cheeao joo-gang
river 河 *hé* he
road 路 *lù* loo
road sign 路标 *lùbiāo* loo-beeao
rock 岩石 *yánshí* yan-sheu
room 房间 *fángjiān* fang-jyen **44, 45**
rosé wine 粉红葡萄酒 *fĕnhóng pútáojiŭ* feun-hong poo-tao-jyo
round 圆形 *yuánxíng* ywan-shing
roundabout 绕行路线 *ràoxínglùxiàn* jao-shing-loo-shyen
rubbish 垃圾 *lājī* la-jee; **to take the rubbish out** 倒垃圾 *dào lājī* dao la-jee
rucksack 背包 *bēibāo* bay-bao
rug 小块地毯 *xiăokuài dìtăn* sheeao-kwhy dee-tan
ruins 遗迹 *yíjì* ee-jee; **in ruins** 废墟 *fèixū* fay-shoo
run out 用完了 *yòng wán le* yong wan le; **to have run out of petrol** 汽油用完了 *qìyóu yòng wán le* chee-yoe yong wan le

S

sad 难过 *nánguò* nan-gwoe
safe 安全 *ānquán* an-chwan
safety 安全 *ānquán* an-chwan
safety belt 安全带 *ānquándài* an-chwan-dy
sail 航海 *hánghăi* hang-hy
sailing 帆船航海 *fānchuán hánghăi* fan-chwan hang-hy; **to go sailing** 去航海 *qù hánghăi* choo hang-hy
sale: for sale 供出售 *gòng chūshòu* gong choo-shoe; **in the sale** 大减价 *dàjiănjià* da-jyen-jya
sales 大减价 *dàjiănjià* da-jyen-jya
salt 盐 *yán* yan
salted 盐腌的 *yán yān de* yan yan de
salty 太咸了 *tài xián le* ty shyen le
same 同样 *tóngyàng* tong-yang; **the same** 同样的 *tóngyàng de* tong-yang de **60**

sand 沙滩 *shātān* sha-tan
sandals 凉鞋 *liángxié* lyang-shyay
sanitary towel 卫生巾 *wèishēngjīn* way-shung-jin
Saturday 星期六 *xīngqīliù* shing-chee-lyo
saucepan 深平底锅 *shēn píngdǐguō* sheun ping-dee-gwoe
save (money) 存钱 *cúnqián* tsoon-chyen
say 说 *shuō* shwoe; **how do you say ...?** ... 怎么说? ... *zěnme shuō?* ... zeun-me shwoe?
scenery 风景 *fēngjǐng* fung-jing
scissors 剪刀 *jiǎndāo* jyen-dao
scooter 小型摩托车 *xiǎoxíng mótuōchē* sheeao-shing mo-twoe-che
scotch (whisky) 苏格兰威士忌 *sūgélán wēishìjì* soo-ge-lan way-sheu-jee
Scotland 苏格兰 *sūgélán* soo-ge-lan
Scottish (adj) 苏格兰人 *sūgélán rén* soo-ge-lan jeun
scuba diving 戴水肺的潜水 *dài shuǐfèi dè qiánshuǐ* dy shway-fay de chyen shway
sea 海 *hǎi* hy
seafood 海鲜 *hǎixiān* hy-shyen
season 季节 *jìjié* jee-jyay
seat 座位 *zuòwèi* zwoe-way **31**
second 第二 *dì èr* dee er
secondary school 中学 *zhōngxué* jong-shway
second class 二等 *èrděng* er-dung
second-hand 二手货 *èrshǒu huò* er-shoe hwoe
secure 安全 *ānquán* an-chwan
security 安全 *ānquán* an-chwan
see 看见 *kànjiàn* kan-jyen; **see you later!** 回头见! *huítóujiàn!* hway-toe-jyen!; **see you soon!** 再见 *zàijiàn!* zy-jyen!; **see you tomorrow!** 明天见 *míngtiān jiàn!* ming-tyen jyen!
seem 看起来 *kànqǐlái* kan-chee-ly
seldom 很少 *hěn shǎo* heun shao
sell 卖 *mài* my **98**
Sellotape® 透明胶带 *tòumíng jiāodài* toe-ming jeeao-dy
send 寄 *jì* jee
sender 寄件人 *jìjiànrén* jee-jyen-jeun
sentence 句子 *jùzi* joo-zeu
separate 分开 *fēnkāi* feun-ky
separately 分开 *fēnkāi* feun-ky
September 九月 *jiǔyuè* jyo-yway
serious 严重 *yánzhòng* yan-jong
several 几个 *jǐ ge* jee ge
sex 性别 *xìngbié* shing-byay
shade 荫凉 *yīnliáng* yin-lyang; **in the shade** 在荫凉地 *zài yīnliángdì* zy yin-lyang-dee
shame 羞愧 *xiūkuì* shyo-kway
shampoo 香波 *xiāngbō* shyang-bo
shape 形状 *xíngzhuàng* shing-jwang
share 分享 *fēnxiǎng* feun-shyang
shave 剃须 *tìxū* tee-shoo
shaving foam 泡沫剃须膏 *pàomò tìxūgāo* pao-mo tee-shoo-gao
she 她 *tā* ta
sheet 床单 *chuángdān* chwang-dan
shellfish 贝类 *bèilèi* bay-lay
shirt 衬衫 *chènshān* cheun-shan
shock 惊愕 *jīng'è* jing-e
shocking 令人震惊 *lìng rén zhènjīng* ling jeun jeun-jing
shoes 鞋 *xié* shyay
shop 商店 *shāngdiàn* shang-dyen
shop assistant 店员 *diànyuán* dyen-ywan
shopkeeper 店主 *diànzhǔ* dyen-joo
shopping 买东西 *mǎi dōngxi* my dong-shee; **to do some shopping** 买点儿东西 *mǎi diǎnr dōngxi* my-dyar dong-shee
shopping centre 购物中心 *gòuwù zhōngxīn* goe-woo jong-shin
short 短 *duǎn* dwan
short cut 近路 *jìnlù* jin-loo
shorts 短裤 *duǎnkù* dwan-koo
short-sleeved 短袖 *duǎnxiù* dwan-shyo
shoulder 肩膀 *jiānbǎng* jyen-bang
show (n) 演出 *yǎnchū* yan-choo **76**

show *(v)* 给 … 看 ***gěi … kàn*** *gay … kan*
shower 淋浴 ***línyù*** *lin-yoo*; **to take a shower** 洗淋浴 ***xǐ línyù*** *shee lin-yoo*
shower gel 浴液 ***yùyè*** *yoo-yay*
shut 关 ***guān*** *gwan*
shuttle 机场大巴士 ***jīchǎng dàbāshì*** *jee-chang da-ba-sheu*
shy 害羞 ***hàixiū*** *hy-shyo*
sick: to feel sick 想吐 ***xiǎng tù*** *shyang-too*
side 侧面 ***cèmiàn*** *tse-myen*
sign *(n)* 标志 ***biāozhì*** *beeao-jeu*
sign: to sign (a cheque) 签（支票） ***qiān (zhīpiào)*** *chyen (jeu-peeow)*
silent 安静 ***ānjìng*** *an-jing*
silver 银的 ***yín de*** *yin de*
silver-plated 镀银 ***dùyín*** *doo-yin*
since 从 … 以来 ***cóng … yǐlái*** *tsong … yee-ly*
single 单人 ***dānrén*** *dan-jeun*
single (ticket) 单程（票） ***dānchéng (piào)*** *dan-chung (peeao)*
sister 姐妹 ***jiěmèi*** *jyay-may*; *(younger)* 妹妹 ***mèimei*** *may-may*; *(older)* 姐姐 ***jiějie*** *jyay-jyay*
sit down 坐下 ***zuò xià*** *zwoe shya*
size *(for shoe/clothes)* 号码 ***hàomă*** *hao-ma*
ski 滑雪 ***huáxuě*** *hwa-shway*
skiing 滑雪 ***huáxuě*** *hwa-shway*; **to go skiing** 去滑雪 ***qù huáxuě*** *choo hwa-shway*
skin 皮肤 ***pífū*** *pee-foo*
skirt 裙子 ***qúnzi*** *choon-zeu*
sky 天空 ***tiānkōng*** *tyen-kong*
skyscraper 摩天大楼 ***mótiāndàlóu*** *mo-tyen-da-loe*
sleep *(n & v)* 睡觉 ***shuìjiào*** *shway-jeeao*; **to sleep with …** 和 … 睡觉 ***hé … shuìjiào*** *he … shway-jeeao*
sleeping bag 睡袋 ***shuìdài*** *shway-dy*
sleeping pill 安眠药 ***ānmiányào*** *an-myen-yao*
sleepy: to be sleepy 困 ***kùn*** *koon*
sleeve 袖子 ***xiùzi*** *shyo-zeu*
slice 片 ***piàn*** *pyen*
slow 慢 ***màn*** *man*
slowly 慢慢地 ***mànmàn de*** *man-man de*
small 小 ***xiăo*** *sheeao*
smell *(n)* 气味 ***qìwèi*** *chee-way*
smell *(v)* 闻 ***wén*** *weun*; **to smell good** 闻起来好 ***wénqǐlái hăo*** *weun-chee-ly hao*; **to smell bad** 闻起来坏 ***wénqǐlái huài*** *weun-chee-ly hwhy*
smile *(v)* 微笑 ***wēixiào*** *way-sheeao*
smoke 抽烟 ***chōuyān*** *choe-yan*
smoker 抽烟人 ***chōuyānrén*** *choe-yan-jeun*
snack 小吃 ***xiăochī*** *sheeao-cheu*
snow *(n)* 雪 ***xuě*** *shway*
snow *(v)* 下雪 ***xiàxuě*** *shya-shway*
so 因此 ***yīncǐ*** *yin-tseu*; **so that …** 这样 … ***zhèyàng …*** *je-yang …*
soap 肥皂 ***féizào*** *fay-zao*
soccer 足球 ***zúqiú*** *zoo-chyo*
socks 袜子 ***wàzi*** *wa-zeu*
some 一些 ***yīxiē*** *ee-shyay*; **some people** 一些人 ***yīxiē rén*** *ee-shyay jeun*
somebody, **someone** 某人 ***mŏurén*** *moe-jeun*
something 某物 ***mŏuwù*** *moe-woo*; **something else** 其他的事 ***qítā de shì*** *chee-ta de sheu*
sometimes 有时候 ***yŏushíhou*** *yoe-sheu-hoe*
somewhere 某地 ***mŏudì*** *moe-dee*; **somewhere else** 其他的地方 ***qítā de dìfang*** *chee-ta de dee-fang*
son 儿子 ***érzi*** *er-zeu*
soon 很快 ***hěn kuài*** *heun kwhy*, 不久 ***bùjiŭ*** *boo-jyo*
sore: to have a sore throat 嗓子疼 ***săngzi téng*** *sang-zeu tung*; **to have a sore head** 头疼 ***tóu téng*** *toe tung*
sorry 令人惋惜 ***lìng rén wănxī*** *ling jeun wan-shee*; **sorry!** 对不起

duìbuqǐ! *dway-boo-chee!*
south 南 *nán nan*; **in the south** 在南部 *zài nánbù zy nan-boo*; **(to the) south of …** 在 … 的南边 *zài … de nánbian zy … de nan-byen*
souvenir 纪念品 *jìniànpǐn jee-nyen-pin*
spare 备用 *bèiyòng bay-yong*
spare part 备用部件 *bèiyòng bùjiàn bay-yong boo-jyen*
spare tyre 备用轮胎 *bèiyòng lúntā bay-yong loon-ty*
spare wheel 备用车轮 *bèiyòng chēlún bay-yong che-loon*
spark plug 火花塞 *huǒhuāsāi hwoe-hwa-sy*
speak 说 *shuō shwoe* **13**, **15**, **17**, **121**, **122**, **134**
special 特别 *tèbié te-byay* **58**
speciality 特产 *tèchǎn te-chan*
speed 速度 *sùdù soo-doo*; **at full speed** 全速 *quánsù chwan-soo*
spell 拼写 *pīnxiě pin-shyay*; **how do you spell …?** … 怎么写? *… zěnme xiě? … zeun-me shyay?*
spend 花钱 *huāqián hwa-chyen*
spice 香料 *xiāngliào shyang-leeao*
spicy 加香料的 *jiā xiāngliào de jya shyang-leeao de*
spider 蜘蛛 *zhīzhū jeu-joo*
splinter 碎片 *suìpiàn sway-pyen*
spoil 毁坏 *huǐhuài hway-hwhy*, 宠坏 *chǒnghuài chong-hwhy*
sponge 海绵 *hǎimián hy-myen*
spoon 勺子 *sháozi shao-zeu*
sport 体育运动 *tǐyù yùndòng tee-yoo yoon-dong*
sports ground 运动场 *yùndòngchǎng yoon-dong-chang*
spot 疱疹 *pàozhěn pao-jeun*
sprain: to sprain one's ankle 扭伤了脚脖子 *niǔshāng le jiǎobózi nyo-shang le jeeao-bo-zeu*
spring 春天 *chūntiān choon-tyen*
square 广场 *guǎngchǎng gwang-chang*
stadium 体育场 *tǐyùchǎng tee-yoo-chang*
stain 玷污 *diànwū dyen-woo*
stairs 楼梯 *lóutī loe-tee*
stamp 邮票 *yóupiào yoe-peeao* **114**
start 开始 *kāishǐ ky-sheu*
state 陈述 *chénshù cheun-shoo*
statement 陈述 *chénshù cheun-shoo*
station 车站 *chēzhàn che-jan*
stay *(n)* 停留 *tíngliú ting-lyo*
stay *(v)* 呆 *dāi dy*; **to stay in touch** 保持联系 *bǎochí liánxì bao-cheu lyen-shee*
steal 偷 *tōu toe* **135**
step 台阶 *táijiē ty-jyay*
sticking plaster 橡皮膏 *xiàngpígāo shyang-pee-gao*
still 无汽的 *wú qì de woo chee de*
still water 无汽的水 *wú qì de shuǐ woo chee de shway*
sting *(n & v)* 叮 *dīng ding*; **to get stung by …** 被 … 叮了 *bèi … dīng le bay … ding le*
stock: out of stock 卖光了 *mài guāng le my gwang le*
stomach 胃 *wèi way*
stone 石头 *shítou sheu-toe*
stop *(n)* 汽车站 *qìchēzhàn chee-che-jan* **36**
stop *(v)* 停 *tíng ting*
stopcock 旋塞阀 *xuánsāifá shwan-sy-fa*
storey 楼层 *lóucéng loe-tsung*
storm 暴风 *bàofēng bao-fung*
straight ahead, **straight on** 一直往前 *yīzhí wǎng qián yee-jeu wang chyen*
strange 奇怪 *qíguài chee-gwhy*
street 街道 *jiēdao jyay-dao*
strong 味道浓 *wèidào nóng way-dao nong*
stuck 走不动 *zǒubudòng zoe-boo-dong*
student 学生 *xuésheng shway-shung* **30**
study 学习 *xuéxí shway-shee*

style 款式 *kuǎnshì* kwan-sheu
suffer 受疼痛 *shòu téngtòng* shoe tung-tong
suggest 建议 *jiànyì* jyen-yee
suit: does that suit you? 那适合你吗？ *nà shìhé nǐ ma?* na sheu-he nee ma?
suitcase 旅行衣箱 *lǚxíng yīxiāng* lu-shing ee-shyang **32**
summer 夏天 *xiàtiān* shya-tyen
summit 高峰 *gāofēng* gao-fung
sun 太阳 *tàiyáng* ty-yang; **in the sun** 在太阳下晒 *zài tàiyáng xià shài* zy ty-yang shya shy
sunbathe 日光浴 *rìguāngyù* jeu-gwang-yoo
sunburnt: to get sunburnt 晒伤 *shàishāng* shy-shang
sun cream 防晒霜 *fángshàishuāng* fang-shy-shwang
Sunday 星期天 *xīngqītiān* shing-chee-tyen
sunglasses 太阳镜 *tàiyángjìng* ty-yang-jing
sunhat 遮阳帽 *zhēyángmào* je-yang-mao
sunrise 日出 *rìchū* jeu-choo
sunset 日落 *rìluò* jeu-lwoe
sunstroke 中暑 *zhòngshǔ* jong-shoo; **to get sunstroke** 中暑了 *zhòngshǔ le* jong-shoo le
supermarket 超市 *chāoshì* chao-sheu **97**
supplement 补充 *bǔchōng* boo-chong
sure 确信 *quèxìn* chway-shin
surgical spirit 消毒酒精 *xiāodú jiǔjīng* sheeao-doo jyo-jing
surname 姓 *xìng* shing
surprise (*n*) 惊讶 *jīngyà* jing-ya
surprise (*v*) 使 … 惊讶 *shǐ … jīngyà* sheu …jing-ya
sweat 汗 *hàn* han
sweater 套头毛衣 *tàotóu máoyī* tao-toe mao-yee
sweet (*n*) 甜食 *tiánshí* tyen-sheu
sweet (*adj*) 甜 *tián* tyen
swim: to go for a swim 去游泳 *qù yóuyǒng* choo yoe-yong
swim (*v*) 游泳 *yóuyǒng* yoe-yong
swimming 游泳 *yóuyǒng* yoe-yong
swimming pool 游泳池 *yóuyǒngchí* yoe-yong-cheu
swimming trunks 男游泳裤 *nányóuyǒngkù* nan-yoe-yong-koo
swimsuit 女游泳衣 *nǚyóuyǒngyī* nu-yoe-yong-yee
switch off 关掉 *guāndiào* gwan-deeao
switch on 打开 *dǎkāi* da-ky
switchboard operator 总机接线员 *zǒngjī jiēxiànyuán* zong-jee jyay-shyen-ywan
swollen 肿 *zhǒng* jong
syrup 糖浆 *tángjiāng* tang-jyang

T

table 餐桌 *cānzhuō* tsan-jwoe **56**, **57**
tablespoon 汤勺 *tāngsháo* tang-shao
tablet 药片 *yàopiàn* yao-pyen
take 拿 *ná* na; **it takes two hours** 花两小时 *huā liǎng xiǎoshí* hwa lyang sheeao-sheu
take off (*plane*) 起飞 *qǐfēi* chee-fay
takeaway 外卖店盒饭 *wàimàidiàn héfàn* wy-my-dyen he-fan
talk 说话 *shuōhuà* shwoe-hwa
tall 高 *gāo* gao
tampon 月经棉条 *yuèjīng miántiáo* yway-jing myen-teeao
tan 黄褐色 *huánghèsè* hwang-he-se
tanned 晒成黄褐色 *shàichéng huánghèsè* shy-chung hwang-he-se
tap 水龙头 *shuǐlóngtóu* shway-long-toe
taste (*n*) 味道 *wèidao* way-dao
taste (*v*) 尝 *cháng* chang
tax 税 *shuì* shway
tax-free 免税 *miǎnshuì* myen-shway

taxi 出租车 *chūzūchē* choo-zoo-che **40**
taxi driver 出租车司机 *chūzūchē sījī* choo-zoo-che seu-jee
team 队 *duì* dway
teaspoon 茶勺 *cháshāo* cha-shao
teenager 少年 *shàonián* shao-nyen
telephone *(n)* 电话 *diànhuà* dyen-hwa
telephone *(v)* 打电话 *dǎ diànhuà* da dyen-hwa
television 电视 *diànshì* dyen-sheu
tell 告诉 *gàosu* gao-soo
temperature 发烧 *fāshāo* fa-shao; **to take someone's temperature** 给某人量体温 *gěi mǒurén liáng tǐwēn* gay moe-jeun lyang tee-weun
temple 庙 *miào* meeao
temporary 暂时 *zànshí* zan-sheu
tennis 网球 *wǎngqiú* wang-chyo
tennis court 网球场 *wǎngqiúchǎng* wang-chyo-chang
tennis shoe 网球鞋 *wǎngqiúxié* wang-chyo-shyay
tent 帐篷 *zhàngpeng* jang-pung **51**
terminal 终点站 *zhōngdiǎnzhàn* jong-dyen-jan
terrace 台阶 *táijiē* ty-jyay
terrible 糟糕 *zāogāo* zao-gao
thank 谢谢 *xièxie* shyay-shyay, 感谢 *gǎnxiè* gan-shyay; **thank you** 谢谢你 *xièxie nǐ* shyay-shyay nee; **thank you very much** 非常感谢 *fēicháng gǎnxiè* fay-chang gan-shyay
thanks 谢谢 *xièxie* shyay-shyay; **thanks to** 由于 *yóuyú* yoe-yoo
that 那 *nà* na; **that one** 那个 *nà ge* na ge
the see grammar
theatre 剧院 *jùyuàn* joo-ywan
theft 失窃 *shīqiè* sheu-chyay
their, **theirs** 他们的 *tāmen de* ta-meun de
them 他们 *tāmen* ta-meun
theme park 主题公园 *zhǔtí gōngyuán* joo-tee-gong-ywan
then 那时 *nàshí* na-sheu
there 那儿 *nàr* nar; **there is** 有 *yǒu* yoe; **there are** 有 *yǒu* yoe
therefore 因此 *yīncǐ* yin-tseu
thermometer 温度计 *wēndùjì* weun-doo-jee
Thermos® flask 热水瓶 *rèshuǐpíng* je-shway-ping
these 这些 *zhèxiē* je-shyay; **these ones** 这些 *zhèxiē* je-shyay
they 他们 *tāmen* ta-meun
thief 小偷 *xiǎotōu* sheeao-toe
thigh 大腿 *dàtuǐ* da-tway
thin 薄 *báo* bao
thing 东西 *dōngxi* dong-shee
think 想 *xiǎng* shyang, 认为 *rènwéi* jeun-way
think about 考虑 *kǎolǜ* kao-loo
thirst 渴 *kě* ke
thirsty: to be thirsty 渴了 *kě le* ke le
this 这 *zhè* je; **this one** 这个 *zhè ge* je ge; **this evening** 今天晚上 *jīntiān wǎnshang* jin-tyen wan-shang; **this is** 这是 *zhè shì* je sheu
those 那些 *nàxiē* na-shyay; **those ones** 那些 *nàxiē* na-shyay
throat 嗓子 *sǎngzi* sang-zeu
throw 扔 *rēng* jung
throw out 扔掉 *rēngdiào* jung-deeao
Thursday 星期四 *xīngqīsì* shing-chee-seu
ticket 票 *piào* peeao **30**, **76**, **77**, **84**
ticket office 售票处 *shòupiàochù* shoe-peeao-choo
tidy 整洁 *zhěngjié* jung-jyay
tie 领带 *lǐngdài* ling-dy
tight 紧 *jǐn* jin
tights 长筒丝袜 *chángtǒng sīwà* chang-tong seu-wa
time 时间 *shíjiān* sheu-jyen **144**; **what time is it?** 几点了？ *jǐ diǎn le?* jee dyen le?; **from time to time** 有时 *yǒushí* yoe-sheu; **on time** 准时 *zhǔnshí* joon-sheu; **three times** 三次 *sān cì* san tseu

time difference 时差 *shíchā* sheu-cha
timetable 时刻表 *shíkèbiǎo* sheu-ke-beeao **30**
tinfoil 锡纸 *xīzhǐ* shee-jeu
tip 小费 *xiǎofèi* sheeao-fay
tired 累 *lèi* lay
tobacco 烟叶 *yānyè* yan-yay
tobacconist's 烟店 *yāndiàn* yan-dyen
today 今天 *jīntiān* jin-tyen
together 一起 *yīqǐ* ee-chee
toilet 厕所 *cèsuǒ* tse-swoe, 卫生间 *wèishēngjiān* way-shung-jyen **13**, **56**
toilet bag 卫生包 *wèishēngbāo* way-shung-bao
toilet paper 卫生纸 *wèishēngzhǐ* way-shung-jeu
toiletries 卫生用品 *wèishēng yòngpǐn* way-shung yong-pin
toll 道路通行费 *dàolù tōngxíngfèi* dao-loo tong-shing-fay
tomorrow 明天 *míngtiān* ming-tyen; **tomorrow evening** 明天晚上 *míngtiān wǎnshang* ming-tyen wan-shang; **tomorrow morning** 明天早上 *míngtiān zǎoshang* ming-tyen zao-shang
tongue 舌头 *shétou* she-toe
tonight 今天夜里 *jīntiān yèlǐ* jin-tyen yay-lee
too (*also*) 也 *yě* yay; (*excessive*) 太 *tài* ty; **too bad** 太糟糕 *tài zāogāo* ty zao-gao; **too many** 太多 *tài duō* ty dwoe; **too much** 太多 *tài duō* ty dwoe
tooth 牙 *yá* ya
toothbrush 牙刷 *yáshuā* ya-shwa
toothpaste 牙膏 *yágāo* ya-gao
top 顶部 *dǐngbù* ding-boo; **at the top of ...** 在 ... 上部 *zài ... shàngbù* zy ... shang-boo
torch 手电 *shǒudiàn* shoe-dyen
touch 触摸 *chùmō* choo-mo
tourist 旅游者 *lǚyóuzhě* lu-yoe-je
tourist office 旅游信息中心 *lǚyóuxìnxī zhōngxīn* lu-yoe-shin-shee jong-shin **82**
tourist trap 旅游者太多的地方 *lǚyóuzhě tài duō de dìfang* lu-yoe-je ty dwoe de dee-fang
towards 向 *xiàng* shyang
towel 毛巾 *máojīn* mao-jin
town 城镇 *chéngzhèn* chung-jeun
town centre 市中心 *shìzhōngxīn* sheu-jong-shin
town hall 市政府 *shìzhèngfǔ* sheu-jung-foo
toy 玩具 *wánjù* wan-joo
traditional 传统 *chuántǒng* chwan-tong
traffic 交通 *jiāotōng* jeeao-tong
traffic jam 交通阻塞 *jiāotōng zǔsè* jeeao-tong zoo-se
train 火车 *huǒchē* hwoe-che **35**, **36**; **the train to Beijing** 到北京去的火车 *dào běijīng qù de huǒchē* dao bay-jing choo de hwoe-che
train station 火车站 *huǒchēzhàn* hwoe-che-jan
tram 有轨电车 *yǒu guǐ diànchē* yoe gway dyen-che
transfer (*of money*) 转帐 *zhuǎnzhàng* jwan-jang
translate 翻译 *fānyì* fan-yee
travel 旅行 *lǚxíng* lu-shing
travel agency 旅行社 *lǚxíngshè* lu-shing-she
traveller's cheque 旅行支票 *lǚxíng zhīpiào* lu-shing jeu-peeao
trip 旅行 *lǚxíng* lu-shing; **have a good trip!** 旅行愉快！ *lǚxíng yúkuài!* lu-shing yoo-kwy!
trolley 手推车 *shǒutuīchē* shoe-tway-che
trouble 麻烦 *máfan* ma-fan
trousers 裤子 *kùzi* koo-zeu
true 真实 *zhēnshí* jeun-sheu
try 试 *shì* sheu; **to try to do something** 试着做某事 *shìzhe zuò mǒushì* sheu-je zwoe moe-sheu
try on 试穿 *shìchuān* sheu-chwan **102**

Tuesday 星期二 *xīngqī'èr* *shing-chee-er*
tube 地铁 *dìtiě* *dee-tyay*
turn *(n)* **it's your turn** 该你了 *gāi nǐ le* *gy nee le*
turn *(v)* 拐 *guǎi* *gwhy*
twice 两次 *liǎng cì* *lyang tseu*
type *(n)* 种类 *zhǒnglèi* *jong-lay*
type *(v)* 打字 *dǎzì* *da-zeu*
typical 典型 *diǎnxíng* *dyen-shing*
tyre 轮胎 *lúntā* *loon-ty*

umbrella 伞 *sǎn* *san*
uncle 叔叔 *shūshu* *shoo-shoo*
uncomfortable 不舒服 *bù shūfu* *boo shoo-foo*
under 在 … 下面 *zài … xiàmian* *zy … shya-myen*
underground 地铁 *dìtiě* *dee-tyay* **35**
underground line 地铁线 *dìtiěxiàn* *dee-tyay-shyen*
underground station 地铁站 *dìtiězhàn* *dee-tyay-jan*
underneath 在 … 下面 *zài … xiàmian* *zy … shya-myen*
understand 懂 *dǒng* *dong* **15**
underwear 内衣 *nèiyī* *nay-yee*
United Kingdom 英国 *yīngguó* *ying-gwoe*
United States 美国 *měiguó* *may-gwoe*
until 到 … 为止 *dao … wéizhǐ* *dao … way-jeu*
upset 胃疼 *wèi téng* *way tung*, 烦恼 *fánnǎo* *fan-nao*
upstairs 楼上 *lóushàng* *loe-shang*
urgent 紧急 *jǐnjí* *jin-jee*
us 我们 *wǒmen* *wo-meun*
use 用 *yòng* *yong*; **I'm used to it** 我习惯了 *wǒ xíguàn le* *wo shee-gwan le*
useful 有用 *yǒuyòng* *yoe-yong*
useless 无用 *wúyòng* *woo-yong*
usually 通常 *tōngcháng* *tong-chang*
U-turn U 形转弯 *yōuxíng zhuǎnwān* *yoe-shing jwan-wan*

vaccinated: I'm vaccinated against （我）接种了 … 疫苗 *wǒ jiēzhǒng le … yìmiáo* *wo jyay-jong le … ee-meeow*
valid 有效 *yǒuxiào* *yoe-sheeao*
valley 山谷 *shāngǔ* *shan-goo*
VAT 增值税 *zēngzhíshuì* *zung-jeu-shway*
vegetarian 吃素 *chīsù* *cheu-soo*
very 很 *hěn* *heun*
view 风景 *fēngjǐng* *fung-jing*
villa 花园住宅 *huāyuán zhùzhái* *hwa-ywan joo-jy*
village 村庄 *cūnzhuāng* *tsoon-jwang*
visa 签证 *qiānzhèng* *chyen-jung*
visit *(n & v)* 参观 *cānguān* *tsan-gwan*
volleyball 排球 *páiqiú* *py-chyo*
vomit 呕吐 *ǒutù* *oe-too*

W

waist 腰 *yāo* *yao*
wait 等 *děng* *dung*; **to wait for somebody** 等某人 *děng mǒurén* *dung moe-jeun*; **to wait for something** 等某事发生 *děng mǒushì fāshēng* *dung moe-sheu fa-shung*
waiter 男侍者 *nánshìzhě* *nan-sheu-je*
wake up 醒 *xǐng* *shing*
Wales 威尔士 *wēi'ěrshì* *way-er-sheu*
walk *(n)* **to go for a walk** 去散步 *qù sànbù* *choo san-boo*
walk *(v)* 走 *zǒu* *zoe*
walking: to go walking 去走路 *qù zǒu lù* *choo zoe-loo*
walking boots 旅行靴 *lǚxíngxuē* *lu-shing-shway*
Walkman® 随身听 *suíshēntīng* *sway-sheun-ting*

wallet 钱夹 *qiánjiā chyen-jya*
want 想 *xiǎng shyang*, 要 *yào yao*; **to want to do something** 想要做某事 *xiǎng yào zuò mǒushì shyang yao zwoe moe-sheu*
warm 暖和 *nuǎnhuo nwan-hwoe*
warn 警告 *jǐnggào jing-gao*
wash (n) **to have a wash** 洗脸 *xǐliǎn shee-lyen*
wash 洗 *xǐ shee*; **to wash one's hair** 洗头 *xǐ tóu shee toe*
washbasin 洗脸盆 *xǐliǎnpén shee-lyen-peun*
washing: to do the washing 洗衣服 *xǐ yīfu shee yee-foo*
washing machine 洗衣机 *xǐyījī shee-yee-jee*
washing powder 洗衣粉 *xǐyīfěn shee-yee-feun*
washing-up liquid 洗洁精 *xǐjiéjīng shee-jyay-jing*
wasp 马蜂 *mǎfēng ma-fung*
waste 浪费 *làngfèi lang-fay*
watch (n) 手表 *shǒubiǎo shoe-beeao*
watch (v) 观察 *guānchá gwan-cha*; **watch out!** 注意！ *zhùyì! joo-yee!*
water 水 *shuǐ shway* **58, 59**
water heater 热水器 *rèshuǐqì je-shway-chee*
waterproof 防水 *fángshuǐ fang-shway*
wave 波浪 *bōlàng bo-lang*
way 方向 *fāngxiàng fang-shyang*
way in 入口 *rùkǒu joo-koe*
way out 出口 *chūkǒu choo-koe*
we 我们 *wǒmen wo-meun*
weak 浑身无力 *húnshēn wúlì hoon-sheun woo-lee*
wear 穿 *chuān chwan*
weather 天气 *tiānqì tyen-chee*; **the weather's bad** 天气不好 *tiānqì bù hǎo tyen-chee boo hao*
weather forecast 天气预报 *tiānqì yùbào tyen-chee yoo-bao* **28**
website 网站 *wǎngzhàn wang-jan*
Wednesday 星期三 *xīngqīsān shing-chee-san*
week 星期 *xīngqī shing-chee*, 周 *zhōu joe*
weekend 周末 *zhōumò joe-mo*
welcome 欢迎 *huānyíng hwan-ying*; **welcome!** 欢迎 *huānyíng! hwan-ying!*; **you're welcome** 欢迎你们 *huānyíng nǐmen hwan-ying nee-meun*
well 好 *hǎo hao*; **I'm very well** 我很好 *wǒ hěn hǎo wo heun hao*; **well done** (meat) 全熟 *quánshú kwan-shoo*
well-known 有名 *yǒumíng yoe-ming*
Welsh (person) 威尔士人 *wēi'ěrshì rén way-er-sheu jeun*; (language) 威尔士语 *wēi'ěrshìyǔ way-er-sheu-yoo*
west 西 *xī shee*; **in the west** 在西部 *zài xībù zy shee-boo*; **(to the) west of** 在 … 的西边 *zài … de xībian zy … de shee-byen*
wet 湿 *shī sheu*
wetsuit 保暖潜水服 *bǎonuǎn qiánshuǐfú bao-nwan chyen-shway-foo*
what 什么 *shénme sheun-me*; **what do you want?** 你要什么？ *nǐ yào shénme? nee yao sheun-me?*
wheel 轮子 *lúnzi loon-zeu*
wheelchair 轮椅 *lúnyǐ loon-yee*
when 什么时候 *shénme shíhou sheun-me sheu-hoe*
where 哪儿 *nǎr nar*; **where is/are …?** … 在哪儿？ *… zài nǎr? … zy nar?*; **where are you from?** 你是哪国人？ *nǐ shì nǎ guó rén? nee sheu na gwoe jeun?*; **where are you going?** 你到哪儿去？ *nǐ dào nǎr qù? nee dao nar choo?*
which 哪个 *nǎ ge na ge*
while 一会儿 *yīhuìr yee-hwayr*
white 白色 *báisè by-se*
white wine 白葡萄酒 *bái pútáojiǔ by poo-tao-jyo*
who 谁 *shéi shay*; **who's calling?** 您是谁 *nín shì shéi? nin sheu shay?*

whole 整个 ***zhěnggè*** *jung-ge*
whose 谁的 ***shéi de*** *shay de*
why 为什么 ***wèishénme*** *way-sheun-me*
wide 宽 ***kuān*** *kwan*
wife 妻子 ***qīzi*** *chee-zeu*
wild 野生 ***yěshēng*** *yay-shung*
wind 风 ***fēng*** *fung*
window 窗 ***chuāng*** *chwang*; **in the window** 在橱窗里 ***zài chúchuāng lǐ*** *zy choo-chwang lee*
windscreen 汽车挡风玻璃 ***qìchē dǎngfēngbōli*** *chee-che dang-fung-bo-lee*
wine 葡萄酒 ***pútáojiǔ*** *poo-tao-jyo* **59**
winter 冬天 ***dōngtiān*** *dong-tyen*
with 和 … 在一起 ***hé … zài yīqǐ*** *he … zy yee-chee*
withdraw 取款 ***qǔkuǎn*** *choo-kwan*
without 无 ***wú*** *woo*
woman 女人 ***nǚrén*** *nu-jeun*
wonderful 好极了 ***hǎo jí le*** *hao jee le*
wood 木头 ***mùtou*** *moo-toe*
wool 羊毛 ***yángmáo*** *yang-mao*
work *(n)* 作品 ***zuòpǐn*** *zwoe-pin*; **work of art** 艺术作品 ***yìshù zuòpǐn*** *yee-shoo zwoe-pin*
work 工作 ***gōngzuò*** *gong-zwoe*
works 著作 ***zhùzuò*** *joo-zwoe*
world 世界 ***shìjiè*** *sheu-jyay*
worse 更坏 ***gèng huài*** *gung hwhy*, **to get worse** 变得更坏 ***biàn de gèng huài*** *byen de gung hwhy*; **it's worse than …** 比 … 更差 ***bǐ … gèng chà*** *bee … gung cha*
worth: to be worth 值 … 钱 ***zhí … qián*** *jeu … chyen*; **it's worth it** 值得做 ***zhíde zuò*** *jeu-de zwoe*
wound 伤口 ***shāngkǒu*** *shang-koe*
wrist 手腕 ***shǒuwàn*** *shoe-wan*
write 写 ***xiě*** *shyay* **16**, **99**
wrong 错 ***cuò*** *tswoe*

XYZ

X-rays *X* 光检查 ***X-guāng jiǎnchá*** *X-gwang jyen-cha*
year 年 ***nián*** *nyen*
yellow 黄色 ***huángsè*** *hwang-se*
yes 是 ***shì*** *sheu*
yesterday 昨天 ***zuótiān*** *zwoe-tyen*; **yesterday evening** 昨天晚上 ***zuótiān wǎnshang*** *zwoe-tyen wan-shang*
you *(sg)* 你 ***nǐ*** *nee*; *(pl)* 你们 ***nǐmen*** *nee-meun*
young 年轻 ***niánqīng*** *nyen-ching*
your, yours *(sg)* 你的 ***nǐ de*** *nee de*; *(pl)* 你们的 ***nǐmen de*** *nee-meun de*
youth hostel 青年旅馆 ***qīngnián lǚguǎn*** *ching-nyen lu-gwan*
zero 零 ***líng*** *ling*
zip 拉链 ***lāliàn*** *la-lyen*
zoo 动物园 ***dòngwùyuán*** *dong-woo-ywan*
zoom (lens) 变焦距镜头 ***biànjiāojù jìngtóu*** *byen-jeeao-joo jing-toe*

GRAMMAR

While Chinese grammar is rather complicated, it is possible to express quite a lot if you know some simple facts about the language, and by using straightforward structures.

Numbers

Singular and plural are not distinguished in Chinese:

> 人 ***rén*** *jeun* a person, some people

Numbers, for example 一 ***yī*** *ee* one, 二 ***èr*** *er* two, 三 ***sān*** *san* three and so on, can be added before the noun to indicate the number involved:

> 两个人 ***liǎng ge rén*** *lyang ge jen* two people; 三个人 ***sān ge rén*** *san ge ren* three people

The 个 ***gè*** *ge* which is inserted between the number and the noun is the most common of the **measure words** used in Chinese, generally with neutral tones (not marked with any tone).

When the numeral 二 ***èr*** *er* two is used with a measure word, the character 两 ***liǎng*** *lyang* is used instead of 二 ***èr*** *er*, for example 两个人 ***liǎng ge rén*** (two people).

Sometimes 们 ***mén*** *meun* is placed at the end of a word (usually only words denoting people) to show the plural when the number is not clear from the context, or when we want to emphasize the fact that several people are being talked about.

> 人们 ***rénmen*** *jeun-meun* people
> 朋友们 ***péngyoumen*** *pung-yoe-meun* friends

There are no **articles** as we understand them in English; Chinese defines the noun in other ways:

> 天气很好 ***tiānqì hěn hǎo*** *tyen-chee heun hao* the weather is very good (no indication, the most common)

GRAMMAR

这个城市 ***zhè ge chéngshì*** *je ge chung-sheu* the city (use of a demonstrative)

We therefore often need to look at the context to see how to translate the noun.

银行 ***yínháng*** *yin-hang* a bank, the bank, banks
我去银行 ***wǒ qù yínháng*** *wo choo yin-hang* I am going to the bank

Adjectives of one syllable are normally placed directly before the nouns they describe:

一个新饭店 ***yī ge xīn fàndiàn*** *ee ge shin fan-dyen* a new hotel
一个大饭馆儿 ***yī ge dà fànguǎnr*** *ee ge da fan-gwanr* a large restaurant

When the adjective has more than one syllable the particle 的 ***de*** *de* is usually placed between the adjective and the noun it qualifies:

古老的修道院 ***gǔlǎo de xiūdàoyuàn*** *goo-lao de shyo-dao-ywan* an old abbey

When the adjective describes the subject the verb "to be" is often omitted:

这个电影很有意思 ***zhè ge diànyǐng hěn yǒu yìsi*** *je ge dyen-ying heun yoe ee-seu* this film is very interesting

Personal pronouns used as the subject of a sentence (I, you, he, she etc) are often omitted when it is obvious who is being talked about. They are usually used for emphasis:

I	我 ***wǒ*** *wo*
you	你/您 ***nǐ/nín*** *nin*
he/she/it	他/她/它 ***tā*** *ta*
we	我们 ***wǒmen*** *wo-meun*
you *(plural)*	你们 ***nǐmen*** *ni-meun*
they	他们 ***tāmen*** *ta-meun*

Note that there is no difference between the third-person masculine and feminine forms in spoken Chinese, but in written Chinese different forms of the characters are used.

Possessive pronouns and adjectives are formed by the addition of 的 ***de*** *de*:

> 她的护照 ***tā de hùzhào*** *ta de hoo-jao* her passport

However, when talking about family members and close relationships the 的 ***de*** *de* is often omitted:

> 我爸爸 ***wǒ bàba*** *wo baba* instead of 我的爸爸 ***wǒ de bàba*** *wo de baba* my father

The most common **demonstrative adjectives** are 这 ***zhè*** *je* this and 那 ***nà*** *na* that.

The structure used is 这 ***zhè*** *je* + measure word + noun:

> 这本书 ***zhè běn shū*** *je beun shoo* this book
> 这个饭店很好 ***zhè ge fàndiàn hěn hǎo*** *je ge fan-dyen heun hao* this hotel is very good

The plural forms are 这些 ***zhèxiē*** *je-shyay* these and 那些 ***nàxiē*** *na-shyay* those.

These demonstrative adjectives are often used where English would use the definite article.

GRAMMAR

Adverbs of place

在 ***zài*** *zy* is usually translated by "in" or "at":

> 我在这个饭店 ***wǒ zài zhè ge fàndiàn*** *wo zy zhe ge fan-dyen* I am at the hotel
> 她在中国 ***tā zài zhōngguó*** *ta zy jong-gwoe* she is in China

从 ***cóng*** *tsong* is translated by "from":

> 我从苏格兰来 ***wǒ cóng sūgélán lái*** *wo tsong soo-ge-lan ly* I came from Scotland

The structure 从 **cóng** *tsong* ... 到 **dào** *dao* ... from ... to is frequently used:

> 我从苏格兰到北京来 **wǒ cóng sūgélán dào Běijīng lái** *wo tsong soo-ge-lan dao bay-jing ly* I came to Beijing from Scotland

Comparison
To make a straightforward comparison between two things, use the structure:
subject of the comparison + 比 **bǐ** *bee* + object of the comparison + adjective:

> 中国比英国大 **zhōngguó bǐ yīngguó dà** *jong-gwoe bee ying-gwoe da* China is larger than Britain

To express the superlative, use 最 **zuì** *zway*

> 中国、英国和俄国，俄国最大 **zhōngguó, yīngguó hé éguó, éguó zuì dà** *jong-gwoe, ying-gwoe he e-gwoe, e-gwoe zway da* of China, Britain and Russia, Russia is the largest

To say something is "a bit more" than something else the expression 一点儿 **yīdiǎnr** *ee-dyar* is added to the comparative:

> 咖啡比茶贵一点儿 **kāfēi bǐ chá guì yīdiǎnr** *ka-fay bee cha gway ee-dyar* coffee is a bit more expensive than tea

When asking **questions**, interrogative adverbs are often placed at the end of the interrogative phrase or sentence:

> 哪？**nǎ?** *na?* which?
> 你是哪国人？ **nǐ shì nǎ guó rén?** *nee sheu na gwoe jeun?* where are you from? (literally: you are which country person?)

> 什么？**shénme?** *sheun-me?* what?
> 你吃什么？ **? nǐ chī shénme?** *nee cheu sheun-me?* what are you going to eat?

> 什么时候？**shénme shíhou?** *sheun-me sheu-hoe?* when?
> 你们什么时候去上海？ **nǐmen shénme shíhou qù Shànghǎi?** *nee-meun sheun-me sheu-hoe choo shang-hy?* when are you going to Shanghai?

多少? **duoshăo?** *dwoe-shao?* how many?/how much?
多少钱? **duōshăo qián?** *dwoe-shao chyen?* how much does it cost?

多长时间? **duō cháng shíjiān?** *dwoe chang sheu-jyen?* how long?
你来北京多长时间了? **nĭ lái Běijīng duō cháng shíjiān le?** *nee ly bay-jing dwoe chang sheu-jyen le?* how long have you been in Beijing?

怎么? **zěnme?** *zeun-me?* how?
你们怎么去北京? **nĭmen zěnme qù Běijīng?** *nee-meun zeun-me choo Beijing?* how will you go to Beijing?

哪儿? **năr?** *nar?* where?
北京饭店在哪儿? **Běijīng fàndiàn zài năr?** *bay-jing fan-dyen zy nar?* where is the Beijing Hotel?

为什么? **wèishénme?** *way-sheun-me?* why?
你为什么来中国度假? **nĭ wèishénme lái Zhōngguó dùjià?** *nee way-sheun-me ly jong-gwoe doo-jya?* why did you come to China for a holiday?

The most common way to express a **negative** is to place 不 **bù** *boo* in front of a verb or adjective:

我不是上海人 **wŏ bú shì Shànghăi rén** *wo boo sheu shang-hy jeun* I'm not from Shanghai

However, with the verb 有 **yŏu** *yoe* to have, the negative can only be formed with 没 **méi** *may*, never with 不 **bù** *boo*:

我没有电影票 **wŏ méi yŏu diànyĭng piào** *wo may yoe dyen-ying peeao* I don't have a ticket for the film

没有 **méi yŏu** *may yoe* is also used to indicate the past tense:

我没有懂 **wŏ méi yŏu dŏng** *wo may yoe dong* I didn't understand

There are several ways to **ask a question** in Chinese. The most commonly used is the structure subject + verb + object + 吗 **ma** ma:

你是苏格兰人吗? **nĭ shì sūgélán rén ma?** *nee sheu soo-ge-lan jeun ma?* are you Scottish?

A question can also be formed by using the structure verb/adjective + 不***bù*** *boo*/没***méi*** *may* + repeated verb/adjective:

你是不是苏格兰人? ***nǐ shì bu shì sūgélán rén?*** *nee sheu boo sheu soo-ge-lan jeun?* are you Scottish?
你有没有火? ***nǐ yǒu méi yǒu huǒ?*** *nee yoe may yoe hwoe?* do you have a light?

Verbs do not change their form regardless of the subject or whether singular or plural. They are often used with a particle, or marker. Tense is often indicated by using an adverb of time, such as yesterday, tomorrow, next week and so on:

昨天下雨了 ***zuótiān xià yǔ le*** *zwoe-tyen shya yoo le* it rained yesterday

The particle 了 ***le*** *le* indicates the past tense or that a new state of affairs has come about.

他知道了 ***tā zhī dao le*** *ta jeu dao le* he knows now
他走了 ***tā zǒu le*** *ta zoe le* he's gone
他去上海了 ***tā qù Shànghǎi le*** *ta choo shang-hy le* he's gone to Shanghai
我来晚了 ***wǒ lái wǎn le*** *wo ly wan le* I'm late

When 了 ***le*** *le* is used with the negative 不 ***bù*** *boo* or 没 ***méi*** *may* the meaning is usually "no longer" or "no more":

现在我不喝酒了 ***xiànzài wǒ bù hē jiǔ le*** *shyen-zy wo boo he jyo le* I no longer drink alcohol
我身上没钱了! ***wǒ shēnshang méi qián le!*** *wo sheun-shang may chyen le!* I don't have any money on me!

了 ***le*** *le* may also be used to indicate an exclamation:

太贵了 ***tài guì le*** *ty gway le* it's too expensive.

过 ***guò*** *gwoe* (which suggests the idea of transition, passing through) is also used to express the past when used as a verbal suffix:

他去过北京 ***tā qùguo Běijīng*** *ta choo-gwoe bay-jing* he has been to Beijing

我学过中文，可是现在都忘了 ***wǒ xuéguo zhōngwén, kěshì xiànzài dōu wàng le*** *wo shway-gwoe jong-weun, ke-sheu shyen-zy doe wan le* I've studied Chinese, but I've forgotten it all now

The **past** can also be formed by adding the negative particle 没 ***méi*** *may* before the verb:

我没吃过北京烤鸭 ***wǒ méi chīguo Běijīng kǎoyā*** *wo may cheu-gwoe bay-jing kao-ya* I have never eaten Peking duck

在 ***zài*** *zy* can also be used as an auxiliary to form the continuous:

我在学中文 ***wǒ zài xué zhōngwén*** *wo zy shway jong-weun* I am studying Chinese

Modal verbs like "should", "can" and "may" in English are used in a similar way in Chinese.

会 ***huì*** *hway* to be able to, to know how to
她会开车 ***tā huì kāichē*** *ta hway ky che* she can drive, she knows how to drive

能 ***néng*** *nung* to be able to
他骨折了，不能开车了 ***tā gǔzhé le, bù néng kāichē le*** *ta goo-je le, boo nung ky-che le* he's got a fracture and can't drive any more

会 ***huì*** *hway* expresses possibility
天气预报说这周会有好天气 ***tiānqì yùbào shuō zhè zhōu huì yǒu hǎo tiānqì*** *tyen-chee yoo-bao shwoe je joe hway yoe hao tyen-chee* the weather forecast says there should be good weather this week

能 ***néng*** *nung* can also be used in a similar way, often in requests:
你能告诉我到北京饭店怎么走吗？ ***nǐ néng gàosu wǒ dào Běijīng fàndiàn zěnme zǒu ma?*** *nee nung gao-soo wo dao bay-jing fan-dyen zeun-me zoe ma?* can you tell me how to get to the Beijing Hotel?

您能在地图上给我指出来吗？ ***nín néng zài dìtú shang gěi wǒ zhǐ chūlái ma?*** *nin nung zy dee-too shang gay wo zheu choo-ly ma?* could you show me on the map?

你能推荐一个好餐馆吗？ ***nǐ néng tuījiàn yī ge hǎo cānguǎn ma?*** *nee nung tway-jyen ee ge hao tsan-gwan ma?* can you recommend a good restaurant?

把 ***bǎ*** *ba* is very commonly used; it stresses the result of an action or gives a sense of intention:

请您把它礼品包装，可以吗？ ***qǐng nín bǎ tā lǐpǐn bāozhuāng, kěyǐ ma?*** *ching nin ba ta lee-pin bao-jwang, ke-yee ma?* could you gift-wrap it for me?

我可以把背包搁在前台吗？ ***wǒ kěyǐ bǎ bēibāo gē zài qiántái ma?*** *wo ke-yee ba bay-bao ge zy chyen-ty ma?* could I leave my backpack at reception?

我把一个东西落在飞机上了 ***wǒ bǎ yī ge dōngxi là zài fēijī shang le*** *wo ba ee ge dong-shee la zy fay-jee* I've left something on the plane

HOLIDAYS AND FESTIVALS

Some of China's holidays are based on the solar calendar and take place on the same date each year, while others, usually older, traditional festivals, are tied to the lunar calendar, and dates vary.

Traditional festivals in the lunar calendar

Chinese New Year or **Spring Festival** (春节 ***chūnjié*** *choon-jyay*), between 21 January and 19 February.
The Spring Festival (Chinese New Year's Day, renamed in 1912 to distinguish it from the Western New Year) falls on the first day of the first month in the Chinese lunar calendar (usually in January or February of the solar calendar), and the day before it is Chinese New Year's Eve 除夕 ***chúxī*** *choo-shee*. The Han people and other ethnic minorities in China all celebrate the Spring Festival, with such activities as setting off firecrackers, pasting 春联 ***chūnlián*** *choon-lyen* (couplets matching each other in sound and meaning, written on red paper) on the door, and performing the *yangge* (literally, "rice seedling song") dance and the lion dance. People give 红包 ***hóngbāo*** *hong-bao* lucky red envelopes containing a few bank notes, especially to children. It can be difficult to get travel tickets at this time, and shops are closed for a couple of days.

Lantern Festival (元宵节 ***yuánxiāojié*** *ywan-sheeao-jyay*), between 5 February and end of February.
The fifteenth day of the first lunar month is the Yuanxiao Festival, also known as the Lantern Festival. The special food for this festive day is called 元宵 ***yuánxiāo*** *ywan-sheeao*, a round dumpling with a sweet meat stuffing. The lanterns originate from the old belief that deceased relatives return over the New Year, and need a light to show them the way back to the afterlife.

Spring Equinox (清明节 ***qīngmíngjié*** *ching-ming-jyay*), 4 or 5 April.
Qing Ming meaning "clean and bright", marks the start of the growing year. It is also the time of year when people go out to their family tombs and to memorials to pay tribute to the dearly departed and national heroes.

Dragon Boat Festival (端午节 ***duānwǔjié*** *dwan-woo-jyay*), Summer Solstice.

This June festival is dedicated to the memory of Qu Yuan, from the state of Choo during the period of the Warring States (475–221BC). According to legend, Qu Yuan drowned himself in protest against the cruel reign of the King. Fearing that Qu Yuan's body might be eaten by the river fish, people wrapped up sticky rice in bamboo leaves, raced each other in their boats to the place where Qu Yuan had died and threw the rice dumplings into the river to feed the fish, so as to keep Qu Yuan's body from harm. Later, the act of wrapping rice in bamboo leaves evolved into the tradition of preparing a special food called 粽子 ***zòngzi*** *zong-zeu* for the festival. The boat race to save Qu Yuan's body was the origin of the dragon boat race, which is held every year on this day.

Mid-autumn Festival (中秋节 ***zhōngqiūjié*** *jong-chyo-jyay*), between 10 September and 10 October.
The Mid-Autumn Festival, which falls on the fifteenth day of the eighth lunar month (September of the solar calendar), is also known as Family Reunion Day. This is a time when the whole family enjoys getting together to eat moon cakes. The full moon indicates togetherness to the Chinese.

National public holidays

Besides National Day (1 October) and International Labour Day (1 May), which are the two major official holidays celebrated all over the country, there are many other traditional holidays and festivals in China.

1 January	New Year (one-day holiday)
Late January/ early February	Chinese New Year (officially three days' holiday, but the celebrations extend over up to a month
8 March	International Women's Day (half a day's holiday for women)
1 May	International Labour Day (one to three days' holiday)
4 May	Chinese Youth Day (half a day's holiday for the over-14s)
1 June	International Children's Festival (one day's holiday for under-13s)
1 August	Festival of the People's Liberation Army of China (one day's holiday for the military)
1 October	National Day (one to three days' holiday)

USEFUL ADDRESSES

Website of the **China International Travel Service (CITS)**: www.cits.net

Website of the **China National Tourist Office**: www.cnto.org

IN THE UK

Embassy of the People's Republic of China, UK
49-51 Portland Place, London W1B 1JL
Tel.: 020-729 94049
Fax: 020-743 69178
Website: **www.chinese-embassy.org.uk**

Consulate General of the People's Republic of China in Manchester
Consular District: Newcastle, Lancaster, Derby, Great Manchester, York, Durham
Denison House, 49 Denison Road, Rusholme, Manchester M14 5RX
Tel.: 0161-248 9304
Fax: 0161-257 2672
E-mail: **chinaconsul_man_uk@mfa.gov.cn**
Website: **http://manchester.chineseconsulate.org/eng/**

Consulate General of the People's Republic of China in Edinburgh
Consular District: Northern Ireland, Scotland
55 Corstorphine Road, Edinburgh EH12 5QG
Tel.: 0131-337 3220
Fax: 0131-337 1790
E-mail: **edinburgh_chineseconsulate@mfa.gov.cn**
Website: **http://edinburgh.chineseconsulate.org/**

IN THE US

Embassy of the People's Republic of China, USA
2300 Connecticut Ave. NW, Washington, D.C. 20008

Tel.: (202) 328-2500/01/02
E-mail: **chinaembassy_us@fmprc.gov.cn hin**
Website: **http://www.china-embassy.org/eng**

IN CHINA

British Embassy, Beijing
11 Guanghua Lu, Jianguomenwai, Beijing 100600
Tel.: (0086) (10) 5192 4000
Fax: (0086) (10) 6532 1937/8/9
E-mail: **commercialmail@peking.mail.fco.gov.uk**
Website: **http://www.uk.cn**

British Consulate-General, Shanghai
Suite 301, Shanghai Centre 1376, Nanjing Xi Lu, Shanghai 200040
Tel.: (0086) (21) 6279 7650
Fax: (0086) (21) 6279 7651
E-mail: **britishconsulate.shanghai@fco.gov.uk**

US Embassy, Beijing
Xiu Shui Bei Jie 3, Beijing 100600
Tel.: (0086) (10) 6532 3831
Fax: (0086) (10) 6532 4153
E-mail: **AmCitBeijing@state.gov**
Website: **http://beijing.usembassy-china.org.cn/**

US Consulate-General, Shanghai
1469 Huai Hai Zhong Lu, Shanghai 200031
Tel.: (0086) (21) 6433 6880
Fax: (0086) (21) 6433 4122
Website: **http://www.usembassy-china.org.cn/shanghai**

EMERGENCY PHONE NUMBERS

Fire brigade: **119**
Police: **110**
Ambulance: **120**